"Should be read by every environmental campaigner"

"Sadly, the population myth has been used to distract attention from the roots of ecological crisis in a destructive economic system and to shift the blame for problems such as climate change onto the poor. This splendid book is an essential read for all of us who are concerned with creating an ecologically sustainable and just future. Buy it, read it, and spread the word!"
—Derek Wall, author of *The Rise of the Green Left*

"Ian Angus and Simon Butler's superb book challenges the 'commonsense' idea that there are too many people. Clearly and concisely they blame a system that puts profit before people and planet, refuting the arguments of the latter day Malthusians. It is a book that should be read by every environmental campaigner, trade unionist and political activist."
—Martin Empson, author of *Marxism and Ecology: Capitalism, Socialism and the Future of the Planet*

"How did apparently progressive greens and defenders of the underprivileged turn into people-haters, convinced of the evils of overbreeding among the world's poor? How did they come to believe the 200-year-old myths of a right-wing imperialist friend of Victorian mill owners? It's a sorry story, told here with verve and anger."
—Fred Pearce, author of *Peoplequake*

"Angus and Butler have written a comprehensive dissection of the arguments surrounding overpopulation. It's a vital and insightful socialist response to the debate and highly recommended to anyone interested in fighting for a better world and avoiding the pitfalls of false solutions."
—Chris Williams, author of *Ecology and Socialism*

"This is an essential subject, and we are in Angus and Butler's debt for treating it with such clarity and rigor."
—from the Foreword by Joel Kovel, author of *The Enemy of Nature*

TOO MANY PEOPLE?
Population, Immigration, and the Environmental Crisis

Ian Angus and Simon Butler

Haymarket Books
Chicago, Illinois

© 2011 Ian Angus and Simon Butler

Published in 2011 by Haymarket Books
PO Box 180165
Chicago, IL 60618
www.haymarketbooks.org
773-583-7884

ISBN: 978-1-60846-140-0

Trade distribution:
In the US, Consortium Book Sales and Distribution, www.cbsd.com
In Canada, Publishers Group Canada, www.pgcbooks.ca
In the UK, Turnaround Publisher Services, www.turnaround-uk.com
In Australia, Palgrave Macmillan, www.palgravemacmillan.com.au
All other countries, Publishers Group Worldwide, www.pgw.com

Cover design by Ragina Johnson. Cover image of rooftops in the Mineira slum in Rio de
Janeiro, Brazil, by Felipe Dana, Associated Press.

Published with the generous support of Lannan Foundation and the Wallace Global Fund.

Printed in the United States on recycled paper containing 100 percent
postconsumer waste in accordance with the guidelines of the Green Press Initiative,
www.greenpressinitiative.org.

Library of Congress cataloging-in-publication data is available.

10 9 8 7 6 5 4 3 2 1

Table of Contents

Appendixes

To the Ogoni people of Nigeria; to the Cree of Alberta, Canada; to the people of the Amazon rainforests; to the farmers of La Vía Campesina; and to the millions of others around the world who are fighting to stop the destruction of their homelands and our common planet. Your struggles inspire us, and show the way forward for humanity

Foreword by Betsy Hartmann

This brilliant book by Ian Angus and Simon Butler comes not a moment too soon. The myth of overpopulation has returned with a vengeance along with the scaremongering and scape-goating that are its hallmarks. A strategic coalition of powerful population and environment organizations and pundits are spreading false messages that poor women's fertility is to blame for critical global problems ranging from climate change to poverty to political instability. Nativists are riding the latest population wave to target immigrants as the cause of environmental degradation: it's the greening of hate.

I have worked on the population issue for over three decades now. As an activist in the international women's health movement, I have fought with many others around the world to advance and protect

---

Betsy Hartmann is the author of Reproductive Rights and Wrongs: The Global Politics of Population Control *and the director of the Population and Development Program at Hampshire College in Amherst, Massachusetts. A longstanding activist in the international women's health movement, she writes and speaks on the intersections of reproductive rights, population, immigration, environment, and security concerns. For more information, visit her website at www.BetsyHartmann.com.*

reproductive rights, including access to safe, affordable abortion. At the same time I have fought against the human rights violations of population control programs, from restrictions on contraceptive choice to coercive sterilization. As a political researcher, scholar, and teacher, I have studied the myth of overpopulation from many different directions, charting how it negatively affects family planning and health programs, environmental movements, and the pursuit of social justice and peace. It is a divisive ideology that plays on racialized fears of people of color whether in the global North or global South. Despite the periodic deployment of feminist language, it views women mainly as wombs.

In the years I have been working on population, the world demographic picture has changed dramatically as birth rates have declined around the globe. Today demographers tend to be much more concerned with the phenomenon of negative birth rates and population aging than they are with rapid population growth. The momentum built into our present numbers means that world population will reach around nine billion by 2050, but after that it is expected to stabilize. Now more than ever, it is clear that the myth of overpopulation is really not about the numbers, but about obscuring the social, economic, and political inequalities at the root of current global crises, including climate change. It is about preserving the power of the rich.

Too Many People? shines a keen light on all these issues and more. With clear prose and careful, cogent analysis, Angus and Butler provide the tools necessary to dismantle the myth of overpopulation step by step. In so doing, they also show the way to a more hopeful, justice-centered environmental and reproductive politics. Like the excellent publications they edit, *Climate and Capitalism* and *Green Left Weekly,* this book makes complex information, ideas, and arguments accessible to a wide variety of readers—activists, students, educators, journalists, policy makers, and indeed anyone who wants to better understand the world.

The resurgent myth of overpopulation stands in the way of global solidarity and progress. This book gives me hope that the myth can be dispelled quickly and decisively so we can get on with the pressing challenges at hand. The urgency of addressing climate change means there is no time to lose. Read this book. It will liberate and embolden you to take action.

Foreword by Joel Kovel

I n the year 2000 I sought the presidential nomination of the Green Party, principally by driving around California in my Saab and visiting party locals. From San Diego to Arcata, from San Luis Obispo to Fresno to Nevada City, I made my rounds and met with people in their homes and town halls, sounding out their needs and presenting myself as the best national candidate to advance the Green Agenda, whose central idea is the preservation, repair, and enhancement of the earth's ecological integrity.

For those who were elsewhere that year, I finished far behind Ralph Nader in the race for the Green Party nomination, who in turn lost by a considerable margin to George W. Bush. I mostly remember my wanderings fondly, setting aside the inevitable irritations of so quixotic a venture. The people were friendly, interesting, and varied. They seemed deeply committed to the integrity of the environment and eager for fundamental change—in a word, *progressive* in all respects. But this was

---

Joel Kovel is the author of The Enemy of Nature: The End of Capitalism or the End of the World? *(Zed Books, 2007) and editor of the quarterly journal* Capitalism Nature Socialism. *He was a coauthor of the first* Ecosocialist Manifesto *and a founder of the Ecosocialist International Network.*

not always satisfactory. There was a darker side to some of my meetings, present at times in those gatherings that engaged people of relative affluence and—for want of a better word—whiteness.

On such occasions the Greens revealed—circumspectly, to be sure—a current of distress and antipathy toward other people, generally speaking, those of a different hue and of the *South*. Needless to say, not the geographic south of, say, Southern California; rather, a South signifying the alien Other, a zone consumed and left behind by the global North of industrial-capitalist countries. Their lands devastated and their lives in ruin, many people from the South come North, driven by the needs of survival. In the Northern metropolis they are strangers and called aliens. In California their presence was felt on street corners early in the morning, where they put their day labor up for sale hoping to be gathered by the Toyota pickups. This image became notorious at this time, as was the fact that they often lived in canyons and gullies out of the sight of the citizenry.

All this made many progressives uneasy, with its implication that the North was continuing the process of exploitation and squeezing yet more surplus value from the bodies of the South. And yet they could not face up to the implications. The continuing presence of the "aliens," indeed the very word, signified a structural rift between peoples, one that the liberals and certain sectors of the Greens could not appropriate within their worldview. Thus its significance became split off and distorted.

We have seen a good deal of racism stemming from this rift. It arises all along the various boundaries of the North-South interface. In the decade since my campaign the racist quotient has risen as the global economic and ecological crises grind on. Thus we have Arizona in the United States and the surging of the radical, anti-immigration right in England, France, Russia, Austria, and elsewhere. All this will worsen unless we rise up to overcome it.

But there is another, linked kind of reaction that appears, often among progressives, including a number of the Green progressives I saw on my travels in California. These people aren't racist—or at least they keep their racism well hidden. Instead, they try to contend with the alienation they feel toward those on the wrong side of the North-South divide with a dispassionate scientific gloss. They worry about the *invasiveness of too many strange creatures*. At times such creatures become labeled as the so-called invasive species of plants and animals; but often enough as well, they are the self-same human strangers, such as those who offensively appeared on California's street corners early in the morning. The categorization now veers away from what is wrong with the alien. Rather, it is that there are just too many of them; and too many people spells doom no matter what the particulars.

The whole argument becomes displaced to the high ground of *population*—displaced over and over, it may be added, because the population question provides such fertile soil for evading the truth about society and its current ecological crisis. It is really quite amazing how many tricky and complicated arguments can be mounted once one abstracts from social reality and converts the human condition into a matter of quantity. This so-called science is an intellectual toadstool that sprouts without end.

It's a good-sized forest, and demands a guidebook equal to its complexities. And Ian Angus and Simon Butler have given us one with *Too Many People?*—a veritable Baedeker of the dark and occult sciences of "populationism," by which is meant the ideological rendering of population science in the service of defending the existing order of things. I like the way Angus and Butler move on past the traditional usage of Malthusianism and its "neo-" version to identify the ideology. It's confusing to base a category on a thinker so bizarre as the Reverend Malthus (Marx calls him a "baboon" in the *Grundrisse*), though we should never forget how vast has been his influence—testimony not to intellectual power but to the value of his mystification to the propertied classes. In any case, it is not Malthus himself who deserves our attention, but his staying power, that ever-recurring impulse of the bourgeois intellectual to conjure rationalizations to put away the wretched of this earth and justify what the dominant society has done to them.

This is an essential subject, and we are in Angus and Butler's debt for treating it with such clarity and rigor. What emerges is a rich and variegated tapestry woven around two deep themes.

First, while population is by no means irrelevant, giving it conceptual pride of place not only inflates its explanatory value but also obscures the essential factors that make for ecological degradation and makes it impossible to begin the hard work of overcoming them.

And second, it is not only possible but also essential to turn the populationist argument on its head. The true question is not numbers of people but the relation of population to a worthwhile society. Declining population is not therefore an unmitigated good. In the midst of worrying about overpopulation, people tend to forget that population is in fact going to decline, and that as it recedes like the tide, it will expose a whole new set of challenges in its wake. If, for example, each woman has but one child—a populationist's dream, however unlikely—then each generation is halved compared to the one that went before. Allowing for certain wrinkles and lags, this predicts a remarkable global drop in the next century, roughly from seven to one billion, with severe repercussions in labor shortages along the way—scarcely a utopian outcome.

Nor is a large population necessarily a bad thing. We need to bear in mind with Angus and Butler, along with the burgeoning community of ecosocialists for whom they speak, that large numbers of people who freely and collectively determine their labor can—and, I should think, will—direct their creative energy to caring for and mending a nature ravaged by capital. Thus an ecosocialist society, in which humanity lives within limits and with deep respect for nature, need not be primarily concerned with numbers of people, so long as the *quality* of their relation to nature, which includes, to be sure, their relation with each other, is worthy.

In all cases, the rational control of population is a direct function of the power women have over their lives. Thus a free ecosocialist society grounded in the empowerment of women will also be free from the compulsion to worry about population. Indeed, the best way to honor *Too Many People?* is to work collectively to put its subject matter into the proverbial dustbin of history.

Acknowledgments

As editors of *Climate and Capitalism* (Ian) and *Green Left Weekly* (Simon) we have met, corresponded with, and learned from more green-left and left-green activists than we can possibly name here. Their insights and advice have helped enormously with all our writing, and with this book in particular.

Jeff White carefully read several drafts of *Too Many People?* and thoroughly checked the reference notes. In addition to providing valuable suggestions on content, he caught and corrected innumerable errors, typographical and otherwise.

Lis Angus, Martin Empson, Betsy Hartmann, Joel Kovel, John Riddell, and Chris Williams read the manuscript at various stages and gave us detailed comments and suggestions that have made the book much stronger.

The scan of the cover of the 1954 *Population Bomb* pamphlet in chapter 9 was shared by Ronald Ladouceur, who maintains the *Textbook History* blog at www.textbookhistory.com.

We are grateful to the following for permission to include complete articles or long excerpts:

The Sustainability Institute (www.sustainer.org) for permission to include "Who Causes Environmental Problems?" by Donella Meadows (appendix 2).

Richard Smith for permission to include a long excerpt from "Beyond Growth or Beyond Capitalism," originally published in *Real-World Economics Review* (chapter 14).

The Climate Justice and Migration Working Group of the Mobilization for Climate Justice, for permission to include their statement on climate justice and migration (appendix 4).

Some parts of this book originally appeared in *Climate and Capitalism* or *Green Left Weekly.* All have been extensively rewritten and updated.

On Terminology

Throughout this book, we use the term *populationism* to refer to ideologies that attribute social and ecological ills to human numbers, and *populationist* for people who support such ideas. We prefer those terms to the more traditional *Malthusianism* and *Malthusian*, for two reasons.

First, because in our experience few people are familiar with the ideas of Thomas Robert Malthus, so labels based on his name aren't informative.

And second, because most modern populationists don't actually agree with what Malthus wrote two hundred years ago. Malthus denied that there are limits to economic growth, didn't believe that any measure could help the poor, and strongly opposed birth control—we don't think it is useful to use his name to identify people who think the opposite.

We frequently use the word *North* as shorthand for the industrialized nations of Europe, Canada, the United States, Japan, New Zealand, and Australia, and *South* for the so-called underdeveloped countries, sometimes called the third world.

We refer to all greenhouse gases as *carbon dioxide* or CO_2. We know that in some cases a term such as *carbon dioxide equivalent* or CO_2e would be more accurate, but the distinction is not critical for this book.

Introduction

If ever there was a measure of the green movement's confusion, it is that so many environmentalists honestly believe that by soberly intoning that there are just "too many people" they somehow cut across all the moral and political agonies of globalization, of rising human migrations, mass extinctions, atmospheric instability and all the rest of it. In fact, "overpopulation" explains none of these things, and as long as we cling to it we remain the confused citizens of an incomprehensible world.

—Tom Athanasiou[1]

We face an environmental crisis of unprecedented scale and scope. Global warming has received the most attention, but human activity is also poisoning rivers, lakes, and seas, exhausting fresh water supplies, destroying fertile soil, killing other species by the thousands, and overwhelming the fundamental ecological processes that have maintained a stable biosphere for millennia. If these trends continue, our world will be irrevocably changed. If they accelerate, as they appear to be doing now, much of human society, and perhaps humanity itself, will be in danger.

One of the world's most respected climate scientists, James Hansen, tells us the time for action is short:

> Our global climate is nearing tipping points. Changes are beginning to appear, and there is a potential for explosive changes with effects that would be irreversible—if we do not rapidly slow fossil fuel emissions over the next few decades . . .

1

Only in the past few years did the science crystallize, revealing the urgency—our planet really is in peril. If we do not change course soon, we will hand our children a situation that is out of their control, as amplifying feedbacks drive the dynamics of the global system.[2]

The harsh truth is that it's already too late to stop climate change completely. Even if all of the greenhouse gas emissions that cause climate change stopped today, humanity would still live with the consequences of past emissions for centuries. The task now is to prevent the crisis from turning into a catastrophe, to head off runaway climate change that could make much of the world uninhabitable. Some scientists believe that we must completely change course by midcentury; others say we have ten or fifteen years at most.

With a few very honorable exceptions, the world's governments have shown little interest in solving this crisis. Politicians make fine speeches, but their inaction speaks much louder than their words. Forty-one years after the first Earth Day, the environmental crisis is worse than ever. Greenhouse gas emissions are higher than ever, and the latest agreement proposed by the world's richest nations is even weaker than the toothless Kyoto Accord.

It is painfully clear that diplomacy and backroom deals aren't working. The powers that be will not act unless they are forced to: the only force that can move them is mass democratic action in the streets—a people's campaign for a sustainable, ecological society. The mass demonstrations in Copenhagen in 2009 and the global meeting of left-greens, indigenous activists, and anti-imperialist movements in Bolivia in 2010 are hopeful signs that such a campaign can be built and win.

To build this movement, climate activists must understand the causes of the environmental crisis and the changes needed to prevent catastrophe. This book focuses on a critically important debate on that subject: the "population question."

Many sincere and dedicated environmentalists believe that a fundamental cause of environmental destruction is population growth—

that there are too many people on the earth and that no real solution is possible unless humans somehow reduce their numbers. The widely circulated "World Scientists' Warning to Humanity," published for the World Earth Summit in 1992, supported that view:

> Pressures resulting from unrestrained population growth put demands on the natural world that can overwhelm any efforts to achieve a sustainable future. If we are to halt the destruction of our environment, we must accept limits to that growth.[3]

In addition, a growing current in the environmental movement in rich countries argues for immigration restrictions on populationist grounds. Noted Australian environmentalist Tim Flannery made that argument during a debate on immigration policy broadcast by the Australian Broadcasting Corporation:

> Growing Australia's population has a much greater impact than growing the population of a poor country. We are the heaviest carbon users in the world, about twenty-three tonnes per capita, so people that come to this country from anywhere on the planet will result almost certainly in an increase in carbon emissions . . .[4]

In *Too Many People?* we argue that the "too many people" and "too many immigrants" explanations for climate change and other forms of environmental destruction are wrong.

Environmentalists who promote birth control and/or anti-immigration policies as solutions to environmental problems profoundly misunderstand the nature of the crisis. Adoption of their proposals would divert the movement from real solutions.

We strongly favor universal access to birth control, abortion, and other maternal health services, and we agree that it's essential to find a balance between natural resources and human needs. We were motivated to write this book by our deep concern about global warming, resource depletion, deforestation, species extinctions, overfishing, expanding deserts, declining water supplies, and all forms of pollution. Those are all major problems, but they are not caused by "overpopulation," and they won't be solved by birth control and immigration restrictions.

As US immigrant rights campaigner Patricia Huang says, "The relationship between population growth and environmental destruction is shaped by how we use our resources, not by the number of people who use them."[5]

This is not an abstract or academic issue: by drawing attention away from the social and economic causes of the environmental crisis, the populationist argument makes it harder to find and fight for genuine solutions. Populationist policies focus on symptoms, not causes. Worse, they shift the blame for climate change, and the burden for stopping it, onto the poorest and most vulnerable people in the world.

They divert attention away from the main challenge, the urgent need to build a new economy based on environmentally sustainable policies and equitable social development.

As renowned US ecologist Barry Commoner once said, populationist solutions to environmental destruction are "equivalent to attempting to save a leaking ship by lightening the load and forcing passengers overboard." Instead, we should ask "if there isn't something radically wrong with the ship."[6]

◇

Debates about populationism are usually framed as disagreements between people who are concerned about the environment and people who are not, between the populationist claim that overpopulation and resource depletion are humanity's biggest problem and the business-as-usual claim that more people will create more wealth and unlock more resources.

We hope *Too Many People?* will help the movement to break away from that sterile framework. Our goal is to promote debate *within* environmental movements about the real causes of environmental destruction, poverty, food shortages, and resource depletion.

To that end, we contribute this ecosocialist response to the new wave of green populationism, in particular as it is expressed today in the United States, Britain, Canada, and Australia. We strongly disagree with the populationists and have had no qualms about expressing our views forthrightly. But we also have tried to present their views fairly and to distinguish between the reactionaries who promote population control to protect the status quo and the green activists who sincerely view population growth as a cause of environmental problems.

Too Many People? is divided into five sections.

- In "Blaming People" we discuss a key debate on population that took place in the early years of the modern environmental movement, a debate that raised issues that remain relevant, and we outline the major currents of populationist thought in the environmental movement today.
- "The Failures of Populationism" critiques key assumptions and arguments of modern populationism.
- "Control and Coercion" holds the human rights record of population control programs up to scrutiny and asks whether non-coercive population programs are possible.
- "Greens versus Immigrants?" examines the supposed ecological arguments for reducing or stopping immigration. We argue that scapegoating immigrants for environmental damage takes the pressure off the real environmental vandals and makes it harder to build strong environmental movements.
- "Production, Consumption, Revolution" looks at the root cause of environmental destruction, an economic and social system that is based on ceaseless growth and that thrives on endless waste. If human civilization is to survive, anti-ecological capitalism must be replaced with a pro-ecological system that can promote sustain-

able human development. Populationist ideas hinder this cause.

The appendixes provide four articles and statements that elaborate on the arguments in this book.

- "The Malthus Myth," by Ian Angus, examines the ideas of Thomas Robert Malthus, the nineteenth-century clergyman and economist who is often described as the founder of populationism.
- "Who Causes Environmental Problems?" by Donella Meadows, lead author of the famous 1972 report *The Limits to Growth*, explains why the frequently cited IPAT formula obscures solutions to ecological problems.
- "We Refuse to Shut the International Door" is a stirring call for solidarity with migrants, written by the great US socialist leader Eugene V. Debs in 1910.
- "Climate Justice and Migration" is an important analysis of and program for the growing climate refugee crisis.

1: Are People the Problem?

We know that the world is burning. The question is how to put out the fire.
—Twilly Cannon, former captain of the Greenpeace ship *Rainbow Warrior*[1]

Other things being equal, a larger population will eat more food, wear more clothes, occupy more shelter, and generate more excrement than a smaller one. That's an indisputable biological fact.

If there is not enough food, fabric, or shelter to go around and the latrines are overflowing, you might conclude that economic, social, or political institutions are faulty, that the system isn't meeting people's basic needs.

Or if you believe that the system is fundamentally sound and that any other system would be worse, you might conclude that the problem is too many people.

Activists have debated those opposing views since the modern environmental movement was born in the 1960s.

The new movement was born as part of the same global radicalization, and involved many of the same people, as the nuclear disarmament and test ban campaigns and the movement against the US war in Vietnam. There had long been wilderness conservationist societies in North America and countryside preservation groups in Europe, but the new movement was very different. It focused on how humanity was affected by environmental destruction rather than on preserving pristine wilderness; it was activist and political rather than charitable.

Above all, where the older groups largely reflected the views of the wealthy and comfortable, the new environmental activists believed that "environmental catastrophe could be avoided only by fundamental changes in the values and institutions of industrial societies."[2]

But what should those changes be? The answer depended on what was causing the environmental destruction, and there was much debate on that.

The longest-lasting and most contentious debate in the environmental movement has focused on whether population growth is a fundamental cause of environmental destruction and whether the movement should support measures to reduce population.

The main issues in that dispute were defined when modern environmentalism was being born. The leading participants in the debate were among the most prominent figures in the new movement: Paul and Anne Ehrlich, authors of *The Population Bomb* (1968),[3] and Barry Commoner, author of *The Closing Circle* (1971). Their disagreements defined a controversy that continues today.

The Population Bomb

Paul Ehrlich came to environmentalism from the conservationist movement. He was a professor, and his wife Anne Ehrlich was a research associate, in the biology department at Stanford University. They initially worked on classifying butterflies, but by the late 1950s they were increasingly focused on human population issues. In 1967, at the urging of the executive director of the venerable Sierra Club, they expanded an article they had written for *New Scientist* magazine into a book. Subsidized by the Sierra Club and published as a mass-market paperback in 1968, *The Population Bomb* became one of the best-selling environmental books of all time.

The arguments in *The Population Bomb* drew heavily on two best-selling books from the late 1940s—*Our Plundered Planet* by Fairfield Osborne and *Road to Survival* by William Vogt—and on the 1967 best seller *Famine—1975!* in which William and Paul Paddock predicted a "time of famines" within a few years and urged the US government to cut off all aid to "can't-be-saved" nations, a category that included India, China, Egypt, and Haiti.[4]

The Ehrlichs' book was a popular presentation of views that were already widely accepted in the preservationist establishment, which tended to be white, rich, and politically conservative. Sierra Club executive director Dave Brower expressed the common view two years before *The Population Bomb* was published: "We feel you don't have a conservation policy unless you have a population policy."[5]

Although the publisher's blurb stressed that Paul Ehrlich was "a qualified scientist," *The Population Bomb* was not a scientific book: it was a political tract aimed at a broad audience. A historian writes: "At a time when an American audience was never more eager to learn about the impending environmental crisis, Ehrlich presented arguably the loudest and most persuasive treatise on the ecological problems of human overpopulation."[6]

The Ehrlichs made three fundamental points.

First, mass starvation was inevitable in the near future. "The battle to feed all of humanity is over. In the 1970s the world will undergo famines—hundreds of millions of people are going to starve to death in spite of any crash programs embarked upon now. At this late date nothing can prevent a substantial increase in the world death rate . . . ." (*Bomb*, 1).

Second, "the progressive deterioration of our environment may cause more death and misery than any conceivable food-population gap" (*Bomb*, 46).

And third, the food and environmental crises had a common cause: "The causal chain of deterioration is easily followed to its source. Too many cars, too many factories, too much detergent, too much pesticide, multiplying contrails, inadequate sewage treatment plants, too little water, too much carbon dioxide—all can be traced easily to *too many people*" (*Bomb*, 66–67).

Why have people insisted on reproducing past the point of no return? The Ehrlichs argued that overpopulation is in our genes.

> Reproduction is the key to winning the evolutionary game. Any structure, physiological process, or pattern of behavior that leads to greater reproductive success will tend to be perpetuated. The entire process by which man developed involves thousands of millennia of our ancestors being more successful breeders than their relatives . . . (*Bomb*, 28)
>
> Billions of years of evolution has given us all a powerful will to live. Intervening in the birth rate goes against our evolutionary values. During all those centuries of our evolutionary past, the individuals who had the most children passed on their genetic endowment in greater quantities than those who reproduced less. Their genes dominate our heredity today. (*Bomb*, 34)

So long as death eliminated people almost as quickly as birth produced them, population rose very slowly, but "the development of medical science was the straw that broke the camel's back." Rich countries exported "instant death control"—wiping out major diseases and causing "plunges in the death rate" in poor countries. The death rate fell, but the birth rate was still driven by our evolved biological urges, so population exploded (*Bomb*, 32–33).

Unlike other populationists of the time (William Vogt, for instance), the Ehrlichs didn't say that medical treatment should be withheld from poor countries, although they did say that "death control in the absence of birth control is self-defeating, to say the least" (*Bomb*, 92).

The Ehrlichs' book described a world in crisis—too many people, too little food, and the environment being destroyed. So their main conclusion wasn't surprising:

A general answer to the question, "What needs to be done?" is simple. We must rapidly bring the world population under control, reducing the growth rate to zero or making it go negative. Conscious regulation of human numbers must be achieved. Simultaneously we must, at least temporarily, greatly increase our food production. This agricultural program should be carefully monitored to minimize deleterious effects on the environment and should include an effective program of ecosystem restoration. As these projects are carried out, an international policy research program must be initiated to set optimum population-environment goals for the world and to devise methods for reaching these goals. (*Bomb*, 131)

But while growing more food would buy time, there would be no solution without drastic measures.

A cancer is an uncontrolled multiplication of cells; the population explosion is an uncontrolled multiplication of people . . . We must shift our efforts from treatment of the symptoms to the cutting out of the cancer. The operation will demand many apparently brutal and heartless decisions. The pain may be intense. But the disease is so far advanced that only with radical surgery does the patient have a chance of survival. (*Bomb*, 166–67)

Unlike many populationists, the Ehrlichs didn't target only population growth in poor countries. Pointing out that per capita resource use in the United States was vastly higher than in other countries, they concluded: "Obviously our first step must be to immediately establish and advertise drastic policies to bring our own population size under control" (*Bomb*, 135).

Still, the policies they proposed for the United States were considerably less drastic than those they advocated for others. For the United States, they suggested tax changes to penalize large families, better sex education, access to birth control and abortion, and a federal Department of Population and Environment. For poor countries, they endorsed compulsory sterilization of men with more than three children and ending food shipments to countries deemed to be "so far behind in the population-food game that there is no hope that our food aid will see them through to self sufficiency" (*Bomb*, 160).

They went further in an article written shortly after *The Population Bomb* appeared, urging the US government to use its political and economic might to force the world into compliance. The United States, they wrote, should "withhold all aid from a country with an expanding population unless that nation convinces us that it is doing everything possible to limit its population." Critics who object that "extreme political and economic pressure" is repressive should "reflect on the alternatives."[7]

Despite their call for drastic population controls, the Ehrlichs were very pessimistic about the possibility of actually making things better.

> Most Americans clearly don't give a damn . . . Our population consists of two groups; a comparatively small one dedicated to the preservation of beauty and wildlife, and a vastly larger one dedicated to the destruction of both (or at least apathetic towards it). (*Bomb*, 66)
>
> By now you are probably fed up with this discussion. Americans will do none of these things, you say. Well, I'm inclined to agree. (*Bomb*, 156)
>
> Many of you are doubtless saying now, "It's too unrealistic—it can't be done." I think you're probably right—as I said earlier, the chances of success are small. (*Bomb*, 174)

The Population Bomb catapulted Paul Ehrlich from local prominence in California to national fame. He appeared more than twenty times on the popular *Tonight Show with Johnny Carson*, and on many other programs. He spoke at conferences and wrote for popular magazines, and he and Anne coauthored a major textbook that went through multiple editions beginning in 1970. Shortly after *The Population Bomb* was published, he and others formed Zero Population Growth (ZPG), which soon had tens of thousands of members and chapters on hundreds of university campuses.

The Ehrlichs never said that population control was the *only* measure needed. In *The Population Bomb* they also advocated increased food production, and in most of their books and articles they argued for improved technology and for reduced consumption in wealthy countries. But they always described population reduction as the top priority. A 1979 article in the journal *Bioscience,* by Paul Ehrlich and frequent collaborator John Holdren, summed up their view:

> It is abundantly clear that in terms of cost, lead time, and imple-mentation on the scale required, technology without population control will be too little and too late . . .
>
> It cannot be emphasized enough that if the population control measures are not initiated immediately and effectively, all the tech-nology man can bring to bear will not fend off the misery to come. Therefore, confronted as we are with limited resources of time and money, we must consider carefully what fraction of our effort should be applied to the cure of the disease itself instead of to the temporary relief of the symptoms. We should ask, for example, how many vasectomies could be performed by a program funded with the 1.8 billion dollars required to build a single nuclear agroindus-trial complex, and what the relative impact on the problem would be in both the short and long terms.[8]

The Closing Circle

Barry Commoner was a biology professor, a socialist, a humanist, and one of the central leaders of the anti–nuclear testing movement in the United States in the 1950s and early 1960s. In 1966 he founded the Center for the Biology of Natural Systems at Washington University in St. Louis, Missouri, which aimed to "adapt our science to the urgent need for understanding the natural biology of the environment and so help to preserve the community of life from extinction at the hand of man."[9]

Commoner strongly disagreed with *The Population Bomb* and said so publicly at a Harvard University teach-in during the first-ever Earth Week in 1970:

> In my opinion, population trends in the U.S. cannot be blamed for the deteriorated condition of the environment . . . Of course, if there

were no people in the country there would be no pollution problem, but the fact of the matter is that there simply has not been a sufficient rise in the U.S. population to account for the enormous increase in pollution levels . . . It is a serious mistake to becloud the pollution issue with the population, for the facts will not support it.[10]

The next day he told a meeting at Brown University, "Pollution begins not in the family bedroom, but in the corporate boardroom."[11]

And in December 1970, during a panel discussion with Paul Ehrlich at a meeting of the American Association for the Advancement of Science: "Saying that none of our pollution problems can be solved without getting at population first is a copout of the worst kind."[12]

Commoner was impressed and inspired by the massive turnout for demonstrations, meetings, and rallies during Earth Week 1970, but he was also disturbed by what he saw as a desire for simplistic explanations and quick fixes. His response was *The Closing Circle: Nature, Man, and Technology*, which he described as "an effort to discover which human acts have broken the circle of life, and why" (*Circle*, 13). Published in October 1971, *The Closing Circle* was by far the most ambitious attempt to date to describe and explain the environmental crisis in the United States.

The Closing Circle included a strong critique of populationism, and its major conclusion directly contradicted the Ehrlichs' views:

Human beings have broken out of the circle of life, driven not by biological need, but by the social organization which they have devised to "conquer" nature: means of gaining wealth that are governed by requirements conflicting with those which govern nature. (*Circle*, 299–300)

After discussing ecology, the ecosphere, and specific examples of major ecological destruction in the United States, Commoner narrowed in on his main concern: why, after millennia in which human beings did little permanent harm to the environment, did major pollution problems either appear for the first time or become very much worse in the years following World War II? Since 1946, Commoner

Profit versus sound energy

"In the last thirty years many thousands of production decisions have been made in the United States. They have determined that automobiles shall be large and sufficiently powerful to travel at a rate of 100 mph; that electricity shall be produced by nuclear power plants; that we shall wear synthetic materials instead of cotton and wool, and wash them in detergent rather than soap; that baseball shall be played on plastic rather than grass; that the beneficent energy of sunlight shall go largely unused.

"In every case, the decision was made according to the 'bottom line'—the expectation of an acceptable profit. More precisely, as we have seen from the behavior of US oil companies, such decisions are based on the marginal difference between existing rates of profit and hoped-for, larger ones.

"It would have been a fantastically improbable statistical accident if most or even a small fraction of these thousands of decisions, made on the basis of a hoped-for marginal increase in profit, happened neatly to fit into the pattern of a rational, thermodynamically sound energy system.

"Such an energy system is a social need, and it is hopeless to expect to build it on the basis of production decisions that yield commodities rather than the solutions to essential tasks; that produce goods which are maximally profitable rather than maximally useful; that accept as their final test private profit rather than social value.

"Thus, the energy crisis and the web of interrelated problems confront us with the need to explore the possibility of creating a production system that is consciously intended to serve social needs and that judges the value of its products by their use, and an economic system that is committed to these purposes. At least in principle, such a system is socialism."

—Barry Commoner, *The Poverty of Power*, 1976

said, population had increased 42 percent, and the US standard of living had not risen much, but pollutants had increased by 200 to 2,000 percent and more. Clearly "more people consuming more" couldn't explain more than a fraction of the problem.

Commoner's key argument was that the pollution explosion was driven not by increased population but by changed industrial and agricultural production—by radical changes in the way things were made and grown, in the raw materials used, and in the products themselves. Those changes were adopted by industry during and after World War II because the new technologies were more profitable than the old ones.

> The crucial link between pollution and profits appears to be modern technology, which is both the main source of recent increases in productivity—and therefore of profits—and of recent assaults on the environment. Driven by an inherent tendency to maximize profits, modern private enterprise has seized upon those massive technological innovations that promise to gratify this need, usually unaware that these same innovations are often also instruments of environmental destruction. (*Circle*, 267–68)

That passage illustrates the most important feature of Commoner's analysis: rather than treating population, technology, and affluence as independent forces, he viewed them as driven by and interacting with wider social processes. A noteworthy example was his discussion of the dynamic factors that underlie what demographers call the "demographic transition"—the process by which population growth in many countries had first accelerated and then leveled off in the nineteenth and twentieth centuries.

> It is sometimes supposed that this self-accelerating interaction between the increase in wealth and technological competence and population growth is bound to set off an explosive "population bomb" unless deliberate steps are taken to control birth rates. In fact, there is strong evidence that the process itself sets up a counterforce that slows population growth considerably. (*Circle*, 118)

The new wealth generated by the agricultural and industrial revolutions of the eighteenth century caused the death rate to fall and population to rise. But as living standards increased further, the birth rate fell and population growth slowed. Child labor was abolished so

children were no longer economic assets. Improved pensions and social services meant that parents didn't need to depend on their children's support in their old age.

> The natural result was a reduced birth rate, which occurred even
> without the benefit of modern methods of contraception. Thus, al-
> though population growth is an inherent feature of the progressive
> development of productive activities, it tends to be limited by the
> same force that stimulates it—the accumulation of social wealth
> and resources. (*Circle*, 119)

But there was nothing inevitable about this process. Population
growth in many third world countries remained high because the
death rate had fallen but the birth rate hadn't followed suit: the demographic transition had been "grossly affected by certain new de-
velopments" (*Circle*, 119).

The wealth produced in the colonies was sent to Europe, which
made possible the increased living standards that led to lower birth rates
but prevented the colonies from going through the same process—
Commoner called this "a kind of demographic parasitism."

Then, after World War II, industry used modern technology to
"replace natural products with synthetic ones," a trend that "exacer-
bated ecological stresses in the advanced countries and has hindered
the efforts of developing nations to meet the needs of their growing
populations" (*Circle*, 246).

In short, poverty was the *cause* of rapid population growth in the
twentieth century, not an effect—and poverty itself was the result of
centuries of colonialist plunder.

Pressuring poor countries into reducing their birth rates without
the improved living standards that enable lower death rates and infant
mortality, Commoner wrote, is a "gigantic and questionable experiment."

> If one's moral convictions and political views regard [that] course
> as dictatorial and corrosive of human values, then one can adopt
> the view that population growth in the developing nations of the
> world ought to be brought into balance by the same means that

have already succeeded elsewhere—improvement of living conditions, urgent efforts to reduce mortality, social security measures, and the resultant effects on desired family size, together with personal, voluntary contraceptive practice. It is this view with which I wish to associate myself. (*Circle*, 242)

The measures Commoner advocated amounted to total restructuring or replacement of the production systems and institutions that had caused the crisis—"something like one half of the postwar productive enterprises would need to be replaced by ecologically sounder ones"—combined with an intensive program to restore damaged ecosystems. He had no illusions that this could be done quickly or cheaply: "Perhaps the simplest way to summarize all this is that most of the nation's resources for capital investment would need to be engaged in the task of ecological reconstruction for at least a generation" (*Circle*, 285).

Head to head

Within weeks of the publication of *The Closing Circle*, Paul Ehrlich and John Holdren were privately circulating a long critique that described Commoner's book as "inexplicably inconsistent and dangerously misleading." An edited version of their critique and an equally long response from Commoner were published in May 1972 in the influential *Bulletin of the Atomic Scientists*.[13]

Large parts of both articles were taken up with "somewhat tedious arguments" (as Ehrlich and Holdren accurately wrote) about mathematics and definitions, along with cheap shots about who had or had not published their research in peer-reviewed journals. In several cases Ehrlich and Holdren identified supposed errors and Commoner replied by pointing out that he had actually said the opposite of what they accused him of saying.

Nevertheless, the exchange reveals two profound differences between the two sides.

1. *Are people always harmful?* Because Commoner's book focused on the rapid acceleration of pollution in the United States after World War II, Ehrlich and Holdren accused him of ignoring the fact that "serious ecological harm has accompanied man's activities ever since the agricultural revolution some 10,000 years ago." They devoted a substantial part of their article to descriptions of earlier environmental disasters.

That was a peculiar criticism: no one actually believed that Commoner was unaware of that history. What Ehrlich and Holdren were really saying was that Commoner didn't agree that *people are always harmful to the environment.* Paul and Anne Ehrlich expressed that view explicitly in a textbook that was also published in 1972: "Each human individual, in the course of obtaining the requisites of existence, has a net negative impact on his environment."[14]

If people are always harmful to the environment, then the only way to save the earth is to reduce the number of people to a point where the damage is less than the maximum the environment can handle. When it comes to population, bigger is always worse.

Commoner argued that humans could change their ways, could realize that "ecological considerations must guide economic and political ones," and could build a new society on that basis. Ehrlich and Holdren didn't agree.

2. *Is the crisis biological or social?* In their critique, Ehrlich and Holdren said not one word about Commoner's clear statement that his goal was to consider "the links between the environmental crisis and the social systems of which it is a part," or about his extensive discussion of the profit-driven system of production that he saw as ultimately responsible for environmental destruction, or about his conclusion that "an economic system which is fundamentally based on private transactions rather than social ones is no longer appropriate."

As pro-capitalist liberals, Ehrlich and Holdren undoubtedly disagreed with Commoner on all of those points, so their failure to comment is significant. By completely ignoring the social and economic framework of Commoner's work, they showed that they viewed such issues as unimportant or irrelevant.

This was fundamental. For Ehrlich and Holdren, the causes of the environmental crisis were *biological and technical,* and so were the solutions. For Commoner, the environmental crisis was rooted in an *economic and social* system that was profoundly anti-ecological.

> Everywhere in the world there is evidence of a deep-seated failure in the effort to use the competence, the wealth, the power at human disposal for the maximum good of human beings. The environmental crisis is a major example of this failure. For we are in an environmental crisis because the means by which we use the ecosphere to produce wealth are destructive of the ecosphere itself. The present system of production is self-destructive; the present course of human civilization is suicidal. (*Circle*, 294–95)

For Ehrlich and Holdren, the problem was growth as such: too much production was overwhelming the ecosphere. The solution was to reduce population so that less production would be needed.

For Commoner, the system of production itself was the problem. So long as it remained in place, ecological crises were inevitable.

◇

Paul and Anne Ehrlich made two explicit predictions in 1968, on the first page of *The Population Bomb.*

1. *Birth rates would not fall unless governments instituted population control,* which they defined as "conscious regulation of the numbers of human beings."

2. *Food production could not possibly expand fast enough to feed everyone,* so massive famines were inevitable in the immediate future. "The battle to feed all of humanity is over ... At this late date nothing can prevent a substantial increase in the death rate."

They were wrong on both counts.

1. *Birth rates fell without population control.* In most developed

countries, birth rates were already falling when *The Population Bomb* was published. The US rate dropped to replacement level (2.1 births per woman) in 1972, continued down to 1.7 by mid-decade, and stayed there through the 1980s. Birth rates in many countries were in decline by the 1980s.

2. *Food production increased dramatically.* Between 1960 and 2000, while the world's population doubled, food production increased by about two and a half times.[15] In the same period, the global death rate (annual deaths per thousand people), which the Ehrlichs said was bound for a "substantial increase," fell from 15.5 to 8.6.[16]

You might think that the Ehrlichs would have analyzed and corrected their mistakes, but you'd be wrong. During the 1970s they published two more editions of *The Population Bomb*, each time pushing the dates for the predicted food catastrophe further into the future but never revising their underlying assumptions. As late as 1990, in *The Population Explosion*, they wrote as though they had been fully vindicated:

> In 1968, *The Population Bomb* warned of impending disaster if the population explosion was not brought under control. Then the fuse was burning; now the population bomb has detonated . . . hunger is rife and the prospects of famine and plague ever more imminent . . .
> *A largely prospective disaster has turned into the real thing.*[17]

In a footnote, the Ehrlichs claimed that their 1968 book didn't make predictions—it only offered possible scenarios. But only one chapter of *The Population Bomb* contained scenarios—the rest of it said that population growth would *definitely* outrun food production and that nothing could be done to avoid a huge increase in the death rate.

For more than four decades they have displayed a remarkable ability to shift ground, maintaining, denying, or minimizing their past errors and adopting new justifications for populationism. That strategy has worked: even today it is rare to read an article or book on population that doesn't mention or quote them. Paul Ehrlich has received at least twelve major medals and awards for his work, and he and Anne have published eight more books and innumerable articles on population-related topics.

In stark contrast, Commoner's radical social-ecological critique of capitalism was cast aside and has been virtually forgotten. The environmental movement that he hoped would challenge capitalism instead became more conservative. By the end of the seventies, protests were out of favor and lobbying was in. Instead of changing the system, the major nongovernmental organizations (NGOs) became part of it, and the population explanation became accepted wisdom among liberal greens.

2: Varieties of Populationism Today

The "population problem" has a Phoenix-like existence: it rises from the ashes at least every generation and sometimes every decade or so. The prophecies are usually the same—namely, that human beings are populating the earth in "unprecedented numbers" and "devouring" its resources like a locust plague.
—Murray Bookchin[1]

I n 1968 and through the 1970s, populationism was defined by two books—*The Population Bomb* by the Ehrlichs and *The Limits to Growth*, sponsored by the Club of Rome.

Today there is no such source, no single article, book, or group that all or even most populationists agree with. Populationism, the social ideology that attributes social ills to the number of humans, takes many forms, and its advocates don't necessarily agree with each other on all questions.

This poses difficulties for critics: in our experience almost any criticism of populationist thought prompts someone to reply that we have misrepresented *real* populationism.

The following brief profiles will provide some idea of the range of views involved.

"Let the people just starve"

As we saw in chapter 1, a key element of populationist ideology is the view that people are always harmful to the environment, so the best way to reduce environmental damage is to reduce the number of people.

Some prominent members and founders of the direct action group Earth First expressed an extreme form of that view in the mid-1980s. They adopted a philosophy known variously as biocentrism, ecocentrism, or deep ecology, holding that "all human decisions should consider Earth first, humankind second"—and they interpreted that credo in deeply reactionary terms.

In 1983, Dave Foreman, the de facto leader of Earth First, argued for denying welfare and food stamps to anyone with more than two children and stopping all immigration to the United States. Even these measures would probably be insufficient, he wrote: "What is really needed is to 1) Give every woman the right to one child. 2) Offer a $20,000 payment to anyone willing to be sterilized without producing any children. 3) Make sterilization mandatory for all women and men after they have parented one child."[2]

Third world people wouldn't be offered those options. In a 1986 interview published in the Australian magazine *Simply Living*, Foreman argued that "the worst thing we could do in Ethiopia is to give aid—the best thing would be to just let nature seek its own balance, to let the people just starve there."

In the same interview he expanded on his argument for keeping immigrants out of the United States:

> Letting the USA be an overflow valve for problems in Latin America is not solving a thing. It's just putting more pressure on the resources we have in the USA. It is just causing more destruction of our wilderness, more poisoning of water and air, and it isn't helping the problems in Latin America.[3]

Even more appalling, in 1987 another Earth First leader, Christopher Manes, using the very appropriate pseudonym "Miss Ann Thropy," wrote in the group's newsletter:

> If radical environmentalists were to invent a disease to bring human population back to ecological sanity, it would probably be some-

thing like AIDS . . . As radical environmentalists, we can see AIDS not as a problem, but a necessary solution . . . To paraphrase Voltaire: if the AIDS epidemic didn't exist, radical environmentalists would have to invent one.[4]

By the end of the 1980s, a majority of Earth First members had rejected such views, and Dave Foreman had left the organization he founded, complaining of "pressure and infiltration from the class-struggle/social-justice left" and "the abandonment of biocentrism in favor of humanism."[5]

The views expressed by Foreman, Manes, and others in the 1980s are outside the populationist mainstream, but they illustrate its anti-human possibilities, and they show clearly that "radical environmentalists" are not necessarily progressive.

PJP: "A progressive, feminist approach"

In a very different part of the populationist spectrum is the Population Justice Project, a US group founded in 2007. The PJP's core views are expressed in two sentences in an "advocacy guide" that it published jointly with Population Action International. "Many environmental problems will be easier to address if world population peaks at 8 billion rather than 11 billion. The good news: there is already a global consensus on how to slow population growth, with programs that improve human wellbeing at very little cost."

We could call this *populationism lite.* They don't propose reducing population, merely slowing its growth. And they don't say this will solve problems—it will just make other problems easier to solve.

Noting that the UN estimates world population will peak after 2050 but that the size of the peak isn't certain yet, they say:

> The impact of population growth on the environment is mediated by consumption, technology, urbanization and other factors. Still, slower population growth could reduce pressure on natural systems that are already over-taxed, and research shows that a host of

environmental problems—including the growth of greenhouse gases, water scarcity, and biodiversity loss—would be easier to address if world population peaks around 8 billion, rather than 11 billion.

How is this to be achieved? PJP and PAI say the best way is to ensure that people have choices, by making contraception and reproductive health services available to all, by providing education and employment, especially for women, and by eliminating gender and economic inequities. They state firmly that they do not advocate "'population control' measures that could become coercive."

Their program is based on what is called the Cairo Consensus—the action plan approved by 179 countries at the UN International Conference on Development and Population in Cairo in 1994. Fifteen years after that agreement, the rich countries have provided less than a quarter of the funding they promised. The Population Justice Project's main goal is to convince politicians in Washington to cough up one billion dollars a year toward keeping the promises that the United States made in Cairo.

Family planning programs, the PAI/PJP advocacy guide says, "are relatively inexpensive, especially when compared to many environmental mitigation efforts."[6]

PJP focuses on the world's poorest women, the 200 million women it says don't have access to birth control today. But if the goal is to reduce emissions by slowing population growth, wouldn't it make more sense to reduce population in rich countries, where each avoided birth would presumably have a greater effect than dozens in the global South?

PJP founder and director Laurie Mazur poses that question herself in her book *A Pivotal Moment*. Her answer:

> The answer lies in the future. The developing countries are where the lion's share of population growth will occur, and they are also where development must occur for half of humanity to escape from grinding poverty. The affluent countries can reduce emissions by reducing the vast amounts of waste in our systems of production and consumption. But the developing countries are not likely to

The Cairo Consensus

The history of modern populationism falls into two periods: before and after the UN International Conference on Population and Development (ICPD) in Cairo in 1994. At that meeting, an unlikely alliance between populationists and liberal feminists, supported by the Clinton administration, won approval for a policy that they presented as the only alternative to the anti-woman policies of the Vatican and other conservative governments.

The Cairo Consensus was a significant defeat for "right to life" forces. Although little of the promised funding for women's health programs actually materialized, the meeting gave women's rights activists in the third world a strong and credible program that conservative governments couldn't easily dismiss. In particular, Cairo's resolutions have aided the fight against anti-abortion laws and for sexual rights.

But the meeting also strengthened the populationists, who came out of it with new credibility and a new way of arguing their case. In Cairo, populationists learned to say "population stabilization" or "demographic transition" instead of "population control," and to always include a sentence opposing coercive programs—but none of those purely verbal shifts changed their underlying assumption that the world's major problems were caused by poor women having too many babies.

See chapter 8 for more on the Cairo Consensus.

raise their standards of living without more intensive use of resources and higher emissions.[7]

Mazur says she advocates "a progressive, feminist approach," and she describes herself as the voice of reason in the "polarized debate" between population extremists like Paul Ehrlich on one side and left-wing feminists like Betsy Hartmann, whom she labels "population deniers," on the other. She calls for "a new conversation about population and the environment," with a goal of "slowing population growth" but doing so without coercion, respecting women's need for reproductive health services and right to make their own choices.[8]

Optimum Population Trust:
"Reduce the number of climate changers"

UK-based Optimum Population Trust (OPT) describes itself as "the leading environmental charity and think tank in the UK concerned with the impact of population growth on the environment."[9]

Founded in 1991, it has an impressive list of patrons, including environmentalists James Lovelock, Paul Ehrlich, and Norman Myers, naturalists Jane Goodall and David Attenborough, former chair of the government's Sustainability Commission Jonathon Porritt, the former UK representative on the UN Security Council, and others. Clearly, OPT is a very well-connected organization.

OPT's view of the issues is summarized on its website:

> *What's the population problem?* Dangerously rapid climate change and rising food, water and fuel scarcity are already threatening human populations. And many other species, on a finite planet. Yet by 2050 world population is expected to grow by another 2.3 billion from today's 6.8 billion—unless urgent action is taken.
>
> *What's the population solution?* GLOBALLY: reduce birth rates. NATIONALLY: reduce or keep birth rates low and/or balance migration to prevent population increase. All countries need environmentally sustainable population policies to underpin other green policies. PERSONALLY: have fewer children and work a few more years before retiring.[10]

OPT literature puts particular stress on environmental issues, especially climate change: "The need to curb man-made climate change is alone a compelling reason for population stabilization and reduction—to reduce climate impacts it helps to reduce the number of climate changers."[11]

OPT says world population growth should be limited to about 1 billion additional people by 2050, compared to the 2.3 billion forecast by the UN. "If the world's mothers reduce the number of children they have, there could be 1.2 billion fewer climate changers in 2050 than projected."

The most effective *personal* climate change strategy is limiting the number of children one has. The most effective *national* and *global* climate change strategy is limiting the size of the population. Population limitation should therefore be seen as the most cost-effective carbon *offsetting strategy* available to individuals and nations—a strategy that applies with even more force to developed nations such as the UK because of their higher consumption levels.[12]

Substantial changes in birth rates in the third world would be achieved by "education and women's empowerment in the area of reproductive and sexual health and the removal of all obstacles to birth control," with special emphasis on developing and delivering "long-acting methods such as injections, intrauterine devices and implants."[13]

Within the UK, OPT wants better birth control education, but its main proposal for reducing population growth is severe immigration restrictions. "As the main force driving current population growth, immigration feeds through into rising greenhouse gas emissions; more crowding, congestion, development; increased pressure on water and energy supplies, farmland and green space."[14]

An article in the *Optimum Population Trust Journal*, cowritten by the journal's editor, argues that all industrialized countries need to reduce immigration. Citing a table that shows immigration as the main cause of rising population in the UK, Italy, the United States, Canada, and Australia, the authors write:

> The degree to which net immigration is preventing the developed nations from achieving a much needed reduction in population is apparent from the table. In all cases, the chief cause is net immigration . . . The need to have balanced immigration can hardly be exaggerated, because few of the less developed nations are showing any inclination to achieve population levels that will be sustainable when fossil fuels become scarce, yet several developed nations have success within their grasp . . . provided only they do not allow their efforts to be overwhelmed by net immigration.[15]

OPT wants the UK government to impose a "zero net migration" policy, under which the number of immigrants permitted to enter each year would be no more than the number of people who emigrate.

Lovelock: "Defend climate oases"

James Lovelock is a patron of Optimum Population Trust, so one might assume that he agrees with its analysis and solutions—but in his books he puts forward a far more extreme position. Lovelock says that we are past the point of no return, that a climate and population catastrophe is inevitable in this century, so our focus should be on preserving islands of civilization in a ruined world, using military force to fend off climate refugees.

Lovelock, who worked with NASA in the 1960s and has made many important contributions to earth science, is best-known for the *Gaia hypothesis*, which speculates that life regulates conditions on earth to keep the physical environment suitable for life to continue. At times Lovelock describes Gaia in ways that imply that earth is a living or even intelligent being.

In Lovelock's view, Gaia now faces a "plague of people," and "we are all the demons." Environmentalists must abandon their concern for people—they should "think again and see that their primary obligation is to the living Earth. Humankind comes second."[16]

With that perspective, it isn't surprising that he can calmly suggest that "we would be wise to aim at a stabilized population of about half to one billion,"[17] a goal that would require the elimination of between 85 and 92 percent of the people in the world today.

Lovelock favors nuclear power, geoengineering, and carbon capture as ways to delay the inevitable catastrophe, but "our greatest efforts should go into adaptation, to preparing those parts of the Earth least likely to be affected by adverse climate change as the safe haven for a civilized humanity."[18]

One such haven—*surprise!*—will be Lovelock's home country. He calls on UK politicians to "make decisions based on our national interest . . . We should not wait for international agreement or instruction. In our small country we have to act now as if we were about to be attacked by a powerful enemy. We have first to make sure our defenses against climate change are in place before the attack begins."[19]

And not just defenses against climate change—he urges more spending on armed forces, especially the navy, to keep desperate people from sharing Britain's wealth.

> Soon we face the appalling question of whom we can let aboard the lifeboats. And whom must we reject? There will be no ducking this question for before long there will be a great clamor from climate refugees seeking a safe haven in those few parts where the climate is tolerable and food is available. Make no mistake, the lifeboat simile is apt; the same problem has faced the shipwrecked: a lifeboat will sink or become impossible to sail if too laden. The old rules I grew up with were women and children first and the captain goes down with his ship. We will need a set of rules for climate oases.[20]

Jeffrey Sachs: "High fertility rates are deleterious to development"

As we saw above in the discussion of PJP, many populationists claim that slowing population in poor countries will reduce *future* greenhouse gas emissions, even though those countries have very low emission rates today. The argument is that the economies in those countries will inevitably grow, causing their per capita emissions to grow—so if there are fewer people, total emissions will be lower.

Ironically, another group of populationists, liberal specialists in global economic development, argue the opposite, that reducing population growth will cause faster and more extensive economic growth. If that's true, then slowing population growth could actually *increase* total emissions.

A case in point is Jeffrey D. Sachs, director of the Earth Institute at Columbia University and, according to *Time* magazine, one of the "100 Most Influential People in the World." In his best-selling 2008 book *Common Wealth: Economics for a Crowded Planet*, Sachs argues: "High fertility rates are deleterious to long-term development."[21] He cites a 2004 study that found a strong correlation between total fertility rate (TFR—the average number of children born to each woman) and economic growth:

> The TFR is shown to have a strong, statistically significant negative effect on economic growth. Consider two countries that are identical in all respects except that one has a fertility rate of 6 and the other a fertility rate of 2 . . . The high-fertility country will have per capita income growth that is 1.3 percentage points per year lower than the growth of the low-fertility country. That's a whopping negative effect of high fertility.[22]

Since "the rapid growth of populations in the poorest countries hinders economic development,"

> the world should embrace a set of policies to help stabilize the global population, through voluntary choices, at a population of roughly eight billion people, rather than the current trajectory, which is likely to take us to nine billion or more by 2050. This may seem like a modest difference, but the consequences would be large, especially since the population control would come mainly in the world's poorest places.[23]

That is, of course, the same goal recommended by PJP and OPT—but they expect very different results to follow.

In 2008, the United Nations projected that in 2050 there could be as many as 10.46 billion people or as few as 7.96 billion. PJP and OPT assumed that per capita emissions would be the same in either case, so the lower figure would mean less global warming. But if Sachs is correct, a smaller population would mean more economic growth and thus (according to populationist logic) *higher* per capita emissions.

Both sides may be wrong about the relationship between population growth and economic growth, but it's hard to see how they can both be right.

SPA: "Reduce population or face chaos"

Sustainable Population Australia (SPA) was founded in 1988 by people who believed that "the major environmental groups were failing to address the issue of population numbers." Although SPA says it is "primarily an environmental organization," five of the six objectives set out in its constitution involve lowering population.[24]

In 2007, in "Global Population Reduction: A 21st Century Strategy to Avoid Human Suffering and Environmental Devastation,"[25] SPA warned: "Without a planned humane contraction, this century will see social chaos and human suffering on an unprecedented scale." If population reduction schemes are not implemented, population reduction will be imposed on us: "So the world faces a stark choice: either act now to reduce population or do nothing and allow this population reduction to be inflicted upon us either directly through famine or indirectly through disease or civil and regional wars motivated by resource scarcity."

SPA supports the introduction of renewable energy and increased foreign aid and has argued that wasteful consumption in the industrialized countries must be reduced. But it insists any gains from such measures will be wiped out if population isn't reduced. Here they support that position by referring the often-used IPAT formula (Impact equals Population times Affluence times Technology), which we will discuss in chapter 3.

> Savings made by implementing renewable technologies (lowering T) and reducing unnecessary affluence (lowering A) would soon be offset by consumption growth due to the rate at which the population (P) continues to expand. The most enduring way to lower total human environmental impact (I) is therefore to lower the value of the population size.

SPA advocates "policies that will initially lead to stabilization of Australia's population by encouraging near replacement fertility rates and low immigration rates."[26] Since Australia's fertility rate of 1.78 is already well below replacement level, SPA focuses on immigration, which it says is responsible for 48 percent of the country's annual population growth. "Ultimately," the SPA Population Policy says, "our immigration program should be no larger than emigration."[27] SPA has also proposed a one-child policy for Australian families, backed by financial penalties.[28]

SPA isn't the only Australian environmental group that supports the "too many people" argument. The Australian Conservation Foundation has said Australia's population growth is a key threat to biodiversity. It calls for Australia's population to be stabilized at no more than 27 million to 30 million people by 2050 (up from about 22 million today).[29] It urges the Australian government "to reduce net migration to a level that is consistent with a goal of environmental sustainability."[30]

◇

As these examples show, populationists hold widely varying views on how serious the overpopulation problem is and on what should be done to solve it. Some believe that a global population catastrophe is inevitable, while others view a modest reduction in birth rates as a way to ease the path to social progress. They all agree, however, that "too many people" is a primary cause of environmental destruction and that reducing human numbers will make things better. As we'll see, that judgment fails on many counts.

3: Dissecting Those "Overpopulation" Numbers

Numbers suggest, constrain, and refute; they do not, by themselves, specify the content of scientific theories. Theories are built upon the interpretation of numbers, and interpreters are often trapped by their own rhetoric. They believe in their own objectivity, and fail to discern the prejudice that leads them to one interpretation among many consistent with their numbers.
— Stephen Jay Gould[1]

Ever since 1798, when the Reverend Malthus claimed that population increases exponentially (2, 4, 8, 16 . . .) while the food supply only grows arithmetically (2, 3, 4, 5 . . .), the populationist argument has depended on numbers. It's rare to read a populationist article, leaflet, or website that doesn't include statements such as these:

- *Optimum Population Trust (OPT):* "Human numbers are still exploding. Our numbers reached 6.8 billion in 2009, and are expected to climb to 9.2 billion in 2050—by more than a third in barely 40 years . . . Every week some 1.6 million extra people are being added to the planet— a sizeable city—with nearly 10,000 arriving each hour . . . On a planet inhabited by 2.5 billion people in 1950—within the lifetimes of many alive today—there are now more than double this number."[2]
- *Global Population Speak Out:* "It took virtually all of human history for our numbers to reach 1 billion in the

1800s. It took only about a century to add the second
billion in 1930. We added the third billion in just 30
years and the fourth in only 15 years. We are now at 6.7
billion with projections of over 2 billion more to come
in the next 40 years. The size and growth of the human
population is linked closely to nearly all forms of environmental degradation we see today."[3]

- *William N. Ryerson, president of the Population Institute*:
  "The world's population is growing by about 80 million
  people annually—the equivalent of adding a new Egypt
  every year. The total population is approaching 7 billion,
  seven times what it was in 1800. Every day approximately 156,000 people die, but 381,000 are born—a net
  daily growth of 225,000 human beings."[4]

- *All Party Parliamentary Group on Population* [UK]: "In
  2005, global population increased by 76 million more
  births than deaths. India has one million more births
  than deaths every three weeks. By 2050, Uganda is projected to grow from 27 million to 130 million; Niger
  from 14 to 50 million; Iraq from 29 to 64 million; and
  Afghanistan from 31 to 82 million. Asia will add 500
  million people in a single decade from 2005."[5]

Such numbers are impressive, but numbers by themselves don't
prove anything, and it is entirely possible to draw inaccurate conclusions from accurate statistics. In this chapter we look at the frequent
misuse (deliberate or not) of numbers and statistics by advocates of
the "too many people" explanation of environmental destruction.

Correlation versus causation

At some point in every introductory statistics course, the instructor
tells students about a European city where increases in the stork pop-

ulation were supposedly matched by increases in the number of new babies. The point being made is that *correlation isn't causation*—storks don't bring babies, no matter what the numbers seem to imply. Stephen Jay Gould explained the issue this way:

> The vast majority of correlations in our world are, without doubt, noncausal. Anything that has been increasing steadily during the past few years will be strongly correlated with the distance between the earth and Halley's comet (which has also been increasing of late)—but even the most dedicated astrologer would not discern causality in most of these relationships. The invalid assumption that correlation implies cause is probably among the two or three most serious and common errors of human reasoning.[6]

Unfortunately, the vital *correlation-or-causation* distinction is rarely observed in arguments that claim to show population growth drives environmental destruction.

No one doubts that the world's population has soared since the Industrial Revolution began in the late 1700s. After millennia in which the number of people grew very slowly, our numbers increased sevenfold in two hundred years, and the growth hasn't stopped. For almost all of human history there were fewer than one billion human beings living on earth: by 2050 there will likely be over nine billion.

And no one doubts that since World War II, economic activity, resource use, and pollution of all forms have also grown at unprecedented rates. "Many human activities reached take-off points sometime in the 20th century and have accelerated sharply towards the end of the century. The last 50 years have without doubt seen the most rapid transformation of the human relationship with the natural world in the history of humankind."[7]

Our debate with populationists is not about the raw numbers. It is about *what the numbers mean*. What are the causes of the environmental crisis, and what does that tell us about the solutions?

People, cars, and population

In his trailblazing book *The Environment: From Surplus to Scarcity*, environmental sociologist Alan Schnaiberg described populationist theory as a "two accounts" model—one set of numbers (e.g., population) is presented as the explanation of another set of numbers (e.g., pollution). The following is based on his real-world illustration of problems with that approach.

Between 1960 and 1970, US population increased by 23.8 million, and private automobile ownership increased by 21.8 million. A populationist model would conclude that more people equaled more cars.

But there is a major logical flaw in that reasoning. Population growth between 1960 and 1970 was almost entirely made up of children born in that decade, none of whom were old enough to buy cars. If population growth is the primary cause, it must involve people born before 1954.

So perhaps we should instead compare the number of cars to the number of households, or families. Did the growth in new households after World War II increase the number of cars?

What cars-per-household figures show is that "the percentage of households with one car actually declines from 62.1 percent to 50.3 percent .... [but] the percentage with two or more cars rose from 13.9 percent to 29.3 percent." So the increase in cars was caused

Populationists isolate one number—population size or growth—and claim it is the underlying cause for all the rest. Population increased; economic activity expanded and environmental degradation increased; so population must have caused the expansion and degradation.

That only shows *correlation*, not *causation*.

Sometimes correlation does indicate causation. For example, the average global temperature and the amount of carbon dioxide in the atmosphere have risen together for decades. Scientists know exactly how an increase in atmospheric CO_2 *causes* temperatures to rise. Since the greenhouse effect is one of the most widely accepted conclusions of modern atmospheric science, it is reasonable—indeed completely logical—to conclude that the increase in CO_2 is causing global warming.

People, Cars, and Population (continued)

not by more people or more families, but by some families buying more than one car. More detailed studies show that families with no car tended to be older, poorer, and urban, while those with two cars tended to be middle aged, better off, and suburban or rural.

Each of these pieces of information changes our sense of how population growth relates to automobile use. Each has different implications for solutions to automobile-related environmental problems.

It is likely, Schnaiberg said, that the rising number of cars was caused not by population growth but instead by the rising number of women who took jobs outside the home in the 1960s. Two-job families that didn't live in large cities with good public transit would often require two cars. "In this simple illustration our evaluation has changed from an initial estimation that up to two-thirds of the growth in autos is due to very recent population growth, to a decision that absolutely none of it can be so attributed . . . . This example illustrates some of the pitfalls of thinking in nonsocial ways about social systems of production and consumption."

To reduce the number of automobiles on the roads, "we need to understand the social system basis of such consumption."

But the fact that global emissions and global population have both increased doesn't, by itself, show that population growth causes emissions growth. The apparent relationship could be a coincidence, or both trends could be the result of a third cause, or the correlation could be an illusion, a result of the way the numbers are presented. (The box above illustrates how correlation can be misleading when one is considering an issue closely related to emissions.)

As Karl Marx wrote 150 years ago, "population" is an abstraction, not a real thing.

> It seems to be correct to begin with the real and the concrete, with the real precondition, thus to begin, in economics, with e.g. the population, which is the foundation and the subject of the entire social act of production. However, on closer examination this

proves false. The population is an abstraction if I leave out, for example, the classes of which it is composed.[8]

That is a profound insight, one that activists who are concerned
about the complex relationship between humanity and the world
we live in must understand. "Population" is just a number, one that
can conceal far more than it reveals. Population statistics are useful
only if we understand how they are determined, what they include
and leave out, and what their strengths and limitations are for any
given purpose.

To determine whether population growth is causing climate
change, we need to dissect the big numbers and examine the real connections and relationships.

Population where?

To begin to explain the relationship between population and climate
change, it's useful to look at differences between rich and poor countries. In 2009, Dr. David Satterthwaite of the International Institute
for Environment and Development did just that—and his findings
exploded the myth that population growth is a major driver of climate change.[9]

His study shows that between 1980 and 2005:

- Sub-Saharan Africa had 18.5 percent of the world's
  population growth and just 2.4 percent of the growth in
  carbon dioxide emissions.
- The United States had 3.4 percent of the world's population growth and 12.6 percent of the growth in carbon
  dioxide emissions.
- China had 15.3 percent of the world's population growth
  and 44.5 percent of the growth in carbon dioxide emissions. Population growth rates in China have fallen very

rapidly while greenhouse gas emissions have increased.

- Low-income nations had 52.1 percent of the world's population growth and 12.8 percent of the growth in carbon dioxide emissions.

- High-income nations had 7 percent of the world's population growth and 29 percent of the growth in carbon dioxide emissions.

- Most of the nations with the highest population growth rates had low growth rates for carbon dioxide emissions, while many of the nations with the lowest population growth rates had high growth rates for carbon dioxide emissions.[10]

In short, the correlation between emissions growth and population growth, a connection that seems obvious when we consider only global figures, turns out to be an illusion when we look at the numbers country by country. Almost all of the population growth is occurring in countries with low emissions; almost all of the emissions are produced in countries with little or no population growth. This leads to three inescapable conclusions.

1. *CO_2 emissions are a problem of rich countries, not poor ones.* The nineteen countries in the G20 produced more than 22,500 million tonnes of CO_2 in 2006. That's 78 percent of the worldwide total—nearly four times as much as all other countries combined. It is more than 770 times as much CO_2 as produced by the nineteen lowest-emitting countries. Per capita CO_2 emissions in the United States are 98 times greater than in Gambia, 132 times greater than in Madagascar, 197 times greater than in Mozambique, and 400 times greater than in Mali or Burkina Faso.[11]

Note that these figures significantly understate the case, because some major emission sources that are concentrated in rich countries, such as military activity and international air travel, are not included in officially reported figures.

So the idea that providing the means for family planning to those who don't have access will somehow slow global warming makes no sense. With few exceptions, birth control has long been widely available in the countries that are doing the most to destroy the earth's climate.

2. *There is no correspondence between emissions and population density.* The high-emitting G20 includes countries such as India, Japan, and South Korea, which are home to high numbers of people per square kilometer—but it also includes countries with very low population density, such as Australia, Canada, and Russia.

Exactly the same is true of the lowest-emission countries, which include some with high population density (Rwanda, Burundi) and some with low population density (Niger, Chad).

So it is clearly possible to have low population density with high emissions, or high population density with low emissions.

It's also worth noting that almost all of the low-emission countries have far fewer people per square kilometer than the United Kingdom, where Optimum Population Trust promotes third world birth control as a means of slowing global warming.

3. *Population growth rates do not correspond to CO_2 emissions.* In fact, there's a negative correlation. Broadly speaking, the countries with the highest emissions are those whose population is growing most slowly or even declining, while the countries with the lowest emissions have the highest population growth rates.

In fact, in most G20 countries the birth rate is at or below replacement level. According to some estimates, by the end of this century the population of Italy (excluding immigration) will fall by 86 percent, Spain will decline 85 percent, Germany 83 percent, and Greece 74 percent.[12]

Only three G20 countries (Saudi Arabia, South Africa, and India) have fertility rates that are clearly above replacement level, and even they are growing far more slowly than the lowest-emitting countries.

If we were to adopt the usual populationist *correlation equals causation* stance, we'd have to conclude that high emissions cause low population growth or that high population growth causes low emissions. Of course that's absurd: both emissions levels and population growth are shaped by other social and economic causes.

This shows that there is something seriously wrong with the argument that more people equals more emissions, and something even more wrong with the idea that third world birth control will slow global warming. As environmental writer Fred Pearce says in *Peoplequake*:

> The poorest three billion or so people on the planet (roughly 45 percent of the total) are currently responsible for only 7 per cent of emissions, while the richest 7 per cent (about half a billion people) are responsible for 50 per cent of emissions.
>
> A woman in rural Ethiopia can have ten children and her family will still do less damage, and consume fewer resources, than the family of the average soccer mom in Minnesota or Manchester or Munich. In the unlikely event that her ten children live to adulthood and all have ten children of their own, the entire clan of more than a hundred will still be emitting only about as much carbon dioxide each year as you or me.
>
> So to suggest, as some do, that the real threat to the planet arises from too many children in Ethiopia, or rice-growing Bangladeshis on the Ganges delta, or Quechua alpaca herders in the Andes, or cow-pea farmers on the edge of the Sahara, or chai-wallas in Mumbai, is both preposterous and dangerous.[13]

Problems with per capita

The flip side of populationist misuse of global numbers is the equally frequent misuse of *per capita* numbers to "prove" the harmful environmental impact of individuals. As ecological sociologist Alan Schnaiberg has shown, per capita figures make it remarkably easy to make *any* social problem look like a population problem: just divide the total population into the number of problem events.[14] It's easy to calculate violent crimes per capita, rainstorms per capita, or even Celine Dion concerts per capita—but that simple arithmetical operation doesn't tell you whether changing the number of people will change the number of crimes, storms, or concerts.

The per capita figure looks like a *rate*, an actual measurement of the number of problem events caused by each person—but it is actually a *ratio*, an abstract comparison of two numbers that may or may not be causally connected. You can't get meaningful results using a ratio as if it were a rate, but we constantly see populationists trying to do just that. Pollution divided by population equals per capita pollution—which leads to the circular claim that per capita pollution times population equals total pollution.

Recently, for example, OPT explained why it favors a "population-based climate strategy":

> The most effective national and global climate change strategy is limiting the size of the population . . . A non-existent person has no environmental footprint: the emissions "saving" is instant and total.
>
> Given an 80-year lifespan and annual per capita emissions (2006) of 9.3 tonnes of CO_2 . . . each Briton "foregone"—each addition to the population that does not take place—saves 744 tonnes of CO_2.

The briefing goes on to quantify the lifetime saving from preventing one birth at £30,000—a "nine million percent" return on a 35-pence investment in condoms.[15]

That might be a feeble attempt at humor, but OPT also published what claimed to be a serious study "proving" that birth control is the most cost-effective way to reduce carbon emissions. The study offered a forecast of the number of unwanted births that might be eliminated between now and 2050 if modern birth control were universally available—and then multiplied the number of nonpeople by the current per capita emission rates in the countries they wouldn't be born in. The result—thirty-four fewer gigatonnes of CO_2, at a cost of only $7/tonne.[16]

(OPT later added an addendum to this report, saying, "The figure of $7 per tonne of carbon abated by investment in family planning is unreliable, and should not be quoted." Despite the fact that "The true figure worldwide remains unknown," OPT reaffirmed its belief that reducing population would be the most cost-effective way of reducing emissions.)

Canadian ecosocialist Jeff White explained the logical fallacy behind such arguments on the *Climate and Capitalism* website.

> It starts with mathematical sleight-of-hand. Representing a country's total emissions as simply the sum of all the per capita emissions helps to create the false impression that total emissions are a direct function of population.
>
> The fallacy lies in the fact that the total emissions must be known before you can calculate the per capita emissions. First you take the total emissions and divide by total population to get a per capita figure; to then multiply that figure by the total population is merely to reverse the calculation back to the original number you started with—total national emissions! It's these total emissions that are the primary data; per capita figures are derived from the total, not the other way around.
>
> Per capita figures are statistical artifacts that tell us the ratio of a country's total emissions to its population. But they don't tell us about individual contributions to the country's total emissions. For example, if I tell you that Canada's annual per capita emissions are 23 tonnes of CO_2 equivalent, it doesn't tell you how much of that 23 tonnes I, as an average Canadian, am personally responsible for. It includes, for example, "my" per capita shares of the emissions caused by the mining of the tar sands in Alberta, the manufacture of cement in Quebec, and the industrialized livestock production in Ontario—none of which I have any personal control over.
>
> If half the population of Canada suddenly disappeared, my per capita share of emissions, and that of every other remaining Canadian, would increase dramatically overnight, without any change being made in my—or anyone else's—personal levels of carbon consumption. The population fetishists would realize their fondest wish (a dramatic reduction in population levels) while per capita emission levels would soar! What could demonstrate more clearly that per capita statistics tell us nothing about "overpopulation"?[17]

The circular reasoning that White exposed appears again and again in populationist works.

- Lester Brown of the Earth Policy Institute predicts that if the world's population by 2050 matches the UN's "low" projection instead of the "medium" projection, we will reduce our energy needs by the equivalent of 2,792 million tons of oil. He arrives at that improbably precise figure by multiplying the difference between the two population projections by per capita energy use.[18]

- Jeffrey Sachs, director of the Earth Institute, extends that error to the entire economy in his best-selling book *Common Wealth*: "The total magnitude of economic activity is calculated by multiplying the average income per person by the number of people."[19]

- American populationist Edward Hartman tells us: "America's *energy use per capita, i.e., per person,* was relatively unchanged between 1970 and 1990, but *total energy use in America increased 24%* . . . In other words, per capita energy conservation was overwhelmed by an increasing number of people."[20] [emphasis in original]

These authors and many others seem unaware that their conclusions are entirely embedded in their assumptions. They use per capita numbers that are derived from total amounts in order to calculate the same total amounts. In Schnaiberg's words, such calculations are "devoid of any substantive meaning."

The IPAT illusion

The most common misuse of per capita ratios in all of ecology involves IPAT, a formula that the Ehrlichs and John Holdren introduced in the 1970s. It states that environmental impact (I) is the product of three factors:

P: the size of the population

A: the affluence or income per person or consumption level, usually expressed as dollars of gross national product (GNP) per person

T: the technological intensity per unit of economic activity, usually expressed as some form of output (CO_2 emissions, for example) per dollar of GNP

So Impact equals Population times Affluence times Technology.

Usually spelled IPAT and pronounced "eye-pat," this formula is a key element of the accepted wisdom of mainstream environmentalism in general and of its populationist wing in particular. Sooner or later, in any discussion of the relationship between population and the environment, someone will claim that the IPAT formula *proves* that "too many people" is the root cause of environmental degradation, global warming, loss of biodiversity, and a host of other problems.

IPAT says that a large number of people who live in luxury, consuming goods that were created using high-pollution technology, will cause more environmental damage than a small number of people who live in poverty and consume goods created with low-pollution technology. It is often cited as proof that to reduce the human impact on the environment, we must reduce the number of people, consume less, use cleaner technology—or some combination of the three.

But IPAT, like many other calculations based on ratios, is circular. Australian socialist Ben Courtice comments:

> It is almost mathematically meaningless, because A and T simply describe averages, per capita. Taken together, they add up to the average ecological footprint of each unit of population (each person, that is). So the total impact equals the average impact multiplied by the number of people. The mathematics of this is as profound as saying that a number equals half of itself multiplied by two.[21]

In fact, IPAT isn't a formula at all—it is what accountants call an *identity*, an expression that is always true *by definition*. Ehrlich and

Holdren didn't *prove* that impact equals population times affluence times technology—they simply *defined* it that way. Not surprisingly, their definition was based on their opinion that population growth is the ultimate cause, the universal multiplier, of other problems: "If population growth proceeds unabated, the gains of improved technology and stabilized per capita consumption will be erased and averting disaster will be impossible."[22]

IPAT is frequently cited by populationist campaigners, but it is rarely used by actual population scientists, even those who otherwise accept populationist explanations, because it doesn't produce meaningful results.

Geographers William B. Meyer and B. L. Turner point out that while "population" is a clearly defined term, "neither 'affluence' nor 'technology' is associated with a substantial body of social science theory."[23] In other words, no one actually knows how to assign values to two of the four terms in IPAT, a fatal problem for anyone who hopes to measure their effects.

Sociologists Thomas Dietz and Eugene Rosa note that while IPAT has "structured much of the debate about the effects of population, affluence and technology on the environment, and has been a widely adopted perspective in ecology . . . . it does not provide an adequate framework for disentangling the various driving forces of anthropogenic environmental change." As a result, there have been few attempts to test IPAT's assumptions. "In particular, social scientists have generally ignored the model, while biological, ecological and other physical and environmental scientists, by generally assuming the model to be true, have not been motivated to test it rigorously."[24]

Brian O'Neill, whose computer modeling study of population change is discussed below, devotes seven tightly argued pages of his book *Population and Climate Change* to an explanation of why IPAT isn't useful. Discussions based on the Ehrlich-Holdren formula, he says, "have provided grist for the population-environment debate, [but] they have done little to help resolve it." Moreover, "taken together, all the difficulties associated with [IPAT-based] decompositions make their results of little value in assessing the importance of population policies relative to other policies to reduce GHG emissions."[25]

One of the most powerful critiques of IPAT is *Taking Population out of the Equation: Reformulating I=PAT*, by Patricia Hynes, who points out that IPAT treats the three elements P, A, and T as equal factors: increasing or decreasing any of them changes the environmental impact proportionately. That mathematical equality ignores the absence of equality in the real world.

> The P of most concern for fertility control—the "poorest of the poor"—are institutionally powerless yet collectively resilient women who have larger numbers of children for complex reasons that range from immediate survival and necessity to lack of appropriate reproductive health services to coercion by a male partner, patriarchal religion, or the state. The T of concern, the highest-polluting industrial processes that provide consumer goods for the wealthiest fifth of humanity, belong almost entirely to men in the most powerful, interlocking institutions, including multinational oil and gas corporations, governments, and industrial giants like car makers and chemical and weapons manufacturers, whose goal is maximizing economic growth and profit . . .
>
> How much imprecision and injustice is built into IPAT when an Indian tribal woman uprooted by state privatization of forests she used for subsistence, or a destitute African woman impoverished by Western "development," is considered comparable in environmental impact to a corporate or government or military person from the wealthiest one-fifth of the world? Within this model, the chasm in equity between the absolute poor and the extravagantly wealthy is invisible and irrelevant.[26]

Hynes also points out that IPAT is based on a "singular view of humans as parasites and predators on the natural environment"—it assumes that human activity always harms the natural world. There is no way, using IPAT, to account for people who devote themselves to "restoring and replenishing their local environment as they use it, and guarding it from maldevelopment projects."[27]

Limits to Growth author Donella Meadows, who had long supported IPAT, heard Hynes articulate these and other criticisms at a conference in 1995 and agreed with them. See appendix 2 for Meadows's article discussing that meeting.

Malthus with a computer

Another approach to quantifying the impact of population growth on the environment involves computer modeling. While some such studies are much more sophisticated than IPAT, they don't do any better at *proving* the connection.

A case in point is a study announced by the Vienna-based International Institute for Applied Systems Analysis (IIASA) in October 2010. Judging by the news release, this study left no doubt: "The study showed that a slowing of that population growth could contribute to significantly reducing greenhouse gas emissions." Following the UN's lowest plausible population growth path could, all by itself, "provide 16 to 29 percent of the emission reductions thought necessary to keep global temperatures from causing serious impacts."[28]

The study, conducted by a team headed by Brian O'Neill, was published in the *Proceedings of the National Academy of Sciences (PNAS)*.[29] Populationist groups in the United States quickly seized on it; within weeks, three had published briefs citing this study in support of their views.[30]

But there is less here than meets the eye. Further down the page, the release says:

Scientists have long known that changes in population will have some effect on greenhouse gas emissions, but there has been debate on how large that effect might be.

The researchers sought to quantify how demographic changes influence emissions over time, and in which regions of the world.

They also went beyond changes in population size to examine the links between aging, urbanization, and emissions.

In short, O'Neill's team didn't *prove* that population growth causes greenhouse gas emissions to grow. They *assumed* that it does and then tried to determine how various demographic changes might affect the process.

That's an important distinction. No computer model can prove facts about the real world. It can only assume facts to be valid and test their implications over time, under a given set of assumptions.

For example, the computer models used by the Intergovernmental Panel on Climate Change don't prove that greenhouse gas emissions cause atmospheric temperatures to rise. That fact has been proved by decades of scientific research and confirmed by theoretical studies that show exactly how the warming process works. What the computer models show are the implications of that information under various assumptions about economic growth, technology development, and so on. As the eminent climate scientist James Hansen points out, "Models, at best, produce answers consistent with the assumptions put into them."[31]

There was an important discussion of that issue following the publication of *The Limits to Growth* in 1972. The authors of that landmark study claimed that their computer model of the global economy predicted that if then-current trends continued, "the limits to growth on this planet will be reached sometime within the next one hundred years," and that the most likely result would be "a rather sudden and uncontrollable decline in both population and industrial capacity."[32]

The Limits to Growth was a monster best seller. Millions of people read it, and its conclusions became part of the accepted wisdom of many environmentalists.

Far less attention was paid to *Thinking about the Future,* a much drier study published ten months later, in which thirteen specialists in different disciplines from the University of Sussex carefully dissected

The Limits of Modeling

"Large-scale computer programs can simulate important aspects of a process, but in the end what we are left with are more numbers. These are often useful for projections as long as nothing important changes. And they are certainly essential in design, where quantitative precision can be crucial. But there is no substitute for qualitative understanding, the demonstration of a relation between the particular and the general understanding that requires theoretical practice distinct from the solving of equations or the estimation of their solutions."

—Richard Lewontin and Richard Levins, *Biology under the Influence*

The Limits to Growth and found it wanting, to say the least. They showed in detail that the computer model was seriously flawed and that the data it used to make predictions were inadequate.

Most important, they argued that using a computer model to predict social trends gave the study a spurious appearance of objectivity, while concealing political, economic, and social biases of which even the scientists concerned might not have been aware.

In the opening essay, "Malthus with a Computer," economist Christopher Freeman wrote:

> The nature of their assumptions is not a purely technical problem. It is essential to look at the political bias and the values implicitly or explicitly present in any study of social systems. The apparent detached neutrality of a computer model is as illusory as it is persuasive. Any model of any social system necessarily involves assumptions about the workings of that system, and these assumptions are necessarily coloured by the attitudes and values of the individual or groups concerned . . .
>
> It cannot be repeated too often that the validity of any computer calculation depends entirely on the quality of the data and the assumptions (mental models) which are fed into it. Computer models cannot replace theory.[33]

Freeman exempted *The Limits to Growth* from the common accusation of "garbage in, garbage out" because the authors had obviously gone to a great deal of effort to get data, adopt reasonable assumptions, and test the model. Rather, the model's weakness was its dependence on assumptions similar to those of early populationist writer Thomas Malthus.

> Although it would be quite wrong to talk of "garbage" in the MIT model, there is a real point in the description: "Malthus in, Malthus out" . . . What is on the computer print-out depends on the assumptions which are made about real-world relationships, and these assumptions in turn are heavily influenced by those contemporary social theories and values to which the computer modelers are exposed.[34]

Today's computers are much more powerful than anything imagined by the authors of *The Limits to Growth*, but Freeman's arguments retain their full force. Indeed, given the increased complexity of the models—and thus the increased possibility of error—it is even more important today that modelers make their assumptions as explicit as possible.

One such assumption in the IIASA study was expressed clearly by Brian O'Neill in an interview with the *Los Angeles Times* on October 10, 2010: "As the economy grows faster, it raises the income for everybody, and people are spending more money and consuming more and emitting more." He said the same thing more formally in the *PNAS* paper: "In the PET model, households can affect emissions either directly through their consumption patterns or indirectly through their effects on economic growth."

The assumption that economic expansion is driven by consumer demand—more consumers equals more growth—is a fundamental part of the economic theories that underlie the model. In other words, *their conclusions are predetermined by their assumptions.*

What the model actually tries to do is to use neoclassical economic theory to predict how much economic growth will result from various levels of population growth, and then to estimate the emissions growth that would result. Unfortunately, as Yves Smith says about financial economics, any computer model based on mainstream economic theory "rests on a seemingly rigorous foundation and elaborate math, much like astrology."[35]

In short, if your computer model assumes that population growth causes emissions growth, then it will tell you that fewer people will produce fewer emissions. Malthus in, Malthus out.

4: Is the World Full?

Overpopulation is . . . a historically determined relation, in no way determined by abstract numbers or by the absolute limit of the productivity of the necessaries of life, but by limits posited rather by specific conditions of production . . . How small do the numbers which meant overpopulation for the Athenians appear to us!

—Karl Marx[1]

Populationists often accuse their critics of being "cornucopians"—of believing that the earth's resources will never run out and that infinite growth is possible or desirable. Some people have indeed argued just that: the best known was Julian Simon, a business professor and best-selling author who denied that there were any limits to growth, because capitalism would always ensure that "just about any environmental and economic trend pertaining to basic human material welfare . . . will show improvement in the long run."[2]

Simon claimed that "the standard of living has risen along with the size of the world's population since the beginning of recorded time. There is no convincing economic reason why these trends toward a better life should not continue indefinitely." He also said that "with present technology and without moving toward the much higher yields found under experimental conditions, the world can more than feed any foreseeable population increase."[3]

In 1984 Simon predicted:

> If present trends continue, the world in 2000 will be *less crowded* (though more populated), *less polluted, more stable ecologically,* and less vulnerable to resource-supply disruption than the world we live in now. Stresses involving population, resources, and environment *will be less in the future than now* . . . The world's people will be *richer* in most ways than they are today . . . The outlook for food and other necessities of life will be *better* . . . life for most people on earth will be *less precarious* economically than it is now.[4] [emphasis and ellipses in original]

Astonishingly, he republished that statement in 1996, without a word changed and with no suggestion that it didn't seem likely to come true in the next four years. Simon's ideological faith in the magic of what he called free markets blinded him to the realities of the world around him.

Simon's cornucopianism led him directly into climate change denial. He seems to have believed that since the market couldn't stop climate change, it must not be a real problem. In 1996, he confidently predicted that "global warming is likely to be simply another transient concern, barely worthy of consideration ten years from now."[5] So much for his crystal ball.

One of Simon's co-thinkers, Jacqueline Kasun, carried the *all growth is good* argument to extremes. She rejected the view that population growth always leads to poverty or environmental damage, simply inverting the populationist claim that big is bad:

> Population growth permits the easier acquisition as well as the more efficient use of the economic infrastructure—the modern transportation and communications systems, and the education, electrification, irrigation, and waste disposal systems. Population growth encourages agricultural investment—clearing and draining land, building barns and fences, improving the water supply. Population growth increases the size of the market, encouraging producers to specialize and use cost-saving methods of large-scale production. Population growth encourages governments, as well as parents, philanthropists, and tax-payers, to devote more resources to education. If wisely directed, these

efforts can result in higher levels of competence in the labor force. Larger populations not only inspire more ideas but more exchanges, or improvements, of ideas among people, in a ratio that is necessarily more than proportional to the number of additional people.[6]

Despite their differences, cornucopians agree with the populationists in one important respect: both say population growth is the primary driver of economic growth. The difference is that the Ehrlichs think that's a bad thing, while Kasun and Simon think it's great.

When populationists accuse all critics of cornucopianism, they are in effect saying that only two positions are possible: either unlimited population growth is possible and desirable, or the human population is nearing (or has passed) an absolute limit that can't be exceeded without causing a catastrophe. They deny, or don't even consider, the possibility that humanity's relationship with the earth can't be reduced to numbers and arithmetic.

When the first wave of modern populationists claimed that certain countries were overpopulated, they were immediately challenged by critics who pointed out that other countries with less space supported more people. Paul Ehrlich's opening chapter in *The Population Bomb*, describing his shock and fear at first seeing a crowded street in New Delhi, led many to point out that there were far more people per square mile in New York City.

Such criticisms caused many populationists to adopt a somewhat more sophisticated concept: *carrying capacity*, which prominent populationist William Catton defines in his best-selling book *Overshoot*.

> An environment's carrying capacity for a given kind of creature (living a given way of life) is the *maximum persistently feasible load*— just short of the load that would damage that environment's ability to support life of that kind. Carrying capacity can be expressed quantitatively as the number of us, living in a given manner, which a given environment can support *indefinitely*.[7]

Depending on which populationist articles you read, the earth's population is now approaching, has reached, or is well past the planet's carrying capacity, making a mass "die-off" possible, likely, or certain in the near future.

The term *carrying capacity* is borrowed from biology, where it is defined as the maximum number of members of a species that can survive indefinitely in a given environment, given the space and resources available. It is used to estimate how many members of a given species—elephants or salmon or bees—can live, eat, and reproduce in a defined area without depleting the environment and forcing a reduction in their numbers. The basic concept was originally developed in 1838 by Belgian mathematician Pierre Verhulst and independently reinvented by US statisticians Raymond Pearl and Lowell Reed in 1920. It holds that the growth of any given population can be described as an S-shaped or logistic curve, growing slowly at first, then speeding up, and then leveling off when it reaches carrying capacity, as in the figure below.

This seems reasonable in the abstract, but as anthropologist David Price points out, "outside of the laboratory, it has been nearly impossible to find examples of logistic growth."

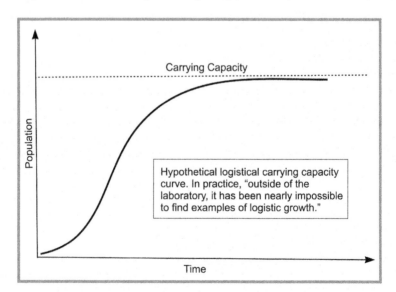

Hypothetical logistical carrying capacity curve. In practice, "outside of the laboratory, it has been nearly impossible to find examples of logistic growth."

Commonly, natural populations fluctuate. Some vary with no apparent regularity, while others, such as lemmings, wax and wane cyclically. Some, such as locusts, are prone to occasional outbreaks in which population skyrockets and then plummets. Populations of many species grow wildly in response to unusually benign conditions, and then collapse. Some populations can even seem stable over considerable periods, but seldom if ever does a natural population rise sharply and then stabilize in the form of [a] sigmoid curve.[8]

Insects behave in very predictable ways and can't choose to live differently; if their population growth can't be accurately described using carrying capacity theory, then it's very unlikely to be a useful guide to human populations that live, produce, and reproduce in a multitude of different ways. After a careful review of attempts by ecologists to use carrying capacity as a guide to human environmental impacts, environmentalist Irmi Seidl and economist Clem Tisdell conclude:

> An academic disservice has been done by those who claim that carrying capacities in applied and human ecology are scientific and objectively determined. Only in controlled conditions does such a claim seem tenable . . . This view is untenable as far as social carrying capacities are concerned and in relation to most applied ecology issues because value judgments inevitably become an integral part of the concept. Carrying capacities alter according to variations in value judgments and objectives. In human society, institutional arrangements are likely to alter the carrying capacities and desired levels of populations, and carrying capacities in the shorter term may differ greatly from those in the longer term. Carrying capacities are far from being universal constants.[9]

The work of demographer Joel Cohen is particularly devastating for the concept of human carrying capacity. In a 1995 article in *Science*, he wrote:

> Human carrying capacity depends both on natural constraints, which are not fully understood, and on individual and collective choices concerning the average level and distribution of material

well-being, technology, political institutions, economic arrangements, family structure, migration and other demographic
arrangements, physical, chemical, and biological environments,
variability and risk, the time horizon, and values, tastes, and fashions. How many people Earth can support depends in part on
how many will wear cotton and how many polyester; on how
many will eat meat and how many bean sprouts; on how many
will want parks and how many will want parking lots. These
choices will change in time and so will the number of people
Earth can support.[10]

And in his book *How Many People Can the Earth Support?*:

The Earth's capacity to support people is determined partly by
processes that the human and natural sciences have yet to understand, and partly by choices that we and our descendants have yet
to make. A numerical estimate of how many people the Earth can
support may be a useful index of present human activities and of
present understanding of how to live on the Earth; it cannot predict
the constraints or possibilities that lie in the future . . .

At any given time, a *current* but changing human carrying capacity is defined by the *current* states of technology; of the physical,
chemical, and biological environment; of social, political, and economic institutions; of levels and styles of living; and of values, pref-
erences, and moral judgments.[11]

Cohen's book includes twenty-six different published definitions
of human carrying capacity. He points out that they "vary very widely
and occasionally contradict one another." Human carrying capacity,
he concludes, "is a collection of concepts with no single generally accepted meaning."[12]

To explain why there cannot be a single answer to the question
"How many people can the earth support?" Cohen lists eleven questions, each of which, he says, could be the topic of a book.

1.   How many at what average level of material well-being?
2.   How many with what distribution of material well-being?
3.   How many with what technology?

4. How many with what domestic and international political institutions?
5. How many with what domestic and international economic arrangements?
6. How many with what domestic and international demographic arrangements?
7. How many in what physical, chemical, and biological environments?
8. How many with what variability or stability?
9. How many with what risk or robustness?
10. How many for how long?
11. How many with what values, tastes, and fashions?[13]

In a 2010 article on demographic trends, Cohen summarized what he learned from studying attempts to quantify the earth's carrying capacity:

> Estimates made in the past half a century ranged from less than one billion to more than 1,000 billion. I learned that these estimates are political numbers, intended to persuade people either that too many humans are already on Earth or that there is no problem with continuing rapid population growth. By contrast, scientific numbers are intended to describe reality. Because no estimates of human carrying capacity have explicitly addressed the questions raised above, taking into account the diversity of views about their answers in different societies and cultures at different times, no scientific estimates of sustainable human population size can be said to exist.[14]

Populationist writers frequently make a logical leap in their arguments. They start with a true but abstract point: infinite growth is impossible on a finite planet. But they jump from there to the conclusion that the environmental crisis proves that we have exceeded the maximum number of people the earth can support, which simply doesn't follow. For example, the amount of CO_2 in the atmosphere has reached a point where dangerous climate change is likely—but that shows human activity has to change, not that there are too many people.

One day, when we have broad agreement on the answers to all of Joel Cohen's questions, and when we have eliminated the gross waste, destruction, and inequities of capitalism, we may be able to measure the earth's carrying capacity scientifically. If so, humanity may then decide to consciously limit its numbers. Since the birth rate is already below replacement levels in much of the world, that probably won't be a difficult task. But today, science provides no support for a populationist program.

5: The Bomb That Didn't Explode

An unlikely bedfellow has slipped under the covers with the
sleeping giant of overpopulation: The new ally stirs under the
namesake of "population implosion."
—Elizabeth L. Krause[1]

For decades, populationists have predicted a population-driven Armageddon caused by exponential growth, which the *McGraw-Hill Online Learning Center Glossary* defines as "growth at a constant rate of increase per unit of time." The basis of this warning is the mathematical truth that small percentage increases, continued over time, produce large totals.

These comments are typical:

- *Paul and Anne Ehrlich*: "Human populations grow in a pattern that is essentially exponential, so we must be alert to the treacherous properties of that sort of growth . . . What begins in slow motion may eventually overwhelm us in a flash."[2]

- *Population Action International*: "It is not physically possible for population growth to continue for long at today's levels . . . There is also the sheer power of continuing exponential growth to consider. One demographer calculated in 1974 that at then-current growth rates, in seven centuries only one square foot of land would be available for each human being."[3]

- *Paul Ekins*: "The unsurprising fact that exponential population growth, combined with increasing per capita
  consumption of resources combined with increasing destruction and exploitation of the natural environment,
  is unsustainable, is already resulting in calamity and will
  result in catastrophe sooner rather than later if current
  trends are not reversed."[4]

One of the most influential modern statements of that warning
(more than two million views on YouTube alone) is Albert Bartlett's
video lecture bombastically titled *The MOST IMPORTANT Video
You'll Ever See*.

Bartlett, a retired physics professor, begins by declaring, "The
greatest shortcoming of the human race is our inability to understand
the exponential function." The first part of his lecture is devoted to
showing how things quickly become very big when they grow exponentially. He includes the famous story of the inventor of chess, who
supposedly asked to be rewarded with one grain of wheat on the first
square of a chessboard, two grains on the second square, four on the
third, and so on through all sixty-four squares, doubling each time.
The total would be over a hundred times greater than the entire
world's current annual production.

But Bartlett's real concern is population growth. In 1999, he says,
the world's population was six billion, and it was growing 1.3 percent
per year, at which rate it would double by 2052. But that's not the
end of it: "If this modest 1.3% per year could continue, the world
population would reach a density of one person per square meter on
the dry land surface of the earth in 780 years, and the mass of people
would equal the mass of the earth in 2400 years."

Since that isn't possible, he reasons that population growth will
stop, whether people plan for it or not. "Zero population growth will
happen . . . Today's high birth rates will drop, today's low death rates
will rise, till they have exactly the same numerical value."

We have to decide what measures are needed to stop population growth, he says, because if we don't, nature will decide for us. He cites the AIDS epidemic in Africa as an example of "nature taking care of the problem."

Bartlett is continuing a long populationist tradition; as long ago as 1798, the Reverend Thomas Robert Malthus said that population grows exponentially (he said geometrically, but he meant the same thing), and his disciples have echoed him in various ways ever since.

There is nothing wrong with Bartlett's arithmetic. He explains the nature and results of exponential growth very accurately. There's just one problem: *the world's population is not growing exponentially.*

Joel Cohen, a leading expert on population trends and growth, says bluntly: "Because of its great simplicity, the exponential model is not very useful for long-term predictions, beyond a decade or two. Surprisingly, in spite of the abundant data to the contrary, many people believe that the human population grows exponentially. It probably never has and probably never will."[5]

The scary populationist forecasts of a sardine-can world assumed that the growth rates of the 1950s and 1960s would continue largely unchanged. Ehrlich, Holdren, and their co-thinkers were certain that only compulsory population control could have any effect, and even that would be too late to avoid mass famine in India and other countries.

Commenting on the 1972 debate discussed in chapter 1, prominent populationist Garrett Hardin ridiculed Barry Commoner's claim that birth rates could slow without compulsion, calling predictions of declining birth rates "fictional" and a "pleasant superstition," while Ehrlich and Holdren said Commoner's argument was fatally flawed because "the developed countries still have high growth rates . . . The reduction in birth rates associated with the demographic transition was not adequate to compensate for the even more dramatic fall in death rates."[6]

In that very year, the US birth rate dropped to replacement level. Within a few years, birth rates in most Northern countries did the same. In those countries the decline, which populationists said couldn't happen, actually happened sooner and faster than Commoner or anyone else expected. Far from growing "at a constant rate of increase per unit of time," the human population's rate of increase has been *slowing down* for almost fifty years. In some countries population growth has stopped, and in most others it is likely to stop in the first half of this century.

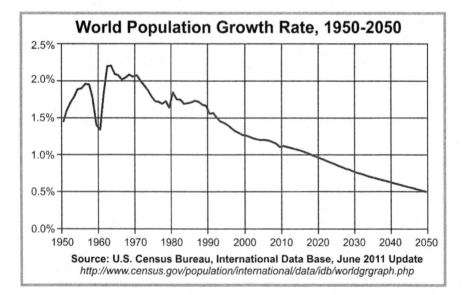

World Population Growth Rate, 1950-2050

Source: U.S. Census Bureau, International Data Base, June 2011 Update
http://www.census.gov/population/international/data/idb/worldgrgraph.php

There is true irony here; global population growth had started to slow down five years *before* Paul Ehrlich published *The Population Bomb*. The world's annual growth rate peaked in 1963, and it has declined since.

The best predictor of long-term trends on population size is the total fertility rate (TFR), the number of live children each woman will have, on average, in her lifetime. The global replacement level averages about 2.3. It is about 2.1 in rich countries where the child mortality rate is low. In poor countries, it is higher. In the long run, population will increase if the rate is higher than the replacement level and will decline if it is lower. In at least 116 countries, representing about half of the world's population, the TFR is now below the replacement level.

It is important to understand that TFR is only part of the story: a country's total population usually continues to grow for decades after the TFR falls below the replacement level. China is a case in point; its fertility level has been below its replacement level since the mid-1990s, but because so many women in China are still in or just reaching their childbearing years, the number of births each year still exceeds the number of deaths. As the population ages, it will start to decline in absolute numbers, but that point is still at least a decade away. This factor, called *demographic momentum*, means that reductions in birth rates will not have a short-term effect on total population.

Some countries have already reached the turning point. This table compares recent US Census Bureau projections for the populations of six countries in 2010 and 2040, in millions.[7]

	2010	2040
Germany	82.3	76.8
Italy	58.1	53.2
Japan	126.8	103.9
Poland	38.5	34.5
Russia	139.4	116.6
South Korea	49.6	48.3

In 1980, twenty-three European countries had fertility rates above replacement level. Today none of them do, and in seven countries fertility is half what it was then.[8] Some demographers believe that by 2060 Europe's population could fall by one-quarter, and Japan's population by half.

The European decline has been so rapid that sensationalist press stories now warn of social crises caused by depopulation. Publishers have rushed out books with titles like *The Birth Dearth: What Happens When People in Free Countries Don't Have Enough Babies?* and *The Empty Cradle: How Falling Birthrates Threaten World Prosperity and What to Do about It.* These books, most of them by right-wing ideologues, offer predictions of imminent depopulation, collapsing tax revenue, and bankrupt pension plans, forecasts that are no more reliable than the warnings of imminent global famines made in *The Population Bomb* and *Famine—1975!* four decades ago. They highlight some current statistics, project them forward as irreversible trends, mix in conservative (often racist) political prejudices, including certainty that no real social change is desirable or possible, and *presto!*—an instant best seller about impending catastrophe.

Contrary to what populationists have been predicting for years, the rate of growth is slowing dramatically. And contrary to what the "birth dearth" crowd now claims, the world's population is still growing, and it isn't likely to fall even to 1990 levels for a very long time.

Projected Population Growth, 2009–2050

	Population (thousands)		Percent
	2009	2050	increase
World	6,829,360	9,149,984	34.0
More developed regions	1,233,282	1,275,243	3.4
Less developed regions	5,596,079	7,874,742	40.7
Least developed countries	835,486	1,672,414	100.2
Less developed regions, excluding China	4,242,768	6,448,481	52.0
Sub-Saharan Africa	842,801	1,753,272	108.0
Africa	1,009,893	1,998,466	98.0

Source: United Nations Population Division World Population Prospects: The 2008 Revision (http://esa.un.org/unpd/wpp/unpp/panel_population.htm)

The United Nations projects that the total world population will be over nine billion in 2050. That's three times as many people as in 1950, so depopulation is obviously not on the agenda.

What really concerns the right-wing birth dearthers is not declining population as such but continuing growth in the South, where birth rates have fallen more slowly. When right-wing demagogue Patrick Buchanan warns of *The Death of the West*, he's actually bemoaning the fact that privileged white Americans like him, always a global minority, will be ever more outnumbered as the twenty-first century proceeds. It's no accident that many American and European birth dearth writers advocate blocking immigration—especially nonwhite immigration—to stave off the decline and fall of the existing imperial order.

If the UN's 2010 projections are correct, the world's population will stabilize by about 2100, but such long-range population predictions are notoriously inaccurate. Even short-term forecasts are subject to frequent revision as new data come in and as the failures of previous forecasts become evident; for more than a decade, each of the UN's biennial forecasts of population growth has been significantly different from the previous one.

In the past some demographers, generalizing on their understanding of European history, claimed that all countries eventually experience a "demographic transition" from high birth and death rates to low birth and death rates, driven by economic development and changing living standards. Further research has shown that even Europe didn't follow the supposed pattern, and it's even less applicable to countries whose development was interrupted and severely distorted by colonialism and continuing Northern plunder.

The drivers of today's falling birth rates are complex and their interactions are not well understood. Economics, politics, religion, education, and family structure all play a part, and the relative impact of each differs from country to country. Most demographers believe that if current trends continue, global population will stabilize in this century, but any more precise forecast than that contains a high level of uncertainty. As Joel Cohen reminds us, "Most professional demographers no longer believe they can predict precisely the future growth rate, size, composition, and spatial distribution of populations."[9]

It is abundantly clear, however, that simply making contraceptives available in the South, the principal action advocated by many populationist groups, won't solve the problems of poverty, oppression, and environmental destruction. As the noted Sri Lankan feminist and scholar Asoka Bandarage has written, such technical solutions to complex social problems go in the wrong direction:

> Neither the population issue nor the broader politico-economic crisis that it represents can be resolved by increased funding for family planning programs and quick-fix contraceptives. Poverty alleviation and the economic empowerment of women must be the cornerstones of population policy. To eradicate poverty and to reduce economic inequality, however, we must move away from the capitalist, competitive, "growth first" model of development and toward a new model that places survival of humans and the environment before the needs of corporate profit and technological advancement. We need sustainable and democratic models of development that honor social, ethical, and ecological principles, including the essential oneness and equality of all human beings.[10]

6: Too Many Mouths to Feed?

Starvation is the characteristic of some people not *having* enough food to eat. It is not the characteristic of there *being* not enough food to eat. While the latter can be a cause of the former, it is but one of many possible causes. Whether and how starvation relates to food supply is a matter for factual investigation.
—Amartya Sen[1]

Lester Brown is nothing if not consistent. Year after year since the 1970s he has warned that population growth will soon outstrip food production. Every time food prices go up or food production falls, the founder of the Worldwatch and Earth Policy institutes announces that *this time* there is no turning back. Humanity must start "improving food security by strategically reducing grain demand"— by which he means "quickly shifting to smaller families."[2]

At the end of 2010, when the UN's food price index reached an all-time high, Brown immediately announced that the price surge "is not a temporary phenomenon," because there are too many people competing for the available food.

> We are still adding 80 million people each year. Tonight, there will be 219,000 additional mouths to feed at the dinner table, and many of them will be greeted with empty plates. Another 219,000 will join us tomorrow night. At some point, this relentless growth begins to tax both the skills of farmers and the limits of the earth's land and water resources.[3]

Of course, Brown isn't the only person issuing such dire warnings. Claims that population growth will outrun food production have been made for two centuries, and they appear in most populationist writing today. Headline writers like such statements, because they offer a simple, easy-to-understand explanation for the bewildering and frightening spectre of food shortages and global hunger.

There is an important element of truth in arguments that link population size and food supply, because there is a direct relationship between the number of people on the planet and the amount of food that is required to sustain them. Each individual needs between two and three thousand calories, including all the necessary nutrients, every day. More people require more food.

The populationists' error is not that they see the number of people as important, but that they assume (often without realizing it) that there is no alternative to society's present ways of producing and delivering food.

Thus in 1967, the Paddock brothers, one of whom was an agricultural expert, failed to foresee (or even imagine possible) that a radical increase in agricultural productivity would take place in the decade following publication of their book *Famine—1975!* For them, the current situation and current trends were immutable: population growth was a "locomotive roaring straight at us" that would inevitably collide with "the unmovable landslide across the tracks . . . the stagnant production of food in the undeveloped nations."

> The present downward trends cannot be reversed, nor can they be dusted under the carpet. Those who say there are too many variables in the future to forecast food deficits ignore the present trends . . .
>
> The amount of food per person will continue to decline in the future as it has been doing the past few years. No panacea is at hand to increase the productivity of the land, just as no miracle will arrest the population explosion.[4]

Seldom has a prediction been refuted so quickly and completely. Today even Lester Brown says the years when the Paddocks wrote

Famine—1975! were part of "the golden age of world agriculture."[5] And since that time, as the Food First Institute pointed out in 1998, "increases in food production during the past 35 years have outstripped the world's unprecedented population growth by about 16 percent."[6]

When there are food shortages, populationists declare the trend irreversible, but when food production grows faster than population, as it has for the past half century, they warn that the surplus can't last long. In the 1990s the Ehrlichs, for example, finally accepted that their *Population Bomb* predictions were wrong—but only in regard to timing. In a 1993 article for an academic journal, they wrote:

> Overall, it may prove difficult even to maintain today's level of pro-duction over the long run, let alone provide a sustainable global harvest two, three, or more times larger . . .
>
> It is impossible to avoid the conclusion that the prudent course for humanity, facing the population-food-environment trap, must above all be to reduce human fertility and halt population growth as soon as humanely possible . . . Success in this area re-mains a *sine qua non* for a sustainable future.[7]

That argument might be valid if the present food production and distribution system were so efficient that the only way to feed a grow-ing population would be to grow bigger crops. But that simply isn't true: most of the food produced today never gets to people at all.

Where's the food?

The Food First Institute, citing UN statistics, points out that the world food supply is characterized by abundance, not scarcity.

> The world today produces enough grain alone to provide every human being on the planet with 3,500 calories a day. That's enough to make most people fat! And this estimate does not even count many other commonly eaten foods—vegetables, beans, nuts, root crops, fruits, grass-fed meats, and fish. In fact, if all foods are con-sidered together, enough is available to provide at least 4.3 pounds of food per person a day. That includes two and a half pounds of

grain, beans and nuts, about a pound of fruits and vegetables, and nearly another pound of meat, milk and eggs.[8]

As we know, that's not what happens. The global cereal crop in 2010 was the third highest ever, but 950 million people were desperately hungry, and over a billion more couldn't get enough nutrients to support good health. Even more shocking, 60 percent of the world's hungry people are small farmers and 20 percent are landless agricultural workers.[9] The global food industry isn't just not feeding the world, it isn't feeding the people who produce food.

This raises a critical question: *where's the food?* If the world produces 3,500 calories per person per day, what happens to it? Population is one factor to consider, but it is only one, and it is far from the most important. A serious analysis of food shortages and hunger has to include at least the following points.

1. *Food follows the money.* The world food system is controlled by a handful of giant agribusiness corporations that maximize their profits by moving food to the places where they can reap the greatest return. As Nicholas Hildyard writes, in the capitalist market, "food goes to those who have the money to buy it . . . people earning $25 a year— if they are lucky—must compete for the same food with people who earn $25 an hour, or even $25 a minute."[10]

As a result, the daily availability of food is about 4,000 calories per person in the North but only 2,500 calories in sub-Saharan Africa.[11] Those are averages: food is distributed even more inequitably *within* regions. Even in the United States, the very richest country, thirty-six million people live in hunger, and 17 percent of children are "at high risk of cognitive and developmental damage as a result of inadequate nutrition due to hunger," because they can't afford food.[12]

2. *Grain is converted into beef.* Forty percent of all grain harvested is used to feed animals rather than people.[13] Most goes to factory farms where cattle are fed corn (maize) instead of the grass they would normally eat. This is nutritionally very inefficient: "a single

half-pound beef burger eaten daily by a consumer in Brazil or the United States uses up enough grain to meet the entire total daily energy and protein needs of three people in India with a combined grain and milk diet."[14] But there's more profit in burgers than in grain, so burgers take priority.

We are not arguing for or against vegetarian or vegan diets. As sustainable farming expert Simon Fairlie points out, "If we stopped feeding grain to animals we would still retain over half of our meat supply and also benefit from about three times as much nutrition in the form of grain as there was in the meat foregone."[15]

3. *Corn is made into fuel.* After being stable or falling since the 1970s, world food prices more than doubled between 2002 and 2008. Why? A World Bank research paper concluded, "The most important factor was the large increase in biofuels production in the U.S. and the EU."[16] In 2007, US vehicles burned enough corn to cover the entire import needs of the eighty-two poorest countries.[17] In 2009, more corn was processed by ethanol makers in the United States than the combined grain production of Canada and Australia.[18]

As Mark Lynas writes, "What biofuels do is undeniable: they take food out of the mouths of starving people and divert [it] to be burned as fuel in the car engines of the world's rich consumers. This is, in the words of the United Nations special rapporteur on the right to food, Jean Ziegler, nothing less than a 'crime against humanity.'"[19]

4. *Huge quantities of food are destroyed, spoiled, or thrown away.* Reliable statistics are difficult to find, but the UN Food and Agriculture Organization says that in developing countries postharvest losses range from 15 to 50 percent of production. Worldwatch, citing agronomist Vaclav Smil, calculates that "if all low-income countries are losing grain at a rate of 15 percent, their annual post-harvest losses amount to 150 million tons of cereals. That is six times as much as FAO says would be needed to meet the needs of all the hungry people in the developing world."[20]

Socially generated scarcity

"Discussions of population and food supply which leave out power relations between different groups of people will always mask the true nature of food scarcity—who gets to eat and who doesn't—and lead to 'solutions' that are simplistic, frequently oppressive and which, ultimately, reinforce the very structures creating ecological damage and hunger . . .

"Globe, Inc. is 'overpopulated.' And as long as access to food and other resources is determined by inequitable power relationships, it will remain so. Because no matter how much food is produced, how few babies are born or how dramatically human numbers fall, it is the nature of the modern market economy remorselessly to generate 'scarcity.' Blaming such socially-generated scarcity and ecological degradation on 'overpopulation' or 'underproduction' has long provided the more powerful with an explanation for human misery that does not indict themselves and that legitimizes various ideologies of exclusion.

"Without changes in the social and economic relationships that currently determine the production, distribution and consumption of food in the world, there will always be those who are judged 'surplus to requirements' and who are thus excluded from the wherewithal to live. The human population could be halved, quartered, decimated even, yet hunger would still remain. So long as one person has the power to deny food to another, even two people may be judged 'too many.'"

—Nicholas Hildyard, "Too Many for What?"

A 2010 study found that 40 percent of all food produced in Canada is wasted—just over half by consumers, and the rest in harvesting, transportation, packaging and processing, food service and restaurants, and retail. Similar figures have been reported for other rich countries.[21]

In *Waste: Uncovering the Global Food Scandal,* Tristram Stuart writes:

Recalculating the potential savings using the most up-to-date FAO data for each and every country, it would appear that if all countries kept their food supplies at the recommended 130 per cent of requirements, and poor nations reduced their post-harvest losses, then 33 per cent of global food supplies could be saved. This level of "unnecessary surplus" would be enough to relieve the hunger of the world's malnourished twenty-three times over, or provide the entire nutritional requirements of an extra 3 billion people.[22]

In short, we are already producing enough food to provide a healthy diet for everyone on earth. By ending production of factory-farmed meat and biofuels, and reducing waste to reasonable levels, we could free up enough food for all the population growth that is expected in this century. If population growth is less than expected, we can return substantial areas of agricultural land to nature.

Blaming food shortages on overpopulation downplays the fact that the existing global food system is grossly inequitable, wasteful, and inefficient. Plenty of food is grown, but it isn't available to hungry people.

Will food destroy the earth?

So we *can* feed everyone, but that leads to another question: should we try? Many populationists argue that we must drastically reduce population anyway, because growing so much food will have disastrous environmental results.

There is much to be said for that argument. Today's high-intensity agriculture produces 13.5 percent of all greenhouse gas emissions, drains aquifers, leaches essential nutrients from the soil, promotes erosion, and poisons rivers with toxic runoffs. Modern farms are so dependent on oil and oil derivatives (particularly nonorganic fertilizers) that one author justly titled his book on the subject *Eating Fossil Fuels*.[23]

Populationists David Pimentel and Mario Giampietro, in an article published by Negative Population Growth, insist that environmentally sound agricultural methods, while needed, can't produce enough food; a sustainable agriculture in the United States could feed only 200 million.[24] When that article was published in 1993, getting to 200 million would have required a 22 percent reduction in US population; today it would require a 35 percent cut. If they are correct, one out of every three Americans must somehow disappear so that the rest can be fed sustainably.

Elsewhere, Pimentel has argued that sustainable agriculture could support a global population of only three billion,[25] less than half the number alive today, and less than a third of the number expected in 2050.

Pimentel's insistence that sustainable agriculture can't grow enough food is also defended, in mirror-image form, by anti-ecology campaigners on the far right. Climate change denier Dennis Avery, head of the Center for Global Food Issues at the right-wing Hudson Institute, defends pesticides, artificial fertilizers, genetically modified foods, factory farms, and other technological marvels as the only way to feed the world. In a 2010 debate on organic farming, Avery claimed:

> We're farming 37 percent of the land area now, and we'll need twice as much food when human populations peak in about 2050. To prevent mass starvation and wildlands destruction we'll need to double yields again—with nitrogen fertilizer, pesticides, and biotechnology.[26]

If Pimentel and Avery are correct, the world faces an impossible choice between industrial farming that destroys the environment but feeds everyone and ecologically sound farming that protects the environment but feeds fewer than half of the world's people.

Fortunately, there is strong evidence that they are wrong. Those aren't the only choices.

The experience of Cuba is particularly telling. Suddenly cut off from supplies of fuel, fertilizer, pesticides, and seeds when the Soviet Union collapsed in 1990, Cuba adopted organic, low-impact agriculture on a broad scale. US agroecologist Peter Rosset says that what happened in Cuba defied conventional wisdom about third world agriculture. After a difficult period in which food production fell drastically, Cuban farming more than recovered, using methods that weren't supposed to work.

> Contemporary Cuba turned conventional wisdom completely on its head. We are told that small countries cannot feed themselves; that they need imports to cover the deficiency of their local agriculture. Yet Cuba has taken enormous strides toward self-reliance since it lost its key trade relations. We hear that a country can't feed its people without synthetic farm chemicals, yet Cuba is virtually doing so. We are told that we need the efficiency of large-scale corporate or state farms in order to produce enough food, yet we find small farmers and gardeners in the vanguard of Cuba's recovery from a food crisis. In fact, in the absence of subsidized machines and imported chemicals, small farms are more efficient than very large production units. We hear time and again that international food aid is the answer to food shortages—yet Cuba has found an alternative in local production.[27]

Cuba's successes are impressive, especially for a small and poor country, but precisely because it is small and poor, it may be questioned whether its experience is directly relevant elsewhere. In fact, a growing body of research by scientists and practicing farmers indicates that ecological farming methods not only can produce as much food as we get today, without the environmental damage caused by industrial agriculture, but can also continue to provide healthy diets for all as the population grows.

A multidisciplinary team at the University of Michigan looked at 293 projects that compared the yields produced by conventional farming and various forms of organic farming, for various types of food and various parts of the world. They assumed no change in the proportions lost or allocated to animal feed. Extrapolating the results of those studies globally, they found that "the estimated organic food supply exceeds the current food supply in all food categories, with most estimates over 50% greater than the amount of food currently produced."[28]

Another major study involved scientists in the UK, Thailand, Sri Lanka, Mexico, and China, studying 286 projects in fifty-seven poor countries where farmers had introduced various sustainable methods, such as more efficient use of water, improved use of organic matter in soil, and reduced use of chemical pesticides and herbicides. Result: the crop yield of more than twelve million farms increased by an average of 64 percent.[29]

Perhaps the most important study to date is the Agrimonde project, organized by France's National Institute for Agricultural Research (INRA) and Center for International Cooperation in Agricultural Research for Development (CIRAD), which issued its final report in January 2011.[30]

The Agrimonde team set out specifically to determine (a) whether the world can produce sufficient food for the nine billion people expected to be on the earth in 2050 and (b) whether they can be fed if the world's agricultural systems are converted to ecologically sustainable methods and technologies by 2050.

The researchers compared two scenarios:

- *Agrimonde GO,* the business-as-usual scenario, is based on the "Global Orchestration" scenario developed by the UN Millennium Ecosystem Assessment. Under it, economic development and agriculture would continue to develop as they have in past decades, and environmental problems would be dealt with reactively, rather than by planning to avoid them.
- *Agrimonde 1* involves "increasing yields by using the ecological and biological functionalities of ecosystems to the greatest possible extent" and moving toward more equitable global food distribution. The research was particularly focused on the "doubly green revolution" concepts developed by ecologists Gordon Conway in the UK and Michel Griffon in France, where the object is to increase agricultural productivity in ways that benefit

the poor directly, are applicable under highly diverse conditions, and are environmentally sustainable.[31]

The study used a massive computer model (they say it incorporates more than thirty billion statistics) of the world's agriculture and food systems, divided into seven regions and 149 geographical units. It allowed the researchers to take into account climate change, increasing scarcity of fossil fuels, the impact of land-use changes, social and cultural issues, technological change, and much more. (Of course, like all computer models this one is only as good as its data and assumptions, but the authors have been very open about what has gone into it and have created tools to allow others to test alternatives.)

The report concludes that both scenarios could produce enough food in 2050, but that under the Agrimonde GO scenario, agriculture would cause significant environmental degradation. Agrimonde 1 would allow production to expand sustainably, if three conditions are met:

1. The prevailing food model in industrialized countries must change and not be extended elsewhere. Major changes include cutting loss and wastage at all levels and reducing beef consumption and calorie intake to healthier levels. A daily average of approximately 3,000 calories per person would be available in each of the seven major regions: this would be a 500 calorie increase for most of the world, and a 1,000 calorie decrease in the North. The authors stress the health benefits of such changes.

2. Agriculture must adopt more ecologically friendly production processes and make much more efficient use of fossil fuels. Agricultural practices and education must take advantage both of the latest scientific advances and of traditional agricultural knowledge.

3. The model assumes that each region will produce food for its own needs first and export only when it has sur-

pluses or import to cover shortages. This will require global trading rules that allow easy movement of food while enabling appropriate protections that promote development and protect the environment.

The Agrimonde study is far from definitive: many technical issues are dealt with superficially, and, as the authors admit, "social, economic, spatial, and political options . . . are not incidental and have probably not been sufficiently explored."[32] They also insist that simply having enough food *available* in each region isn't enough.

> Food security is above all a problem of access to food by the poorest populations. It is not only a question of production. The situation of the poorest, especially in rural areas, must be seen as a priority for both research and action, especially since they are going to be the first to be affected by the deterioration of the environment and climate change.[33]

These are important issues. The fact that we *can* feed the world doesn't mean that everyone will actually be fed. The giant corporations whose profits depend on ever-increasing sales of fertilizer, pesticides, and patented seeds will resist conversion to ecological agriculture, and if we don't slow global warming, changing conditions will harm many crops. Nevertheless, Agrimonde and the other studies offer reason for optimism: they show that demography isn't destiny, that it is possible for humanity to feed itself without destroying the world in the process.

7: The Populationist War against the Poor

> Whenever a theory of overpopulation seizes hold in a society
> dominated by an elite, then the non-elite invariably experience
> some form of political, economic, and social repression.
> —David Harvey[1]

Most supporters of population control today say it is meant as a kindness—a benevolent measure that can empower women, help avert climate change, and lift people out of poverty, hunger, and underdevelopment. But population control has a dark past that must be taken into account by anyone seeking solutions to the ecological crisis.

This past is important because it shows that when governments have enforced measures to control people's reproduction, the poorest people have lost their freedoms, and poor women of color have suffered most. This has been the case regardless of whether the policies impose restrictions on the fertility of poor women or stop the poor from migrating to the rich world. Population control schemes inevitably treat the victims of social and economic injustice as obstacles to a sustainable society.

The history of the modern population control movement shows what happens when powerful, influential groups decide that other groups of people are "excess." Historian Matthew Connelly calls the history of twentieth-century population control "a story of how some people have tried to control others without having to answer to anyone. They could be ruthless and manipulative in ways that were, and are, shocking." The population controllers "diagnosed political problems as pathologies that had a biological basis. At its most extreme, this logic has led to sterilization of the 'unfit' or ethnic cleansing. But even family planning could be a form of population control when proponents aimed to plan *other people's* families."[2]

Population control is a socially conservative response to social and ecological problems, one that treats some of the world's poorest and most powerless people as the biggest problem. As Asoka Bandarage has pointed out, population programs reinforce the political status quo because they are carried out as an alternative to the far-reaching social and economic changes that are needed to overcome poverty and environmental decay. "The goal of the population control establishment is not socioeconomic development, but the achievement of [low population growth] without social transformation in poor countries."[3]

For the same reason, Ugandan academic Mahmood Mamdani, in his classic 1974 study *The Myth of Population Control*, wrote that the populationist approach of promoting population reduction without social change is "a weapon of the political conservative."[4]

The population control establishment has been challenged by "pro-life" fundamentalist religious groups that oppose contraception and abortion as a matter of principle. This has allowed population controllers to present their agenda as progressive, enlightened, and even pro-feminist.[5] Further complicating matters, religious conservatives often clothe their opposition to family planning in anticolonial rhetoric. But despite their differences, population controllers and religious extremists share a common outlook on women's reproductive rights. Both, as Bandarage notes, "attempt to wrest reproductive decisions and power from women and hand them to external authorities, whether they be patriarchal religious entities or state and medical hierarchies."[6]

Denial of women's right to control their fertility amounts to population control, whatever form it takes. State-run programs to artificially boost birth rates are also contemptible. Our focus in this chapter, however, is the policies, influence, and actions of those who organized to slow population growth in the name of social progress—the "history of how some people systematically devalued *both* the sanctity of life *and* the autonomy of the individual."[7]

Population control as official policy

Radical socialists and feminists led the birth control movement in the early twentieth century in the United States and Europe, as part of their broader agenda to win social and economic rights for women. By the 1920s, however, the leadership had been taken by the medical profession and eugenicists, supporters of selective human breeding to improve racial purity and individual intelligence.

After World War II, the population control movement began to win real influence in the halls of power, and by the time Ehrlich wrote *The Population Bomb*, anxiety in ruling circles about global population growth had merged with Cold War anticommunism.

What feminist writer Michelle Goldberg has dubbed "the great Cold War population panic"[8] took hold in elite circles in the North. The rise of colonial liberation movements after World War II increased support for population control among the wealthy rulers of the North, many of whom believed that cutting third world population would reduce poverty and thus weaken revolutionary movements. For example, in 1949 the then US secretary of state Dean Acheson attributed the success of the communists in China to overpopulation:

> The population of China during the eighteenth and nineteenth centuries doubled, thereby creating an unbearable pressure upon

The original *Population Bomb*

Paul Ehrlich's 1968 best seller borrowed its title from this pamphlet, published by Hugh Moore, the multimillionaire inventor of the Dixie Cup. Moore financed the printing and distribution of more than 1.5 million copies of the sixteen-page tract between 1954 and 1968. In the late 1960s, Moore founded the Population Crisis Committee and promoted the slogan "people pollute." But this pamphlet didn't mention environmental issues at all. Its focus was expressed clearly in its opening headline "War, Communism, and World Population."

In 1954, Moore explained his real concern in a letter to an even richer populationist, John D. Rockefeller III: "We are not primarily interested in the sociological or humanitarian aspects of birth control. We are interested in the use which Communists make of hungry people in their drive to conquer the Earth."

The pamphlet Moore published stressed that issue:

> Hundreds of millions of people are hungry. In their desperation they are increasingly susceptible to Communist propaganda and may be enticed into violent action . . . .
> The experience of the technical assistance programs during the past years has shown that few—if any—of the underdeveloped

The original *Population Bomb* (continued)

countries are able to produce enough to raise their level of living—confronted as they are with their present rate of population growth.

Improvement of living standards in underdeveloped areas is impossible without a slow-down in population growth. Birth rates must somehow be brought into balance with death rates . . .

The economy of the Free World, moreover, is dependent for many of its vital raw materials [on] these restless, impoverished peoples.

Peril is imminent. The peoples of these areas are dissatisfied and are wondering who will help them most to improve their lot. As long as two thirds of them go to sleep hungry every night the odds favor Communism . . .

Today the population bomb threatens to create an explosion as dangerous as the explosion of the H bomb, and with as much influence on prospects for progress or disaster, war or peace.

The pamphlet illustrated its point with a graphic that said 170 million people were "dominated by communism" in 1937, 1 billion in 1957, and predicted 2.5 billion in 1977 as a result of the addition of "impoverished, overpopulated areas, now threatened."

the land. The first problem which every Chinese Government has had to face is that of feeding this population. So far none has succeeded. The Kuomintang attempted to solve it by putting many land-reform laws on the statute books. Some of these laws have failed, others have been ignored. In no small measure, the predicament in which the National Government finds itself today is due to its failure to provide China with enough to eat. A large part of the Chinese Communists' propaganda consists of promises that they will solve the land problem.[9]

The leaders of the capitalist world needed an explanation for why they had "lost China," and they couldn't admit, even to themselves, that the government and social system they had long supported in China were corrupt and unreformable. Population was an easier explanation, and population control seemed to promise an easier way to avoid "losing" other countries than actually ending exploitation, supporting democratic rights, or solving the agricultural crisis through genuine land reform.

By the 1960s, groups such as the Population Council and the International Planned Parenthood Federation (IPPF) were attracting substantial private and government funding for programs that promoted contraception as a solution to the problems of poor countries. Two of the biggest private sponsors were the Ford and Rockefeller Foundations; John D. Rockefeller III served as the Population Council's first president.

In an essay published in *Ramparts* magazine in 1970, Steve Weissman wrote that in the absence of a serious commitment to "greater economic security, political participation, elimination of gross class division [and the] liberation of women," population control simply masked a new "welfare imperialism of the West." He concluded: "In the hands of the self-seeking, humanitarianism is the most terrifying *ism* of all."[10]

Ruling elites in several third world countries also embraced the population control agenda. For them, contraception and mass sterilization appeared to offer a shortcut to modernization and development. Like populationists in the North, they embraced population control as an alternative to actually dealing with poverty and misery.

The patient is expendable

Flush with funds and political clout, populationists searched for suitable methods of mass population control. In the early 1960s, Western-sponsored population control programs in rural India and Pakistan distributed contraceptive pills, but the programs failed because the poor saw no reason to cooperate. As Mahmood Mamdani showed, bigger families made economic sense in very poor agricultural communities that had no social security benefits or reliable medical care: having fewer children "would have meant to willfully court economic disaster."[11] Most Western populationists failed to understand this essential link between poverty and high birth rates.

After these early failures, the populationists turned to more intrusive methods, in particular intrauterine devices (IUDs) and injected contraceptives such as Depo-Provera, which women could not easily remove or choose not to use.

IUDs were widely criticized in medical circles, because they often caused infection, pain, and bleeding. But J. Robert Willson, chair of obstetrics and gynecology at Temple University, told the 1962 Population Council conference that IUDs should be used despite the dangers.

> We have to stop functioning like doctors . . . In fact, it may well be that the incidence of infection is going to be pretty high in the patients who need the device most . . . Again, if we look at this from an overall, long-range view (these are the things I have never said out loud before and I don't know how it is going to sound), perhaps the individual patient is expendable in the general scheme of things, particularly if the infection she acquires is sterilizing but not lethal.[12]

Willson's fellow obstetrician, Alan Guttmacher, an influential figure in the Population Council and IPPF, defended IUDs in a similar way:

> No contraceptive could be cheaper, and also, once the damn thing is in the patient cannot change her mind. In fact, we can hope she will forget it's there and perhaps in several months wonder why she has not conceived.[13]

Frederick Robbins, an early researcher of the contraceptive pill, also argued that potentially harmful population control methods served a greater good. "The dangers of overpopulation are so great that we may have to use certain techniques of contraception that may entail considerable risk to individual women."[14]

Malcolm Potts, medical director of the IPPF, blithely dismissed safety concerns about the contraceptive drug Depo-Provera. "We are not going to know whether Depo-Provera is safe, until a large number of women use it for a very long time . . . You cannot prove a drug is safe until you use it."[15] While Depo-Provera was being given to millions of women in the third world, it was banned in the United States due to health concerns.

Members of the population control establishment thought individual patients were expendable because they firmly believed their programs would save millions of lives. Many sought justification in what Goldberg calls "cold demographic utilitarianism." Potts said the population control movement was divided into two broad groups. It had "one group, which is sincerely regulated by human beings' sufferings, and talks about rights and individuals' stories." He claimed the other group was more effective because it "had a sense of scale, that says a million people suffering is worse than a thousand people suffering."[16]

Frank admissions of deliberate human rights abuse hardly made for a sound public relations strategy, so in promotional material written for Northern consumption, population control groups portrayed their "family planning" programs as a compassionate way to overcome poverty and promote women's rights. Still, as Connelly notes: "The most effective propaganda for population control in the period did not threaten or cajole, or invoke poor victims. It played on the anxieties about crime, contagion and mass migration, but without actually naming them. It made people feel, viscerally, that it was already too late, and that they were living in a nightmare."[17]

By the mid-1960s, population control had become official US government policy. President Lyndon Johnson openly tied aid to India to population control programs: "I'm not going to piss away foreign aid in nations where they refuse to deal with their own population problems."[18] Johnson's successor, Richard Nixon, declined to make foreign aid conditional on the adoption of democratic freedoms but said "population control is a must . . . population control must go hand in hand with aid."[19]

A new phase of population control had opened. Sterilization of the "expendables," rather than contraceptives, IUDs, or other methods, became the most used method, with horrendous results.

War against the poor

Western populationist groups had been active in India for decades, and by the early 1970s they had won over much of the country's wealthy political elite. The government adopted a goal of reducing the birth rate by 40 percent by 1972 and allocated a remarkable 59 percent of the health budget to family planning programs. In the mid-1970s, the Indira Gandhi government declared the country to be on a "war footing" to stop population growth. She was unapologetic about the undemocratic measures this would involve: "Some personal rights have to be kept in abeyance for the human rights of the nation, the right to live, the right to progress."[20]

Minister of planning Asoka Mehta warned that the Indian government considered individuals expendable during its population drive: "It is war that we have to wage, and, as in all wars, we cannot be choosy, some will get hurt, something will go wrong. What is needed is the will to wage war so as to win it."[21]

Connelly describes what happened:

> Sterilization became a condition not just for land allotments, but for irrigation water, electricity, ration cards, rickshaw licenses, medical care, pay raises, and promotions. Everyone from senior government officials to train conductors to policemen, was given a sterilization quota. This created a nationwide market, in which people bought and sold, sometimes more than once, the capacity to reproduce. Of course, for the very poorest, with no money and nothing else to sell, sterilization in such conditions was not really a choice.[22]

The central government made funding to state governments partly conditional on meeting population control targets.[23] In the impoverished state of Uttar Pradesh, people from the lowest caste composed 29 percent of the population but were 41 percent of those vasectomized.[24] When incentives and disincentives didn't achieve the ever-rising sterilization targets, more repressive measures were adopted. In 1976, the state of Maharashtra proposed jailing parents with more than three children who refused sterilization. The central government said it would not block the plan. A village in the state of Haryana "was surrounded by police, hundreds were taken into custody, and every eligible male was sterilized."[25]

India's state teachers were also conscripted into the hysterical population campaign—they "like everyone else could be demoted, fired, or threatened with arrest. Teachers, in turn, sometimes expelled students whose parents did not submit to sterilization."[26]

At the campaign's height in 1975 and 1976, more than eight million Indians were sterilized. A later government inquiry found that at least 1,774 people died due to botched sterilizations in the emergency period. As late as 1988 the Indian press reported, "In a sterilization camp in Rajasthan an ordinary bicycle pump was used to pump air into women's bodies," leading to the deaths of forty-four women.[27]

Despite the human rights abuses, Western-led institutions held up the Indian emergency period population control campaign as a model. World Bank president Robert McNamara praised "the political will and determination shown by [India's] leadership at the highest level in intensifying the family planning drive with a rare courage of conviction."[28] The UN Fund for Population Affairs awarded Indira Gandhi its World Population Prize in September 1983.

Incentives and repression

Gandhi shared that award with Qian Xinzhong, who, as China's minister for family planning, presided over an equally cruel and coercive population control program.

After decades of promoting an artificially high birth rate, the ruling Chinese bureaucracy reversed itself, embarking on a coercive population control program in 1979. For many years, couples had to apply
to the state for permission to have a child. One permit from the 1980s
said: "Based on the nationally issued population plan targets combined with the need for late marriage, late birth, and fewer births, it
is agreed that you may give birth to a child during [198_]; the quota
is valid for this year and cannot be transferred."[29]

Each Chinese province worked out its own system of incentives
and disincentives to meet its population control quota. Connelly gives
an example from Hubei province:

> If parents had only one child, they were to be given subsidies for
> health care, priority in housing and extra retirement pay. The child
> was also favored with preferred access to schools, university and
> employment. But if the parents had another child, they were re-
> quired to repay these benefits. As for those who had two or more
> children, both mother and father were docked [up to] 10% of their
> pay for a period of 14 years.[30]

As in India, population control in China relied heavily on repressive force. In the "most coercive phase in the whole history of China's
one-child policy [in the 1980s] all women with one child were to be
inserted with a stainless-steel tamper-resistant IUD, all parents with
two or more children were to be sterilized, and all unauthorized preg-
nancies aborted."[31]

Population control programs in Chinese-occupied Tibet were
equally barbaric. A Western doctor who in 1987 worked in a Lhasa
hospital said "women who refuse[d] to 'volunteer' for abortion or sterilization [were] later 'coerced' into doing so and [were] subjected to
'inhumane surgery' without anesthetics or painkillers." Bandarage
cites an account by journalist John Aveden, who "confirmed that it is
typical for a woman who arrives at a hospital for childbirth without
a pass granting permission to have a child to awake after labor to find
that her child is dead and that she has been sterilized."[32]

Bangladesh, one of the world's most densely populated nations, also became a special focus for the population control establishment. In the 1970s and 1980s, state-sponsored sterilization programs offered payment for "acceptors." Overwhelmingly, it was the poorest Bangladeshis who "accepted," compelled by economic insecurity. Each year, the number of sterilizations rose sharply during the months between harvests, when rural unemployment was high.

As in India, a policy of paying for referrals created a sterilization market in Bangladesh. The referral payments "resulted in fostering a large array of unofficial, self-employed agents specializing in recruiting sterilization acceptors among poor, uninformed people." Some women "were not even told that sterilization is an irreversible procedure." In at least one "poor tribal community the [Bangladeshi] army carried out forced sterilizations of women with more than three children after making them sign 'informed consent' papers."[33]

In the Western Hemisphere, the Peruvian government of Alberto Fujimori adopted its own population control policy in the mid-1990s. When sterilization was first made legal in Peru, many hailed it as a breakthrough for women's access to birth control in a country with a Roman Catholic majority. But in the late 1990s it was revealed that the government had resorted to widespread coercion in a bid to lower Peru's birth rate quickly. Some 330,000 women and 30,000 men, most from the Quechuan and Aymaran indigenous minorities, were sterilized against their will.

In addition to trampling on women's rights, population control programs have reinforced existing gender inequality. It's no exaggeration to say that in some countries an entire generation of women has gone missing, largely as a result of increases in female infanticide and sex-selective abortion. By 1991, there were about 100 million fewer women in China, India, Pakistan, Bangladesh, Nepal, West Asia, and Egypt than would otherwise be expected.[34] A survey of 1.1 million Indian households, published in the medical journal *The*

Lancet in 2006, concluded that at least half a million sex-selective abortions take place in India every year.[35] The natural birth ratio is 105 male births for every 100 female, but in the Indian state of Punjab no district exceeds 82 girl births for every 100 males. Some Punjabi districts report ratios as low as 63 girls for every 100 boys. Eighty-five Chinese girls were born for every 100 boys in 2006. For second children, just 65 girls were born.[36]

An imperialist chapter

We are not suggesting that everyone who thinks population growth is an ecological issue would support compulsory sterilization or human rights abuses. Most modern-day populationists reject the coercive programs of the twentieth century, but that doesn't mean that they have drawn the necessary lessons from those experiences.

Population control, even when carried out in the name of empowering women, had the opposite effect. The population controllers assumed that women bore children because they did not understand their own interests, so they denied those women the right to choose. They promised to alleviate poverty, but their programs had no discernible impact on underdevelopment and actually increased inequality. Population control was supposed to save millions from disaster, but it caused disaster for millions.

> The great tragedy of population control . . . was to think that one could know other people's interests better than they know it themselves . . . The essence of population control, whether it targeted migrants, the "unfit," or families that seemed either too big or too small, was to make rules for other people without having to answer to them. It appealed to the rich and powerful because, with the spread of emancipatory movements and the integration of markets, it began to appear easier and more profitable to control populations than to control territory. That's why opponents were correct in viewing it as another chapter in the unfinished history of imperialism.[37]

The Ehrlich-Commoner debate reflected a great political divide over how to respond to the ecological crisis. Ehrlich wanted greater control by governments and institutions over individuals, especially individual reproduction. Commoner wanted greater collective control over governments and institutions and a radical restructuring of the entire production system.

Ehrlich and others who supported population control at the height of the Cold War population panic ignored or denied the human rights implications of their ideas. They never questioned what it meant, in a society divided along class and ethnic lines, for one group to decide that another was "surplus to requirements." For the planet-destroying rulers of the world, the excess people are never themselves. The excess people are always somebody else.

Marxist geographer David Harvey warned environmentalists in the 1970s that ignoring the political consequences of populationism would ensure ever more repression:

> If we accept a theory of overpopulation and resource scarcity but insist upon keeping the capitalist mode of production intact, then the inevitable results are policies directed toward class or ethnic repression at home and policies of imperialism and neo-imperialism abroad. Unfortunately this relation can be structured in the other direction. If, for whatever reason, an elite group requires an argument to support policies of repression, then the overpopulation argument is most beautifully tailored to fit this purpose.[38]

Can the lessons be learned, the mistakes corrected, and enlightened, noncoercive population reduction policies implemented? Most populationists today think so, but as we'll see, coercion takes many forms.

8: Control without Coercion?

Although "coerced sterilization" in its grossly offensive conventional form may have seen its day, a much more insidious pattern of social engineering has come to replace it.
—Mondana Nikoukari[1]

Many contemporary populationists argue that population growth can be slowed or stopped in ways that respect the human rights of women and the poor. The horrors of the Cold War population control panic of the twentieth century need not be repeated. Laurie Mazur says: "We can fight for population policies that are firmly grounded in human rights and social justice."[2]

These activists argue that the debates about population and environment are unnecessarily polarized, that we don't have to choose between population control and social justice—to build an ecological society, we must do both.

Contradictory strategies

But that's easier to say than do. The idea that population control can be merged with a social justice agenda assumes that populationist policies don't contradict the goal of fundamental social change. In reality, far from making sustainable social change easier, populationist policies add divisive tensions and problems to environmental campaigns. In practice, it is just about impossible to "do both."

There are just two broad policy options open to populationists: they can urge individuals to have fewer children, or they can support government-backed coercion. As Andrew Feenberg writes:

> The dilemma of population politics is the absence of any significant realm of action other than appeals to individual conscience and coercion by the state. There is not much else to be done at the political level except attacking public opponents of birth control and lobbying for repressive legislation. One cannot very well demonstrate against babies or even against parents. Unless the state intervenes (as it has in China), the issue is private, each couple choosing how many children it wants as a function of its own values. This explains why Ehrlich's political program wavered between moralistic voluntarism and more or less harsh state action.[3]

As we saw in chapter 7, coercive state action to cut population cannot be reconciled with human rights. It directly contradicts efforts by social activists to increase people's control over governments and institutions, by giving the state more power over individuals' lives and sexuality.

But if calling upon the state to cut population is ruled out, the option of appealing to individuals has its own problems. Past campaigns to convince individuals to have fewer children have had little success. Women's decisions to have children are influenced by a wide range of cultural, social, economic and personal factors, none of which are addressed by calls for smaller families on environmental grounds.

The population establishment isn't a neutral force: it has a specific political agenda, and when it provides funds, it wants to see results. If voluntary programs don't produce the desired demographic outcome, there's likely to be pressure to introduce sterner measures. As Amara Pérez writes in the evocatively titled book *The Revolution Will Not Be Funded*:

> The reality is foundations are ultimately interested in the packaging and production of success stories, measurable outcomes, and the use of infrastructure and capacity-building systems. As non-

profit organizations that rely on foundation money, we must embrace and engage in the organizing market. This resembles a business model in that the consumers are foundations to which organizations offer to sell their political work for a grant .... Over time, funding trends actually come to influence our work, priorities, and direction as we struggle to remain competitive and funded in the movement market.[4]

This is not an abstract issue. Family planning programs that raise government and foundation money by promising to reduce the birth rate will face demands for measurable results—and those that want to keep their grants will find themselves pressured to shift from offering reproductive choices to pressuring women to make the "right" choices.

Experience with family planning in third world countries shows that programs motivated by a desire to cut population tend to use coercive measures, regardless of the desires of their supporters in the North.

Gradations of coercion

An approach that's often counterposed to coercion involves offering incentives and rewards for "accepting" birth control. In practice, many poor women lack the power to make choices about many aspects of their lives, and incentives to use contraception can make it difficult for them to say no. When a woman's family is hungry, the offer of money if she agrees to be sterilized or accepts some form of long-lasting contraceptive is really no choice at all.

Supporters of incentives to lower population point out that incentives and disincentives are routine in everyday life—from traffic regulations to tax systems. These measures help society function. So what could be wrong with giving poor women incentives if it means they get access to family planning services they lacked before? Betsy Hartmann replies:

Such an argument avoids the central question of why people need to be persuaded or forced to have fewer children in the first place. Isn't it because of the very absence of the most powerful incentive of them all: the economic and social security of having fair access to the fruits of development? This is not something that can be handed out in local currency when a person is sterilized; instead it involves major social restructuring. When incentive schemes are substituted for social change, the result invariably discriminates against poor people, especially women, if it does not outright coerce them.[5]

Coercion doesn't just mean forced sterilization: it can take many forms. In some Indian states, people with more than two children are not eligible for government jobs. In Indonesia, entire communities have been denied benefits if an insufficient number of couples used birth control. In Singapore, large families lost child tax credits and priority access to subsidized housing.

A 2006 study by James Oldham found that staff in projects motivated by demographic goals frequently pressured women to accept sterilization or unsafe long-lasting contraceptives. Supposedly noncoercive programs included elements such as denying women access to other services for failing to attend family planning lectures. Oldham concluded:

> When NGOs arrive with predetermined agendas, the danger is that these will be imposed on local communities. As long as a Malthusian [population] narrative is part of the program vision, such a narrative is likely to be communicated to, and potentially imposed upon, target communities . . .
>
> Organizations promoting the funding and provision of reproductive health/family planning services in the global south should refrain from using environmental and population arguments to promote their goals. The distortions of Malthusian arguments cannot be justified simply because they are effective in winning partners or funding; they need to be replaced with rights-based arguments in favor of making reproductive health/family planning available to all women.[6]

The overtly coercive population programs in India and China have been widely publicized. Much less attention has been paid to the decades-long sterilization program in the US colony of Puerto Rico, a program that was officially voluntary but in practice allowed little choice to women who needed jobs on an island with very high unemployment, which US authorities attributed to overpopulation.

> In the 1940s light manufacturing industries began to move in from the U.S. mainland, attracted by cheap labor and low taxes. Young women were a key and "docile" part of that labor force, but subject to "loss" (from the employer's point of view) due to pregnancy. The result was a massive sterilization campaign carried out by the local government and the IPPF [International Planned Parenthood Federation], with U.S. government funding. Women were cajoled and coerced into accepting sterilization, often not even being told that the process wasn't reversible. The result was that by 1968 one-third of the women of childbearing age had been sterilized. The combination of mass sterilization and heavy out-migration due to a declining economy caused the population of Puerto Rico to actually drop—with no resultant improvement in living standards, or the environment.[7]

Feminist lawyer Mondana Nikoukari points out that in the United States, "there is little doubt that women of color, as a group, face disproportionate and coerced sterilization."

> Statistics show that in 1982, fifteen percent of white women were sterilized compared to twenty-four percent of black women, thirty-five percent of Puerto Rican women and forty-two percent of Native American women. By region, the numbers are even more astounding. On Native American reservations nearly 50 sterilizations occurred in one month in the 1970's with the rate of sterilization doubling by the close of the decade. Sterilization rates as high as sixty-five percent have been reported among Latino women in the Northeast, while in the South black women have undergone the highest rate of hysterectomy and tubal ligation in the nation.[8]

In her view, in many cases informed consent has been replaced by "gradations of coercion" imposed by medical practitioners, courts, welfare agencies, and others. If that's true in the United States, how can we imagine that in countries where legal protections are much weaker, population-environment programs will truly respect women's rights?

The "Cairo Consensus"

As these examples show, it can be hard, based on descriptions alone, to distinguish programs that truly empower women from those that only pay lip service to women's rights, since even hard-line population controllers now routinely include some feminist-sounding language in their statements.

Almost every group that promotes birth control for third world women claims adherence to the policies adopted by the 1994 UN population conference in Cairo. Mazur says the Cairo Consensus was a big step forward because it united feminists and populationists. "[In Cairo] feminists and populationists joined forces *because their interests were aligned*. If the best way to slow population growth is by ensuring reproductive rights and empowering women, then this is a win-win for both groups"[9] (emphasis in original).

The Cairo Consensus also has many feminist critics. Hartmann describes it as "a strange brew of feminism, neoliberalism, and population reduction."[10] In a position paper written immediately after the meeting, Indian feminists Vandana Shiva and Mira Shiva wrote that at Cairo "women's rights" were reduced to just "reproductive rights." Those who support the consensus "end up ignoring the fact that women are human beings, not just reproductive beings and have political, economic and environmental rights, not just reproductive rights." Many women's groups at Cairo "unwittingly became promoters of the agenda of demographic fundamentalists who believe that all problems—from ecological crisis to ethnic crisis, from poverty to social instability—can be blamed on population growth, and as a corollary, population control is a solution to all problems facing humanity."[11]

In the context of the human rights abuses endorsed by the twentieth-century population establishment and the misogynist policies supported by anti-choice religious groups, Cairo's emphasis on women was a big step in the right direction. Wider provision of sexual and reproductive health services is a goal that deserves universal support, and the Cairo Consensus has provided a framework for women in many countries to fight restrictions on birth control and abortion.

But the picture isn't all positive. By treating women's rights instrumentally, as a means to achieve demographic ends, the Cairo Consensus gave new credibility to an agenda that has long been used to block social change. Populationist groups in the North have adopted Cairo's vocabulary and have seized on Cairo's call for governments to "formulate and implement population policies and programs" as justification for their long-standing goal of reducing birth rates in the third world.

Rosalind Petchesky points out that populationist influence can also be seen in the contradiction in the Cairo document "between the rhetoric of reproductive and sexual health/rights and an approach to resources still focused on prioritizing family planning within publicly supported services and relying on the market for everything else." The Cairo Action Plan proposed a budget in which the funds allocated to birth control exceeded the funds for all other health services combined.[12] In poor countries, implementing the Cairo program has often meant shifting health care budgets heavily toward birth control, while substantially reducing spending on basic health care.

Hartmann writes that population publications often present women as "an undifferentiated mass which needs to be empowered, with little recognition of the many differences between them—poor or rich, rural or urban, black or white." But acknowledging these differences is crucial because they "impact on their survival and repro-

Using the Users?

Some feminists argue for using populationist prejudices as a way to win gains for women. Michelle Goldberg, for example, writes that the population question can be used "to force the world to pay attention to reproductive justice." In her view, "men in power will rarely work to advance women's rights for their own sake, but they will do so in the service of some other grand objective, be it demographic or economic," so women's rights activists should take advantage of that.[15]

Similarly, Laurie Mazur argues that progressives must preempt right-wing populationists: "If there is no left/progressive voice on this issue, environmentalists and others who are legitimately concerned about population growth will be driven into the arms of the neo-Malthusians."[16]

But the real danger is that liberal environmentalists and feminists will strengthen the right by lending credibility to reactionary arguments. Adopting the argument that population growth causes global warming endorses the strongest argument the right has against the social and economic changes that are really needed to stop climate change and environmental destruction.

If environmentalists and others believe that population growth is causing climate change, then our responsibility is to show them why that's wrong, not to adapt to their errors.

ductive strategies."[13] Lumping the world's women together in this way also downplays significant social and political differences between women.

> Although one can find common agendas among the world's women (for example, most women would probably support an end to domestic violence and forced prostitution), there are also major political differences between them, which includes perspectives on population. How many women of color, for example, support the position of many rich, white women environmentalists that high fertility is the main cause of the environmental crisis? There is no consensus here, even by the wildest stretch of the imagination.[14]

Combining population control policies and social justice campaigns just doesn't work. Population policies not only don't pave the way for progressive social and economic transformation, they raise barriers to it. The Cairo focus on sexual and reproductive rights is welcome, but the price was that the wider issues facing the people of the South were placed on the back burner indefinitely.

Too little, too late

A fundamental objection to the Cairo Consensus is that it "mainly regards women's empowerment as a means to reduce population growth rather than as a worthy end in and of itself."[17]

But even if that were an acceptable approach, attempts to fight environmental destruction by providing birth control services in the South fail on practical grounds. The plans proposed by populationist groups in the North cannot achieve their stated goals. Just providing contraception is unlikely to have a significant effect on population or emissions—and even if it did everything the populationists claim, the effect would be far less than is required to slow climate change or to turn back the environmental crisis more generally.

Many populationist groups say population growth and greenhouse gas emissions can be slowed substantially just by filling the "unmet need" for birth control and abortion, so coercion isn't necessary. For example, Optimum Population Trust promises that "successful population policies, which answered the unmet need for family planning, could mean nearly three billion fewer people in 2050, a difference equivalent to 44 per cent of current world population (6.8 billion)."[18]

But there are at least three reasons to doubt such claims. These are virtually certain:

1. "Unmet need" programs won't produce the promised reductions in population.

2. The population reductions they do achieve won't have an equivalent impact on greenhouse gas emissions.
3. Any impact on greenhouse gas emissions will be too little and too late to slow global warming.

First, the claim that simply making modern contraception available to women who aren't now using it will have a significant effect on birth rates in third world countries ignores essential social and economic factors. As demographer George Martine writes: "This perspective overlooks well-documented arguments that rapid reductions in fertility depend at least as much on speeding up economic development and social transformations, as well as on empowering women and meeting individuals' needs in sexual and reproductive health."[19]

> Family planning programs alone, without some minimal social transformation that motivates people to perceive that limiting fertility would yield some increment in well-being, and that empowers women to take control over their lives, are unlikely to reduce fertility rapidly. This is especially true in countries that still have a predominantly rural population. Throughout history, rural families have had more children in order to work the land. Practically all the least-developed countries still have a large majority of their population residing in rural areas, where family planning programs are more difficult to implement and have understandably had a lesser impact—unless some form of coercion was applied.[20]

In Hartmann's words: "The best population policy is to concentrate on improving human welfare in all its many facets . . . Take care of the population and population growth will go down. In fact, the greatest irony is that in most cases population growth comes down faster the less you focus on it as a policy priority, and the more you focus on women's rights and basic human needs."[21]

Second, since the women whose unmet need for birth control is being targeted are the poorest women in the poorest countries, their greenhouse gas emissions are minimal.

The actual magnitude of the impact that future fertility declines will have on the mitigation of climate change is far from being proportional to the number of people who are "not born" under a scenario of rapid fertility decline. Enormous differences in social organization and in consumption patterns between regions and social groups translate into highly differentiated impacts of additional numbers.[22]

As demographer Wolfgang Lutz points out:

Within each country the rich have fewer children and emit significantly more than the poor. India, for example, has a per capita carbon emission of only 0.21 tons. Although this is one of the lowest in the world there is every reason to assume that the richest 10 percent in India emit at least 10 times more than the bulk of the population and that the expected future population growth of India comes almost entirely from the poor segments of the population. If this is true, the actual impact of population growth on carbon emissions will be much less than national averages would imply.[23]

Equally, the actual impact of population *reduction* on carbon emission will be much less than national averages would imply.

And the third reason for doubting the value of population programs is timing. As George Martine notes, "Even rapid fertility declines would not quickly produce the stabilization or reduction of population sizes . . . [because] a country's population continues to grow in absolute numbers for some decades after it has reached below-replacement fertility."[24] This is the issue of *demographic momentum* discussed in chapter 5: population keeps growing because the number of births, though below the long-term replacement rate, is still greater than the number of deaths.

This is a critical issue, because we don't have decades to solve the climate crisis.

Analysis by a team led by US climate scientist James Hansen shows that the current level of CO_2 in the atmosphere, now 390 parts per million, "is already in the danger zone" for catastrophic climate change. They argue convincingly that we must phase out coal by 2030, and by 2050 we need to have *negative emissions*—that is, we must remove more CO_2 from the atmosphere than is added every year. That can't be achieved without a very rapid reduction in emissions, beginning now.[25] Hansen argues that any increase in the average global temperature greater than one degree will have potentially tragic consequences. "The last time Earth was 2 degrees warmer so much ice melted that sea level was about twenty-five meters (eighty feet) higher than it is today."[26]

Demographer Martine writes:

> The limitations of the "demographic solution" must be made clear. Sheer numbers do not tell the whole story. The world is already on the threshold of a major climactic threat, with or without population growth. Family planning simply does not have retroactive capabilities. Even if humankind failed to produce a single baby during the next generation, its quality of life on Planet Earth would still be endangered by climate change.[27]

However sincere its advocates may be, the "reduce the birth rate" solution to climate change blames third world women for a problem they didn't cause and opens the door to more subtle forms of coercion. Under even the most optimistic (read: unrealistic) assumptions, its impact on emissions will be too little, too late: a fraction of what's needed, decades after dramatic changes must be in place.

In the past, populationists were justly accused of exaggerating the imminence of famine and chaos, so it's ironic that now their proposals ignore the urgency of the environmental crisis. Demographic change is slow, but the climate emergency demands rapid, transformative action. Setting population targets for 2050 is like setting emission cut targets for 2050: it allows the politicians and polluters to do nothing. The real question is what to do now, not a generation from now.

9: Lifeboat Ethics

It may surprise the many who imagine environmentalism to be always
on the liberal side of the political spectrum, but within the context set
by nativism and immigrant bashing, environmentalism has become a
wellspring of xenophobic resentment.
—Tom Athanasiou[1]

In January 1972, the British magazine *Ecologist* devoted an entire
issue to "A Blueprint for Survival," a manifesto that became one of
the most influential statements of environmentalism in Britain.
Reissued as a book, it sold more than 750,000 copies and is often
credited as the document that led to the creation of the Ecology
Party, later renamed the Green Party.

The *Blueprint*'s central thesis was that "if current trends are allowed to persist, the breakdown of society and the irreversible dis-
ruption of the life-support systems on this planet, possibly by the end
of the century, certainly within the lifetimes of our children, are inevitable." A substantial part of the document was devoted to an argument that Britain's population was "well in excess of the carrying
capacity of the land" and so should not be just stabilized but reduced.

> Our task is to end population growth by lowering the rate of re-
> cruitment so that it equals the rate of loss . . . Governments must
> acknowledge the problem and declare their commitment to ending
> population growth; this commitment should include *an end to im-
> migration*.[2] (emphasis added)

The idea that immigrants were a threat to the pristine wilderness was common among US conservationists before World War II, but the "Blueprint" was one of the first documents of the new environmental movement to advocate a "gated community" approach. Instead of defending the global environment and decent living conditions for humanity, the authors of the "Blueprint" urged defense of Britain's environment for the British, by keeping others out.

A parallel movement to restrict immigration on populationist and environmental grounds emerged at about the same time in the United States.

Guarding the American lifeboat

It is often assumed that all environmentalists hold progressive political and social views, but Garrett Hardin disproves that belief. He called himself an "eco-conservative," but *reactionary* would be a better term. Before he adopted the label "human ecologist," he was a eugenicist who wrote:

> Studies indicate that as long as our present social organization continues, there will be a slow but continuous downward trend in the average intelligence—there seems to be little danger of society's being deprived of something valuable by the sterilization of all feeble-minded individuals—more spectacular results could be obtained by preventing the breeding of numerous members of the sub-normal classes higher than the feeble-minded.[3]

Hardin's most famous article, "The Tragedy of the Commons,"[4] is usually cited for its claim that commonly owned resources will always be overused, but Hardin actually wrote it to promote compulsory measures to reduce population. The "pollution problem," he wrote, "is a consequence of population," a result of too many people "using the commons as a cesspool."

The most important aspect of necessity that we must now recognize, is the necessity of abandoning the commons in breeding. No technical solution can rescue us from the misery of overpopulation. Freedom to breed will bring ruin to all . . .

The only way we can preserve and nurture other and more precious freedoms is by relinquishing the freedom to breed, and that very soon.[5]

Hardin denied that voluntary birth control programs could end population growth. He criticized the slogan "Every child a wanted child" because "women want more children than the nation needs to achieve zero population growth . . . if only wanted children are born the population will grow out of control."[6]

In "Lifeboat Ethics: The Case against Helping the Poor," published in 1974, Hardin compared the United States to a lifeboat with little space to spare. Admitting more people would cause everyone to drown. "World food banks move food to the people, hastening the exhaustion of the environment of the poor countries. Unrestricted immigration, on the other hand, moves people to the food, thus speeding up the destruction of the environment of the rich countries."[7]

Giving foreigners access to American food would just help them win the breeding race:

Every day we [Americans] are a smaller minority. We are increasing at only 1 percent per year; the rest of the world increases twice as fast. By the year 2000, one person in 24 will be an American; in 100 years, only one in 46 . . .

If the world is one great commons, in which all food is shared equally, then we are lost. Those who breed faster will replace the rest . . . In the absence of breeding controls, a policy of "one mouth, one meal" ultimately produces one totally miserable world. In a less than perfect world, the allocation of rights based on territory must be defended if a ruinous breeding race is to be avoided. It is unlikely that civilization and dignity can survive everywhere; but better in a few places than in none. Fortunate minorities must act as the trustees of a civilization that is threatened by uninformed good intentions.[8]

The logic of lifeboat ethics

"Sending food to Ethiopia, for instance, does more harm than good . . . The more we encourage population growth by sending more and more food, the more damage is done to the production system. Every time we send food to save lives in the present, we are destroying lives in the future . . .

"Our best chance of solving these problems is to let each country produce as many babies as the government decides is appropriate. This means each country must take care of the babies it produces. No rich country should be an escape hatch for a poor country . . .

"The quickest, easiest, and most effective form of population control in the U.S., that I support wholeheartedly, is to end immigration."

—*Garrett Hardin, from an interview published in* OMNI *magazine, June 1992*

Barry Commoner condemned Hardin's argument in *The Closing Circle*: "Here, only faintly masked, is barbarism. It denies the equal right of all the human inhabitants of the earth to a humane life . . . Neither within Hardin's tiny enclaves of 'civilization,' nor in the larger world around them, would anything that we seek to preserve—the dignity and the humaneness of man, the grace of civilization—survive."[9]

In the United States in the 1970s, Hardin's anti-immigration argument had very concrete implications. As historian Robert Gottlieb points out, the growth of anti-immigration sentiment in the environmental movement paralleled and was influenced by the US government campaign against undocumented workers from Mexico.

By 1973, the new head of the Immigration and Naturalization Service (INS), former Marine commandant Leonard Chapman, would initiate in conjunction with other border control advocates a militaristic-sounding campaign against "illegal aliens" from Mexico, claiming the country was being overrun by poor Mexicans in search of jobs and economic benefits. This campaign not only increased INS budgets but helped lay the groundwork for the emergence of a new and powerful anti-immigrant coalition that prominently included mainstream environmental population control advocates.

By the late 1970s, population control was becoming synonymous with efforts to control the flow of Mexican migrants.[10]

In that political context, Hardin's lifeboat ethics were popular with the right wing of the environmental movement, but his "let them all starve" rhetoric repelled progressive greens. It was left to Paul and Anne Ehrlich to promote a more acceptable environmental argument against immigration.

"The world can't afford more Americans"

The Ehrlichs didn't mention immigration in *The Population Bomb*, but by the late 1970s it had become central to their thinking about US population. In 1979, they and historian Loy Bilderback published a book on US-Mexico border issues, *The Golden Door*, which argued that the problem with Mexican immigrants was not that they were different from Americans but that they wanted to be the same:

> If native Americans continue unrepentantly in their traditional "prosperity," that is, a resource-gobbling, environment-destroying life-style, then America will continue to attract immigrants, legal and illegal, who will strive to do the same. If the past is any guide, most immigrants will sooner or later achieve a standard of living that is not significantly different from that of the native-born. After all, this is what attracts most immigrants in the first place. Thus, adding people to the United States population by migration would increase the total American impact on global resources and environment, as well as contributing to domestic problems, just as adding people by natural increase would.[11]

They repeated that argument in *The Population Explosion* in 1990.

> Migration from poor to rich nations represents a very different kind of threat, however. To the degree that immigrants adopt the lifestyles

of their adopted countries they will begin consuming more resources per person and to do disproportionate environmental damage . . .

The flow of immigrants into the United States should be damped, simply because the world can't afford more Americans.[12]

In 2004 they added the claim that immigrants are actually *more* damaging to the environment than "native Americans" because they reproduce faster and because by immigrating they reduce incentives for improvements in their homelands.

> Migrants understandably move towards jobs and financial rewards, and overall they appear to find them. That means that, on average, they better their condition, become more affluent, consume more, and thus add more to the overall environmental impact of human beings than if they had stayed home. International migrants may also import high-fertility habits from poor nations into rich nations, raising birthrates among the more affluent—and environmentally more destructive—people of the world. And they often bring great economic benefits to rich economies, contributing to the ability of affluent local people to consume more . . .
>
> To the degree that migration as a "safety valve" keeps poor nations from squarely facing their own demographic problems while swelling the numbers of higher-income consumers, migration will have a negative influence on the chances of reaching global sustainability.[13]

Danish environmentalist Inge Røpke calls such reasoning ethically problematic, "implying that the already established citizens of the affluent countries have more right to maintain high consumption levels than newcomers have to approach a high standard . . . Restrictive immigration policies appear as an egoistic defense of privileges rather than a contribution to sustainability."[14]

Eric Neumayer, a professor of environment and development at the London School of Economics, is much harsher: "I would define eco-fascism as a position that holds that some people have the right to consume a lot of resources and pollute much based on nationality, citizenship or race, but all the rest, which is the vast majority of people, do not have this right. And to ensure this, they need to be kept where they are."[15]

As the Sierra Club's Carl Pope wrote, this anti-immigration argument amounts to telling the world: "We know that our way of life is fatal to the biosphere, but we don't plan to change it, and we can't afford to have you join us. Please don't imitate us back in your own countries either."[16]

That position has become standard populationist fare in the United States, Canada, Britain, Australia, and elsewhere.

The greening of hate

- *Federation for American Immigration Reform (FAIR)*: "The United States will not be able to achieve any meaningful reductions in CO_2 emissions without serious economic and social consequences for American citizens unless immigration is sharply curtailed."[17]
- *Center for Immigration Studies (CIS)*: "Continued American population growth is incompatible with sustainability, nationally or globally. Therefore environmentalists committed to sustainability should support reducing current high levels of U.S. immigration."[18]
- *NumbersUSA:* "There are 305 million people in the U.S. today. We're on track, with current immigration numbers, to add another 135 million in just 40 years. That means more stress on the environment. More roads. More cars. More oil."[19]

The three organizations quoted above are Garrett Hardin's direct political heirs in the United States today. Although they appear to be separate, they are, according to the Southern Poverty Law Center, "fruits of the same poisonous tree."

> FAIR, CIS, and NumbersUSA are all part of a network of restrictionist organizations conceived and created by John Tanton, the "puppeteer" of the nativist movement and a man with deep racist roots . . . He has met with leading white supremacists, promoted anti-Semitic ideas, and associated closely with the leaders of a eugenicist foundation once described by a leading newspaper as a "neo-Nazi organization." He has made a series of racist statements about Latinos and worried that they were outbreeding whites. At one point, he wrote candidly that to maintain American culture, "a European-American majority" is required.[20]

Tanton chaired the Sierra Club's Population Committee in the early 1970s and was president of Zero Population Growth (ZPG) from 1975 to 1977. After ZPG refused to endorse his proposal for an anti-immigration campaign, he founded FAIR in 1978; the founding directors included Garrett Hardin and Paul Ehrlich. Since then he has initiated and funded many other anti-immigration groups, each designed to appeal to a specific audience, each presented as independent of the others.

It's tempting to dismiss Tanton and his associates as marginal cranks, but their influence is significant and growing. FAIR, which focuses on lobbying federal and state governments, claims to have been invited to testify before congressional committees more often than any other organization, and in association with NumbersUSA it has successfully used mass lobbying to derail legislative proposals to give legal status to undocumented workers.

FAIR's legal affiliate, the Immigration Reform Law Institute (IRLI), assisted in drafting SB1070, the anti-immigrant law approved in Arizona in 2010. FAIR president Dan Stein describes SB1070 as "a law that both represents the interests of legal Arizonians and serves as model legislation for other states."[21] Elected politicians in forty-one states are members of FAIR's legislative arm, State Legislators for Legal Immigration (SLLI); in May 2010 it was reported that SLLI-affiliated politicians had proposed Arizona-style laws in at least seven other states.[22]

CIS provides intellectual ammunition for the anti-immigration movement. Although it claims to conduct "independent, non-partisan" research, it has, as Mark Potok comments, "never found any aspect of immigration that it liked."[23]

A frequently cited CIS research paper attempts to assign hard numbers to the argument that by coming to the United States immigrants increase global greenhouse gas emissions. The authors claim:

> If the current stock of immigrants in the United States had stayed in their countries of origin rather than migrating to the United States, their estimated annual CO_2 emissions would have been only 155 metric tons, assuming these immigrants had the average level of CO_2 emissions for a person living in their home countries. This is 482 million tons less than the estimated 637 tons they will produce in the United States. This 482 million ton increase represents the impact of immigration on global emissions. It is equal to approximately 5 percent of the increase in annual world-wide CO_2 emissions since 1980.[24]

They reach those conclusions despite their admission that "one obstacle to estimating annual immigrant and native-born per capita CO_2 emission rates is that there are no data that disaggregate rates of these two population cohorts."[25] In place of real numbers, they use their own estimates, which they base on per capita income figures that are themselves estimates.

NumbersUSA, the populist voice of the Tanton network, blames immigration for unemployment, low wages, urban sprawl, congestion, overcrowded schools, lost open spaces, and more. Its president, Roy Beck, says such problems are caused by "bad recent public policies that raised the volume of national immigration above social, economic, educational, cultural, and environmental thresholds."[26]

The group's website promotes the idea that US citizens of foreign ancestry aren't real Americans. For example, a graph headed "Question:

If Congress doesn't change immigration policies, what will happen by the end of the century?" claims to show that *immigrants* will outbreed *Americans*—but the "immigrants" section includes several generations of people born in the United States, all of whom are citizens under the US constitution.

Greening the anti-immigrant right in Canada

The Canadian Centre for Immigration Policy Reform (CCIPR), launched in September 2010, calls itself a "not-for-profit national organization of citizens who believe that major changes must be made to our immigration policies if they are to serve the best interests of Canadians."[27]

It is headed by former Canadian ambassador to Sri Lanka, Martin Collacott, now a senior fellow with the right-wing Fraser Institute, and former Conservative Party candidate Margret Kopala. Its advisory council includes Derek Burney, a longtime Conservative Party strategist who was chief of staff to Prime Minister Brian Mulroney from 1987 to 1989 and who headed Prime Minister Stephen Harper's transition team in 2006.

Like anti-immigrant groups in other countries, CCIPR uses environmental arguments to give its views credibility.

On its Overview page: "Our high immigration levels make it more difficult to achieve Canada's environmental objectives and inhibit efforts to reduce the extraordinary size of our ecological footprint."

And on its Immigration Myths page, CCIPR repeats the "by immigrating they increase environmental damage" argument—but it refers to "ecological footprint" rather than emissions.

> Immigration currently accounts for most population growth in Canada, and population growth is by far the major pressure on the environment. In addition, immigration to Canada from developing countries (which is where most of our immigrants now come from)

has significant negative effects on the environment in the world as a whole because, according to some estimates, such immigrants have an ecological footprint four times that which they had in their countries of origin. It is worth noting in this regard that, while Canada is often criticized for the environmental consequences of its oil sands development, the impact on the environment of our immigration intake is significantly greater. Immigration in fact has major environmental consequences.

The site gives no source for any of these claims, and its Links page includes only seven "organizations with useful analyses of immigration and refugee issues"—three of which are the Tanton groups FAIR, CIS, and NumbersUSA.

The immigration wedge

At the Conservative Political Action Conference in Washington in February 2010, a young right-winger challenged Mark Krikorian, executive director of the Center for Immigration Studies, asking why CIS publishes papers that support the global warming hoax. An observer reports: "Krikorian nonchalantly answered . . . that CIS publishes articles that are in favor of global warming to force a wedge between different people on the Left."[28]

Right-wing groups in the United States have repeatedly used immigration as a wedge to split the environmental movement.

They have used the wedge directly, by creating pseudo-green groups whose real goal is to draw sincere environmentalists into the morass of nativist politics. Groups such as Apply the Brakes, Population-Environment Balance, and Carrying Capacity Network (CCN) have a light green veneer over a hard core of anti-immigrant ideology that verges on outright racism.

For example, the chair of CCN is Garrett Hardin's longtime associate Virginia Abernethy, who calls herself an ethnic separatist. She is also on the editorial advisory board of the *Occidental Quarterly*, a magazine whose statement of principles says, "The European identity of the United States and its people should be maintained. Immigration into the United States should be restricted to selected people of European ancestry."[29] She is also on the editorial advisory board of the official magazine of the Council of Conservative Citizens, formerly known as the White Citizens' Council.

Historian David Reimers explains that environmentalism can provide political cover for racists: "The population-environmental issue offers the possibility of avoiding the racist issue. By making the environment and overpopulation the issues and not who is coming, anti-immigrant voices can say they are not racists and at the same time can tie their crusade to a relatively popular issue."[30]

The far right has also used the immigration issue as a wedge to split or capture genuine environmental groups. The best-publicized case was the attempt, coordinated by a coalition of anti-immigrant groups, to take over the oldest and largest environmental organization in the United States, the Sierra Club. After losing a 1998 membership vote on their proposal to commit the Sierra Club to an immigration restriction program, a secretive group called Sierrans for United States Population Stabilization (SUSPS) launched a multiyear campaign to win a majority on the club's board. The campaign culminated in the 2004 board elections, when anti-immigrant groups across the United States urged their supporters to join the Sierra Club to vote for three SUSPS-endorsed candidates.

The SUSPS candidates were defeated, but not without a time-consuming and divisive battle that diverted attention and effort from Sierra Club's ongoing environmental programs. If they had won, anti-immigration forces would have had effective control of an environmental organization with 750,000 members and over $100 million in assets.

These wedge campaigns show why it's important for environmental activists to understand the nature and background of groups such as FAIR, CIS, and NumbersUSA. These pseudo-green organizations, and the anti-immigrant program they promote, undermine and weaken our efforts to build mass democratic movements to confront and defeat the real causes of environmental destruction.

The US Center for New Community, which has helped organize against attempts by far-right groups to infiltrate environmental movements and groups, has explained the dangers posed to the real environmental movement by anti-immigration groups:

> This environmentalism represents a new and dangerous form of eco-politics. It is an eco-politics that acknowledges energy constraints, resource depletion, and climate change as scientific phenomena, but its response—to keep out immigrants—denies the possibility of effective solutions. Border fences, racial profiling, and mandatory identity cards will not cap carbon or prevent oil spills. Nor will they bring about the necessary transition to renewable energy and a green economy. Instead, this version of environmentalism desperately wants to promote an American dream of unlimited consumption—for whites only.[31]

Unfortunately, the Sierra Club weakened its own position by continuing to support populationist policies and by declaring a position of neutrality on immigration. Instead of actively defending the rights of immigrants, Sierra voted "to take no position on U.S. immigration levels and policies." Whatever the political realities that led to that position, its real effect is to leave a wedge between greens and immigrants.

10: Allies, Not Enemies

Like the ecosphere itself, the peoples of the world are linked through
their separate but interconnected needs to a common fate. The world
will survive the environmental crisis as a whole, or not at all.
—Barry Commoner[1]

History will judge greens by whether they stand with the world's poor.
—Tom Athanasiou[2]

For the right-wing forces who created and lead the anti-immigrant groups we discussed in the last chapter, concern for the
environment is just a ploy—they'll say anything to justify keeping immigrants out. They are engaged in what's been justly called
"the greening of hate—blaming environmental degradation on poor
populations of color."[3]

But in recent years activists and writers who are sincerely concerned about global warming and other forms of ecological destruction have also adopted the argument that cutting immigration will
protect the environment. A report published by the Australia Institute, for example, concludes, "A high immigration policy would result
in Australia's energy-related emissions being 16% higher than they
would be with zero net immigration."[4]

In the United States and Canada, some prominent environmentalists have endorsed restricting immigration.

Leading ecological economist Herman Daly describes himself as "'anti-immigration,' or more precisely 'pro-immigration limits,' without in the least being anti-immigrant."[5] Agronomist David Pimentel and nutritionist Marcia Pimentel argue that US population should be "stabilized," which they say could be achieved if legal immigration levels were cut to pre-1945 levels and all illegal immigration stopped.[6] Canadian ecologist William Rees, cocreator of the ecological footprint concept, argues not only that immigration harms the destination country's environment but that the money immigrants send home to their families will increase consumption and so "contribute to net resource depletion and pollution, both local and global," and "short-circuit negative feedback from the local environment that might otherwise lead to domestic policies that would moderate population growth and ecological decay."[7]

"Immigration harms the environment" is just another way of saying "population growth harms the environment"—except that it targets a particularly vulnerable and powerless group of people. "We need fewer immigrants" puts the blame on "them," on "the others." No matter how sincere and liberal the defenders of that view may be, what they are really doing is defending "our" privileges against encroachments by outsiders.

As Larry Lohmann of The Corner House writes, the anti-immigration argument "relies on the premise that changing Northern lifestyles is a lower priority, or less achievable, than preventing others from sharing them."[8]

Environmental justice

In 1987, the landmark study *Toxic Wastes and Race in the United States* "found race to be the most potent variable in predicting where commercial hazardous waste facilities were located in the U.S., more powerful than household income, the value of homes and the estimated amount of hazardous waste generated by industry."[9] That report

"A simplistic and dangerous argument"

"Many climate groups who call for a sustainable population rely on the fact that when migrants come to Australia they often adopt Australia's carbon-intensive lifestyles, which increases domestic emissions. We suggest that this is a simplistic and dangerous argument. To begin with, by merely restricting the movement of people into Australia we do nothing to stop unsustainable levels of consumption by Australians that cause environmental damage.

"But more importantly, we must recognize that our way of living in Australia, which is a rich so-called 'first world' nation, has created the conditions where people want to escape poverty, labor exploitation, and environmental problems in poorer 'third world' nations by migrating. Yet it is this very process of 'first world' development that has caused the climate crisis. We cannot then turn our backs on the very people that we have exploited to build our carbon intensive lifestyles; we must recognize our carbon debt and act in global solidarity to stop the global problem of climate change.

"As a huge emitter both historically and presently, Australia has an enormous ecological debt to pay. By reducing migration we're penalizing migrants for a problem that Australians have caused. To challenge over-consumption and social inequity, we must target the social structures that are at the root of the problem, not the individuals who are victimized by them.

"Furthermore, often arguments for population control overlook the fact that Australia is a colonized nation. The urge to protect 'our' food and water reserves fails to recognize that we are colonizers. We must remember that we are part of a culture that has [disrespected] and continues to disrespect Indigenous peoples and their lands and waters. We cannot demand population control—or *any* action in the name of climate change—that does not provide space for traditional owners to make decisions about their lives, lands, and waters.

"Because of climate change there is even more imperative to confront over-consumption and share the world's resources. What we need to talk about is how to share these resources equitably and sustainably."

—Friends of the Earth Sydney,
"A Statement on Population and Climate Change"

played a central role in the emergence of the environmental justice movement in the United States in the 1990s.

As the principal author of the 1987 report later wrote, the new movement was based on the idea that defense of the environment and the fight for social justice cannot be separated, because environmental destruction weighs most heavily on people of color.

> Communities are not all created equal. In the United States, for example, some communities are routinely poisoned while the government looks the other way. Environmental regulations have not uniformly benefited all segments of society. People of color (African Americans, Latinos, Asians, Pacific Islanders, and Native Americans) are disproportionately harmed by industrial toxins on their jobs and in their neighborhoods. These groups must contend with dirty air and drinking water—the byproducts of municipal landfills, incinerators, polluting industries, and hazardous waste treatment, storage, and disposal facilities.[10]

Historically, in the United States and other wealthy countries, the mainstream environmental movement has ignored or excluded people of color: indigenous people, African Americans, and immigrants have been radically underrepresented in the membership and absent from leadership positions and decision-making bodies. The widespread adoption of populationist and anti-immigration policies by green groups in the 1970s drove a long-lasting wedge between fighters for civil and human rights on one side and environmental activists on the other. In the United States, the assumption that "environmental issues were simply not significant issues for communities of color" was "embedded in mainstream environmental activities and policy making."[11]

The rise of the environmental justice movement in the United States in the 1990s challenged that assumption in practice by mobilizing African American, Native American, and immigrant communities into important and often successful campaigns against environmental destruction, particularly on a local basis. In doing so, it also posed a challenge to the mainstream environmental movement.

Scapegoating divides us

"We would like to see a real partnership among immigrant community groups, neighborhoods, and activists with the environmental movement, identifying and struggling for resolutions to the serious problems immigrant-based communities continue to face. But to develop this partnership, we need to grapple with the need to have mutual education, develop political trust, cultural sensitivity, and racial and nationality integration.

"For immigrant-based communities, and for the immigrant and refugee rights movement, there will be a real problem in creating these linkages if the scapegoating of immigrants for over-taxing our resources and for environmental degradation becomes a key component of an environmental protection strategy.

"Instead, I would like to see us work, if not together, at least in cooperation to develop and to promote a more comprehensive understanding of the relationship of immigration, population and the environment, that dispels the myths and lies, and gets beyond the historic scapegoating of immigrants for economic and environmental inequities and injustices . . .

"A simple starting point is to agree that in seeking environmental justice, the 'we' and 'us' includes people of color, includes the foreign born, includes immigrants and refugees without immigration documents. You'd better believe that today's immigrants may have a different view of population than a group predominantly composed of people of European heritage."

—Cathi Tactaquin, director of the [US] National Network
for Immigrant and Refugee Rights, 1993[14]

By challenging the whiteness of the environmental movement, environmental justice advocates have successfully raised the question of constituency and the limits of the existing environmental agenda . . . The rise of the environmental justice groups and their challenge concerning environmental racism suggests that reconstituting environmentalism in order that it become more than just a white movement remains a central organizing task.[12]

In 1991, the First National People of Color Environmental Leadership Summit met in Washington, DC, "to build a national and international movement of all peoples of color to fight the destruction and taking of our lands and communities." It proposed a framework for an inclusive environmental justice movement.

> The Principles of Working Together require affirmation of the value in diversity and the rejection of any form of racism, discrimination, and oppression. To support each other completely, we must learn about our different cultural and political histories so that we can completely support each other in our movement inclusive of ages, classes, immigrants, indigenous peoples, undocumented workers, farm workers, genders, sexual orientations, and education differences.[13]

What we see in this and other statements from environmental justice activists is a profoundly important insight that never appears in the writings of the anti-immigration greens—that the *victims* of environmental destruction can and should play central roles as leaders of the fight for change, and that those victims include the very immigrants that populationists would turn back at the border.

The anti-immigration greens appear to be either unaware of or indifferent to the extent to which the policies they favor divide and weaken the environmental movement. How can we possibly win support from the most exploited working people if we accuse them of responsibility for polluting the environment and urge the government to bar them and their families at the border? That's a recipe for defeat.

Protecting plunder

As we've seen, populationists commonly argue that immigration to rich countries increases global warming, because the standard of living and thus the level of greenhouse gas emissions is so much higher in the countries of the North. Setting aside the fact that most immigrants

Socialists and immigration

In 1910, the great US socialist Eugene Debs responded to a proposal by right-wing members of the Socialist Party of America to adopt a policy against Asian immigration.

Nothing, Debs wrote, "could move me to turn my back upon the oppressed, brutalized and despairing victims of the old world, who are lured to these shores by some faint glimmer of hope that here their crushing burdens may be lightened, and some star of promise rise in their darkened skies."

He continued: "Away with the 'tactics' which require the exclusion of the oppressed and suffering slaves who seek these shores with the hope of bettering their wretched condition and are driven back under the cruel lash of expediency."

Debs' stirring defense of international solidarity is directly relevant to the environmental movement today, so we have included it, in full, as appendix 3.

end up in low-paying jobs that don't allow them to be super-emitters, it's noteworthy that the supporters of that theory rarely ask *why* the countries of the North use so much more of the world's resources.

In 1750, average living standards in the North and the South were about the same; now they aren't even close. That change didn't just happen—as the famous liberal economist Robert Heilbroner explained, the primary cause was "the drainage of wealth from the underdeveloped Periphery to the developed Center . . . The widening gulf between rich and poor nations is undoubtedly not just a measure of the superior performance of the capitalist world but also an indication of its exploitative powers."[15]

Similarly, historian Robert Biel writes:

It is not just that there is one group of countries in the world which happens to be developed and another which happens to be poor. The two are organically linked; that is to say, one part is poor *because* the other is rich. The relationship is partly historical—for colonialism and the slave trade helped to build up capitalism and this provided the conditions for later forms of dependency—but the link between development and underdevelopment is also a process that continues today.[16]

Instead of the "trickle down" economics we're often told about, the South has for centuries been the victim of "flood up" economics— a flow of wealth from the poorest countries to the richest that has not been offset by investment and aid. In the last decades of the twentieth century, the imposition of neoliberal "free trade" policies turned the flood into a torrent.

> Since the beginning of the crisis in the 1970s, the world has experienced a series of major changes that have progressively eroded living conditions for a majority of the inhabitants of the planet. Mass unemployment has settled in, the unequal distribution of wealth has intensified, and workers' wages have fallen sharply. In addition, there are the disastrous consequences of closing the borders of industrialized countries to migrants, increasing recourse to violence in case of conflict, destroying the environment (the greenhouse effect, pollution, massive deforestation, etc.), and deregulating food production.[17]

The wealth of the Northern countries is based, in large measure, on centuries of systematic plunder of the South, a process that continues to this day. Part of that process has been the transfer of polluting industries to the South, where they aren't subject to environmental protection regulations. A 2010 study by scientists at the Carnegie Institution found that the United States outsources about 11 percent of its total consumption-based emissions, primarily to the developing world, especially China. Over a third of the carbon dioxide emissions linked to goods and services consumed in many European countries were actually emitted elsewhere.[18]

In short, the North is richer because it plunders the South, and its immediate environment is often less polluted because it exports dirty industry to the South. In this context, the idea of protecting "our" environment by keeping "them" out is deeply hypocritical.

Our fight is global

Northern activists and commentators often view the people of the global South as passive victims of climate change and environmental disasters, not as leaders and agents of sustainable change. They ignore the powerful environmental movements in the South that in many cases are more active and larger than those in the North.

In Nigeria, oil drilling has caused immense damage to the Niger Delta, home to about thirty million people. Each year, more oil is spilled in the delta than was spilled in the Gulf of Mexico oil disaster of 2010. The *Guardian* has described Nigeria as "the world capital of oil pollution."[19] In 1993, environmentalist Ken Saro-Wiwa helped organize protest marches of 300,000 Ogoni people—about half of the entire Ogoni population—to demand change, an action that led to the trial and execution of Saro-Wiwa and eight other activists on trumped-up charges. Despite this history of repression, Nigerian groups such as Environmental Rights Action have continued the campaign and spread it internationally.

In Ecuador, thirty thousand indigenous people are suing oil giant Chevron for $113 billion to clean up the shocking damage done to the Amazon rainforest, devastation that's been called a "Rainforest Chernobyl." Over three decades, Chevron dumped billions of liters of contaminated water into the area's rivers and left behind about a thousand open pits of toxic waste. The rainforest ecosystem has been irreparably damaged and the groundwater polluted. Cancer, birth defects, and miscarriages have reached epidemic proportions in nearby indigenous communities. The affected communities have launched an international campaign to bring the multibillion-dollar company to justice.[20] They won an important court victory in February 2011, but Chevron says it will appeal the ruling.

In China, rapid industrialization has resulted in equally rapid environmental decay. Deserts are encroaching on agricultural land, ancient forests are being clear-cut, soil fertility is in decline, water shortages are reaching a crisis point, and cities are choking on smog

Support environmental refugees

The Climate Justice and Migration Working Group, an international coalition of human rights and immigrant rights groups, estimates that between 25 and 50 million people have already been displaced by environmental change, and that could rise to 150 million by 2050. It calls for recognition of the right of human mobility across borders as an essential response to the climate change threat. Their statement, which includes a seven-point program in defense of the rights of environmental refugees and migrants, is published in full in appendix 4.

and pollution.[21] Walden Bello of Focus on the Global South reports that more than fifty thousand "environment-related riots, protests, and disputes" took place in China in 2005 alone.[22]

India, too, has witnessed a growing number of struggles on environmental issues in recent years, ranging from local land disputes between peasants and agribusiness to the huge mobilizations of India's anti-dam movement. International Rivers reported in December 2010 that protests against big dams in northeast India have been a regular feature in the headlines. What started as a student movement against big dams in Arunachal Pradesh has now snowballed into a major political issue in Assam.[23]

One of the largest and most effective environmental justice groups in the world is La Vía Campesina, an alliance of peasant and small farmer groups that stretches across more than fifty countries and five continents. It was among the first to promote the concept of food sovereignty, the notion that healthy, sustainable food is a basic human right and that farmers must have democratic control over their land and their products. Hundreds of groups responded to La Vía Campesina's call for demonstrations during the 2010 UN climate conference in Cancún, Mexico, where the peasant-farmer group issued a call to assume collective responsibility for Mother Earth, proposing for ourselves to change production and consumption patterns that have provoked the crisis on this planet; to defend the commons and stop their privatization; to redouble efforts, to work intensively to inform, educate, organize and articulate to build a social force that can stop the tendency to convert the grave problems of the climate crisis into business opportunities and that can promote the thousands of people's solutions; to revise and construct new spaces for international alliances; to prepare ourselves for the global referendum for the rights of Mother Earth and the real alternatives to the Climate Crisis . . .[24]

These are just a few examples of a struggle that extends far beyond the boundaries of any country. Far from being just part of the problem, the people of the South are leading the global fight against ecological destruction. They are our allies, not our enemies, and if we are serious about working with them, then no part of our work should involve efforts to turn immigrants from their countries away at our borders.

Support for immigration controls strengthens the most regressive forces in our societies and weakens our ability to deal with the real causes of environmental problems. It gives conservative governments and politicians an easy way out, allowing them to pose as friends of the environment by restricting immigration, while continuing with business as usual. It hands a weapon to reactionaries, allowing them to portray environmentalists as hostile to the legitimate aspirations of the poorest and most oppressed people in the world.

Immigrants are not pollution. Anti-immigration policies divide the environmental movement along race, class, and gender lines, at a time when the broadest possible unity is essential.

11: Too Many Consumers?

> The world with its billions does not have too many people,
> but it does have too many in their thousands who think that
> they are worth a million others.
> —Daniel Dorling[1]

Closely related to the claim that "too many people" are destroying the world is the assertion that the problem is "too much consumption." That concept is embedded in the IPAT equation—the Ehrlichs themselves tell us that "'consumption' is in some ways a more accurate term than 'affluence,' but PAT is a much handier acronym than PCT."[2]

The concept is often expressed in terms of ecological overshoot or in the number of "earths" required to support our excessive lifestyles. A report from Britain's New Economics Foundation puts it this way:

> In 1961 . . . the UK's consumption patterns were roughly aligned with one planet living—that is, one planet's worth of resources would be needed to support the whole global population at the UK's level of consumption. By 2009, this grew to 3.1 planet living. In other words, we would need an additional 2.1 Earth-like planets if every human were to replicate the same levels of consumption in the UK.[3]

That is an important statement about the nature of the global economy. The countries of the North use a grossly disproportionate share of the world's resources, including both physical materials (water, minerals, food) and ecological services such as the atmosphere's ability to absorb greenhouse gases. Simple justice—not to mention human survival—demands that the earth's resources be shared fairly. The North must use less, so that the South can escape poverty.

In the words of Bolivia's president, Evo Morales, "the United States and Europe consume, on average, 8.4 times more than the world average. It is necessary for them to reduce their level of consumption and recognize that all of us are guests on this same land; of the same Pachamama [Mother Earth]."[4]

But problems arise when populationists attempt to trace the obvious disparity between North and South to the behavior of individual consumers in the North.

- *Alan Durning, Sierra Club*: "The consumer society's exploitation of resources threatens to exhaust, poison, or unalterably disfigure forests, soils, water, and air. We, its members, are responsible for a disproportionate share of all the global environmental challenges facing humanity."[5]
- *A PBS television special*: "Even though Americans comprise only five percent of the world's population, in 1996 we used nearly a third of its resources and produced almost half of its hazardous waste. The average North American consumes five times as much as an average Mexican, 10 times as much as an average Chinese and 30 times as much as the average person in India."[6]

The conclusion usually drawn from such statements is that the world can be saved only if the "average American" can be persuaded to cut back drastically, to eat less, drive less, spend less. "Unlimited production and consumption are at the root of our current environmental decay: people will have to lead more ecological lives and will have to consume less in order to achieve a green environmentally safe and sound society."[7]

In recent years, growing numbers of people in the North have indeed been trying to reduce their personal ecological impacts. Every day more people are driving less, rejecting bottled water, turning down their thermostats, and switching from incandescent to fluorescent light bulbs. Any effort to tread more lightly on the earth deserves approval and encouragement, and the fact that so many people are trying to do so is evidence that we can win a majority in the fight for an ecologically sustainable future.

But important as those actions are, it is essential to recognize that individual consumption is not a major cause of environmental destruction and that changes in individual behavior can make at most a marginal difference.

The argument that the world is threatened by "overconsuming Americans" (or Canadians, or Australians, or . . .) rests on two fundamental errors about the nature of the problem: it confuses two different kinds of consumption, and it ignores substantial inequalities *within* the rich countries. We'll discuss each in turn.

Confusing two kinds of consumption

In a 2008 *New York Times* article, best-selling author Jared Diamond wrote:

> The average rates at which people consume resources like oil and metals, and produce wastes like plastics and greenhouse gases, are about 32 times higher in North America, Western Europe, Japan and Australia than they are in the developing world . . . Americans might object: there is no way we would sacrifice our living standards for the benefit of people in the rest of the world. Nevertheless, whether we get there willingly or not, we shall soon have lower consumption rates, because our present rates are unsustainable.[8]

Diamond, like other populationists who make the "too many consumers" argument, is confusing two very different processes: the "consumption" of raw material and environmental resources in the production and distribution of goods and the "consumption" of goods and services by individuals and households. As Victor Wallis points out: "It is remarkable . . . how little effort is routinely made to disaggregate the 'consumption' category. Common parlance, reinforced by the typical framing of cross-national statistics, links consumption to the satisfaction of individual needs or wants, whereas in fact, as an ecological category, it refers to all throughput of materials and energy, for whatever purpose."[9]

The great majority of "consumption" (throughput) does not involve individual product users at all. For example, the average rate at which people produce waste, mentioned above by Diamond, is calculated by dividing the total population into the total waste. But since 99 percent of all solid waste in the United States today comes from industrial processes, eliminating all household waste would have little effect on per capita waste.[10] Diamond's "average rate" is meaningless.

The case of greenhouse gas emissions is similar. The following summary of emission sources is for Canada in 2007,[11] but the breakdown is similar in other super-emitting industrialized countries.

Passenger transportation	19%
Commercial transportation	17%
Industrial	34%
Residential	15%
Commercial/institutional	13%
Agriculture	3%

Only two of those categories can be reasonably attributed to consumers—passenger transportation and residential, a total of 34 percent of Canada's emissions. Although that is not a small proportion, it shows that individual consumers aren't the biggest problem.

But 34 percent substantially overstates the actual emissions that end-customers have any control over, because about 90 percent of "residential" emissions are not produced in residences at all—they are produced by electrical and natural gas providers and statistically *at-tributed* to residences in proportion to use, even though residential customers have no control over how electricity is made.

A very different picture emerges when emissions are calculated, as the Stern Review on *The Economics of Climate Change* did in 2007, "according to the sector from which they are directly emitted . . . as opposed to end user/activity."[12]

Energy emissions

Power	24.8%
Industry	13.7%
Transport	13.5%
Buildings	7.7%
Other	5.0%

Non-energy emissions

Land use	18.3%
Agriculture	13.7%
Waste	3.4%

In short, the great majority of greenhouse gas emissions originate in industrial and commercial operations. Attributing those emissions to consumers is, to say the least, misleading.

Ignoring inequality in the North

No one can deny that most people in the global North enjoy material living standards far higher than those of most people living in the South. It's often pointed out, for example, that a poverty-level income in the North would support a middle-class standard of living in much of the South. Overcoming such gross inequality is a key task facing any movement that aims to build a better world.

But that does not mean everyone in the North lives a lifestyle that endangers the earth's future. Talk of the "American standard of living" (or Canadian, or Australian . . .) obscures substantial inequalities *within* the countries of the North. For example, Australian author Clive Hamilton writes:

> Most people are prosperous beyond the dreams of their parents and grandparents. The houses of typical families are bigger than ever and are filled with big-screen TVs and DVDs and racks of unused clothes. They are centrally heated and air-conditioned; many have swimming pools or pool tables; most have unused rooms; expensive cars are parked outside. It is nothing for an average parent to spend several hundred dollars on a present for a child or to buy them a personal mobile phone . . . Despite the availability of free education, large numbers of households with no more than average incomes choose to outlay tens of thousands of dollars to send their children to private schools and then to universities.[13]

Hamilton is right to draw attention to the social and ecological costs of mass consumerism. Western capitalist economies depend on continual expansion of mass consumption. Multibillion-dollar industries feed off and constantly reinforce the drive to sell more: automobiles, cosmetics, film and television, mass media, professional sport, fast food, leisure and travel, pharmaceuticals, alcohol and tobacco, personal computers, mobile phones, household appliances, supermarkets, and more. Central to the story is the rise of the evil twins of capitalist marketing: advertising and planned obsolescence. We discuss this in chapter 12.

But Hamilton's conclusion, that this has resulted in a new economic order he calls "consumer capitalism," ignores other important trends. Advertising and mass consumption have grown spectacularly, but they have been outpaced by the military and by the fossil fuel, mining, and petrochemical industries. The influence of those organizations, not consumers, has been the decisive factor in preventing effective action to cut greenhouse gas emissions.

Hamilton, like many other critics of consumerism, describes consumption patterns that only a minority of privileged families can afford. Compare his description of the lifestyles of those he calls "most people," "typical families," and "average parents" with Barbara Ehrenreich's account of the actual lives of her coworkers at the Hearthside restaurant in Florida:

> Gail is sharing a room in a well-known downtown flophouse for $250 a week . . .
>
> Claude, the Haitian cook, is desperate to get out of the two room apartment he shares with his girlfriend and two other, unrelated people . . .
>
> Annette, a twenty-year-old server who is six months pregnant and abandoned by her boyfriend, lives with her mother, a postal clerk . . .
>
> Marianne, who is a breakfast server, and her boyfriend are paying $170 a week for a one-person trailer . . .
>
> Billy, who at $10 an hour is the wealthiest of us, lives in the trailer he owns paying only the $400-a-month lot fee . . .
>
> Tina, another server, and her husband are paying $60 a night for a room in the Days Inn. This is because they have no car and the Days Inn is in walking distance of the Hearthside . . .
>
> Joan, who had fooled me with her numerous and tasteful outfits (hostesses wear their own clothes), lives in a van parked behind a shopping center at night and showers in Tina's motel room.[14]

Those real people aren't "prosperous beyond the dreams of their parents and grandparents." They are struggling to survive, in a society in which the cards are stacked against all but a fortunate few.

Much literature on "consumerism" demonstrates little actual contact with the world; it typically retails the distorted images of everyday life that are promoted on television and in advertising but that have little to do with most people's reality. Ehrenreich's coworkers have no chance of living the life of high material consumption that Hamilton and others describe.

In 2009, 43.6 million Americans lived on incomes below the official poverty line. If anyone is consuming the world into ecological catastrophe, it isn't them.

The problem of inequality doesn't stop at the official poverty line. Indeed, it's hard to reconcile claims of profligate spending with the reality of what has happened to the incomes of most Americans (and their counterparts in other countries) in the past forty years. Economist Michael Perelman calculates that the average income of the bottom 90 percent of the population, in constant dollars, fell 4.5 percent between 1970 and 2002.

> This estimate does not mean that everybody in the bottom 90 percent fell behind but that the losses among the vast majority of these people were sufficient to counterbalance the gains of the more fortunate members of the bottom 90 percent. So probably 80 percent of the population was worse off in 2002 than in 1970.[15]

During that period, while most people's incomes were stagnant or declining, the price of housing, the single largest item in any working family's budget, went through the roof. According to the US Census, the median price paid for a new home in the United States, adjusted for inflation, rose from $27,600 in 1970 to $169,000 in 2000—and that's *before* the housing price bubble![16]

Since individual incomes didn't keep pace, house buying has increasingly become possible only for two-income families.

> The typical middle-class household in the United States is no longer a one-earner family, with one parent in the workforce and one at home full-time. Instead, the majority of families with small children now have both parents rising at dawn to commute to jobs so they can both pull in paychecks . . .
>
> Today the median income for a fully employed male is $41,670 per year (all numbers are inflation-adjusted to 2004 dollars)—nearly $800 less than his counterpart of a generation ago. The only real increase in wages for a family has come from the second paycheck earned by a working mother.[17]

Usually, keeping two jobs requires two cars. And that usually means the new home has to be in the suburbs, where lots are big enough for two-car garages. Suburban houses tend to be a little larger; in Canada, the average household's living space increased 10 percent, from about 116 to 126 square meters (1,250 to 1,356 square feet) between 1990 and 2007.[18] So most house buyers aren't moving into the monster homes of superconsumer mythology, but they are getting a little more room—and so their heating and air conditioning bills are higher.

Family incomes are up, but as a result of rising house costs, unavoidable family expenditures are up even more, as this table shows. These figures are adjusted for inflation:

	Early 1970s, one-income family	Early 2000s, two-income family
Total income	$42,450	$73,770
Fixed costs	$22,890	$55,660
Discretionary income	$19,560	$18,110

After fixed costs (mortgage, child care, insurance, car, taxes) were deducted, the average two-income family in the United States in the early 2000s actually had $1,500 *less* discretionary income than a single-income family in the early 1970s.[19]

Of course, these figures are *averages*, with all the limitations of other averages we have discussed. Working families with higher incomes or fewer children will generally have more discretionary income than this table suggests, while those with lower incomes or more children will have less. But on the whole, the statistics show that most working families live on the edge, with not much income for extras. Many can only maintain their standard of living by going into debt, as the authoritative *State of Working America, 2008–2009* reports:

> Debt is a more important feature of the household economy than at any time in modern history. Over the last decade especially,

many American households have become dangerously overlever-aged . . . Wages and income have largely stagnated, and without being able to count on these means for maintaining living stan-dards, many families have taken advantage of often extremely low interest rates to finance consumption through debt. More families than ever before now live with the insecurity of knowing that a fi-nancial emergency such as a serious illness, loss of employment, or even an increase in interest rates could mean being unable to maintain debt repayments.[20]

There's no question that most working people in the North have more material wealth than those in the South, but as these figures show, the idea that all or most working people in the North are af-fluent is an illusion:

> Meager livelihoods are a *typical* condition, an *average* circumstance in the United States, not an extreme condition. You don't need to earn especially low wages in the United States to face spare cup-boards. The average hourly wage will serve you just fine . . .
>   Millions of American households work and live on the edge. There is no cushion. Even a small decline in wages, at the margin, can hurt severely and force considerable sacrifices.[21]

Populationist arguments typically ignore the huge income dis-parities *within* the countries whose overconsumption they decry. In the largest and richest such country, the United States, the wealthiest 20 percent of the population receives and spends more than 60 percent of all income. In 2006, people in the richest 20 per-cent had a *minimum* income of $97,000 and an *average* income of $258,000 a year—13 times the average received by the poorest 40 percent.[22]

The environmental implications of such inequality are profound. A recent Canadian study found that "the ecological footprint of the richest 10 percent of Canadian households is several times the size of the footprint of lower- and lower-middle-income Canadians."[23] As the report's publisher commented: "When it comes to environ-mental impact, it really is a case of the rich and the rest of us."[24]

The real superconsumers

Perhaps the most frequently misused word in all populationist discussions of the developed countries is *we*. James Lovelock, for example, writes:

> When we drive our cars and listen to the radio bringing news of acid rain, we need to remind ourselves that we, *personally*, are the polluters. We, not some white-coated devil figure, buy the cars, drive them, and foul the air. We are therefore accountable, *personally*, for the destruction of the trees by photochemical smog and acid rain. We are responsible for the silent spring that Rachel Carson predicted.[25]

To paraphrase Bob Dylan, *it ain't we, babe.*

Since 1970 the incomes of most working people in the North have stagnated or declined. Far from engaging in an orgy of consumerist overspending, they have struggled, even gone into debt, to maintain a 1970s standard of living.

The wealthy had no such problem. The incomes and wealth of the rich minority soared during the same years, pushing inequality to extremes not seen since the 1920s. This table, based on US Congressional Budget Office figures, shows the contrast between how the rich and the rest of us fared in the last three decades of the twentieth century.

	Annual income		
	1979	**1987**	**1997**
Average household in lowest 20%	$9,300	$8,800	$8,700
Average household in middle 20%	$31,700	$32,000	$33,300
Average household in top 1%	$256,400	$431,500	$644,300

The trend toward greater inequality—the rich getting much richer while everyone else loses ground—accelerated in the 2000s.

According to US tax data, in 2007 the average pretax income of people in the bottom 90 percent of households was about $900 less than in 1979, while the average person in the top 1 percent took in over $700,000 more than in 1979.[27]

The disproportionate share of income taken by the very rich in the United States, UK, Australia, and Canada has led analysts at one of the world's largest banks, Citigroup, to define those countries as *plutonomies*—economies "where economic growth is powered by *and largely consumed by* the wealthy few"[28] (emphasis added).

Journalist Robert Frank summarized the implications of the plutonomy theory in his book about the extremely wealthy, *Richistan*:

> [Citigroup chief equity strategist Ajay] Kapur figured that the top 20 percent of income earners account for as much as 70 percent of consumption in the United States. Like it or not, he said, spending by the rich was propping up the economy, even as the middle and lower classes were struggling . . .
>
> So rather than trying to figure out why the average American consumer was still spending despite rising oil prices, Kapur focused on the wealthy. He found that since the wealthy had so much disposable income, they were largely unconcerned and unaffected by the rise in oil prices. The continued spending by the rich was, in fact, propping up the rest of the consumer economy. As one yacht owner said when I asked him if he worried about rising fuel costs: "So it costs me $60,000 to fill up instead of $40,000. That's nothing for a boat that costs $5 million a year to maintain."[29]

Merrill Lynch and Capgemini, companies that serve the very rich, publish an annual *World Wealth Report* that focuses on those they call High Net Worth Individuals (HNWI)—people with more than $1 million in investable assets, not counting their primary residence, collectibles, consumables, or consumer durables. The 2010 edition reported that about 0.15 percent of the world's population—ten million people in all—qualify for HNWI status, and that their combined wealth totals $39 trillion.[30]

Within the HNWI group, the *World Wealth Report, 2010* identifies ninety-five thousand *Ultra* High Net Worth Individuals who have more than $30 million in investable assets. Although they constitute less than 1 percent of the HNWI group, the Ultras hold more than 35 percent of HNWI wealth.

And even they aren't the richest group. In the entire world, according to *Forbes* magazine, there are just 1,011 billionaires—individuals with over $1,000 million in assets. Their combined wealth is $3.5 trillion, an average of $3.5 billion each.[31]

If populationists really want to look for superconsumers, they should study the people who have far more money than any human being needs and who, according to Citigroup's analysts, spend far more of their income than they save or invest. Stories of profligate spending by the super-rich are legion.

- David and Frederick Barclay, owners of hotels and newspapers in England, bought an island in the English Channel and hired Prince Charles's favorite architect, Quinlan Terry, to build them a £60 million (US$94 million) castle with thick granite walls, battlements, an 80-meter-long dining hall, two swimming pools, and a helicopter pad.

- British retailer Philip Green flew three hundred guests to the south of France and put them up in a $1,600-a-night hotel so they could attend his son's bar mitzvah. He also flew in stonemasons and other craftsmen to build a 300-seat synagogue on the hotel's grounds. The event featured an evening concert by Italian tenor Andrea Bocelli and another by pop star Beyoncé and Destiny's Child.

- Microsoft founder Bill Gates lives in a custom-built, 66,000-square-foot, super-high-tech house called Xanadu, overlooking Lake Washington in Medina, Washington. Its assessed value in 2009 was $147.5 million. Every door handle was custom made, at a cost of $2,000 each.

- In 2003, another Microsoft billionaire, Paul Allen, purchased the world's longest pleasure boat, the 414-foot
yacht *Octopus*. It has been bypassed by the 531-foot
Dubai, built for United Arab Emirates sheikh Mohammed bin Rashid Al Maktoum. And that boat in
turn is now second to the 533-foot *Eclipse*, built for
Russian billionaire Roman Abramovich, a yacht that
reportedly includes a missile defense system and an escape submarine.
- Petrochemicals billionaire Mukesh Ambani, ranked by
Forbes as the fifth-richest man in the world, lives with his
wife and three children in the world's most expensive private home: a $2 billion, 22-story mansion that features
nine elevators, a movie theater, a swimming pool, a yoga
studio, an artificial snowfall room in which the family can
escape the heat, and 600 servants. All this in downtown
Mumbai, a city where six million people live in slums.

And we could go on. As Daniel Dorling points out, the lifestyles
of the super-rich can be justified only if we somehow believe that each
of them is worth hundreds or thousands of ordinary working people.

Individually these people take up the space that used to house hundreds; they consume fossil fuels and other resources far less sustainably than thousands of others collectively consume, and they
demand the time and labor and subservience of tens of thousands
of others in mining for their needs, manufacturing for them and
servicing them in a way that deprives millions more of the potential
benefits of that labor. Just think of all the human work required to
create the materials and technology needed to furnish a grand
mansion, to kit out a large yacht, or construct a private plane, and
then you can begin to comprehend how just one of the world's
many hundreds of billionaires, someone who can spend a couple
of million dollars a day on leisure time outgoings, harms millions
of other human beings who in total get by on less than that for all
they need.[32]

The "global sect of greedy gluttons," as journalist Hervé Kempf calls the super-rich,[33] occupies global ecological space and generates pollution vastly out of proportion to its numbers. Any attempt to attribute the environmental crisis to "American consumption" (or British, or Australian, or Canadian, or . . .) misses the target if it doesn't recognize:

- The richest 1 percent of Americans take in and spend more than the bottom 40 percent.
- The richest 5 percent of Americans own more than everyone else in the United States combined.[34]
- The bottom 80 percent of Americans account for less than 40 percent of consumer spending.[35]
- In Australia, eleven very rich individuals own more than the country's 800,000 poorest households combined.[36]
- The 147 individuals who topped the 2002 *Forbes* "World's Richest People" list had total wealth equal to the total annual income of three billion people, half of the world's population.[37]

In the face of these facts, overpopulation pales as a social issue. To quote *Guardian* columnist George Monbiot: "It's time we had the guts to name the problem. It's not sex; it's money. It's not the poor; it's the rich."[38]

12: The Myth of Consumer Sovereignty

[The market] rarely has anything to do with choice or freedom, since those are all determined for us in advance, whether we are talking about new model cars, toys, or television programs: we choose among those, no doubt, but we can scarcely be said to have a say in actually choosing any of them.

—Fredric Jameson[1]

Whenever an environmental disaster occurs, someone blames it on consumers.

After the supertanker *Exxon Valdez* spilled eleven million gallons of crude oil in 1989, Greenpeace produced ads that featured a picture of the captain and the headline "It wasn't his driving that caused the Alaskan oil spill. It was yours." The ad continued: "It would be easy to blame the *Valdez* oil spill on one man. Or one company. Or even one industry. Too easy. Because the truth is, the spill was caused by a nation drunk on oil."[2]

Similarly, during the BP oil disaster in the Gulf of Mexico in 2010, the British *Guardian* published an article headlined "We're all to blame for the oil spill."

> Moreover, and perhaps most important, we should not only con-sider responsibility for oil production but also for oil consump-tion. Business and finance are not isolated from our own choices. Companies such as BP can only do what they do because we want what they sell. We're all too happy with cheap oil . . .

As consumers, we continue to depend on oil in various ways and therefore maintain the oil-hungry system that makes oil companies drill in deep water and undertake other risky activities.[3]

We could cite many more examples, all promoting the same simple lesson: If only "we" would kick our addiction to oil, then "they" would stop destroying the environment. If "we" would just use less oil, then "they" wouldn't have to drill in environmentally sensitive areas like the Gulf of Mexico.

Such views rest on the implicit assumption that corporations—indeed the capitalist economy as a whole—are driven by consumers' desires and choices, as displayed in the market. Economist Mark Perry of the right-wing American Enterprise Institute explains:

> Consumers are the kings and queens of the market economy, and ultimately they reign supreme over corporations and their employees . . . In a market economy, it is consumers, not businesses, who ultimately make all of the decisions. When they vote in the marketplace with their dollars, consumers decide which products, businesses, and industries survive—and which ones fail."[4]

This view, usually called *consumer sovereignty*, is widely held not just by conservative economists but by commentators of many political stripes. Indeed, it is the core concept of mainstream economic theory.

> The concept of consumer sovereignty is of central importance to neo-classical economic theory: it is the cornerstone around which the whole edifice of consumer and production theory is constructed. It embodies the main principle of neo-classical economics, namely, that the satisfaction of consumers' wants directs the purpose of all economic activity. Production is the means, consumption is the end . . .
>
> To be sovereign means to have sole power and the view associated with consumer sovereignty sees the consumer as having sole power in the economy to decide what is produced, how much is produced and how the produced goods are allocated. Only those things are produced that consumers want, and the quantity produced is determined by how much consumers want them.[5]

Although it is seldom made explicit, the concept of consumer sovereignty is a cornerstone of all populationist accounts of the environmental crisis. As consumers, we get what we want through the responsive market. We are destroying the environment because we want too much of the wrong things. If forests are cut down, it's because consumers want more wood products, or more of the products that will grow where forests used to be. If oil companies destroy ecosystems, it's because more consumers want more gasoline.

That's why corporations are rarely mentioned in populationist writing: the producers of ever-increasing quantities of goods are simply acting to fulfill consumer demand, which is growing because the number of consumers is increasing.

If that's true, then the entire super-polluting system results from consumer decisions, and we have only three options: reduce the number of consumers, or persuade consumers to consume less, or both.

The manipulated market

The concept of consumer sovereignty rests on the absurd idea that manufacturers and others simply wait for us to declare our desires and then hasten to do as we demand. In mainstream economic theory, the essential business functions of marketing and advertising exist only to inform us about possible choices we might make to satisfy our independently determined wants.

Ecosocialist Michael Löwy writes:

> Contrary to the claim of free-market ideology, supply is not a response to demand. Capitalist firms usually create the demand for their products by various marketing techniques, advertising tricks, and planned obsolescence. Advertising plays an essential role in the production of consumerist demand by inventing false "needs" and by stimulating the formation of compulsive consumption habits.[6]

As the liberal economist John Kenneth Galbraith wrote more

than fifty years ago in his classic book *The Affluent Society*, the theory of consumer sovereignty ignores the "central function" of advertising and marketing, which is "to bring into being wants that did not previously exist." Far from just responding to consumer desires, marketing "creates the wants it seeks to satisfy."

This, Galbraith wrote, "would be regarded as elementary by the most retarded student in the nation's most primitive school of business administration." Only economists refuse to understand it: "they have closed their eyes (and ears) to the most intrusive of all economic phenomena, namely, modern want creation."[7]

Later, in *The New Industrial State*, Galbraith elaborated on the vital importance of marketing—which he called the *management of demand*—to modern capitalism.

> The control or management of demand is, in fact, a vast and rapidly growing industry in itself. It embraces a huge network of communications, a great array of merchandising and selling organizations, nearly the entire advertising industry, numerous ancillary research, training, and other related services and much more. In everyday parlance, this great machine and the demanding and varied talents that it employs are said to be engaged in selling goods. In less ambiguous language, it means that it is engaged in the management of those who buy goods.[8]

To suggest that this effort has no effect on buyers would mean, Galbraith wrote, that industry was knowingly wasting billions of dollars, increasing prices, and lowering profits, for no purpose at all. He called that idea nonsense.

Galbraith argued that even when advertising doesn't persuade some individuals to buy specific products, it performs a more general function on behalf of the system as a whole:

> Along with bringing demand under substantial control, it provides, in the aggregate, a relentless propaganda on behalf of goods in general. From early morning until late at night, people are informed of the services rendered by goods—of their profound indispensability . . .

The consequence is that while goods become ever more abundant, they do not seem to be any less important. On the contrary, it requires an act of will to imagine that anything else is so important. Morally we agree that the supply of goods is not a measure of human achievement; in fact, we take for granted that it will be so regarded.[9]

In *The Consumer Trap*, Michael Dawson argues that advertising has to be understood as part of a much larger *marketing* process that aims "to make commoners' off-the-job habits better serve corporate bottom lines."

> Big businesses in the United States now spend well over a trillion dollars a year on marketing. This is double Americans' combined annual spending on all public and private education, from kindergartens through graduate schools. It also works out to around four thousand dollars a year for each man, woman, and child in the country.

Dawson calls this process a form of "class struggle from above."

> On our side of such struggles, within broad limits—for example, we must eat, drink, and sleep—we have the power to choose what we do with our free time, and we fight to make that time as fulfilling as possible. Meanwhile, big businesses have the power to implant objects, images, messages, and material infrastructures in our off-the-job behavior settings, and, thereby, to influence the choices we make in our personal lives.[10]

This is not to suggest that we are just helpless victims of all-powerful marketing monsters. It is always possible for some individuals to refuse to be influenced by the marketing process or even opt out entirely from the system it serves. As Galbraith argues, such actions have little effect on the system as such, because demand management aims to influence not individual buyers but masses of people, the entire potential market.

> Any individual of will and determination can contract out from its influence. This being so, no case for individual compulsion in the purchase of any product can be established. To all who object there is a natural answer: You are at liberty to leave! Yet there is slight

danger that enough people will ever assert their individuality to impair the management of mass behavior.[11]

Buyers frequently resist being manipulated, and specific advertising campaigns do fail. But by spending a trillion dollars a year on marketing, corporations don't just promote individual products: they set the terms under which the market operates, define the range of permissible choices, and promote the constant expansion of needs and purchases that their profits depend on. They wouldn't spend the money if it wasn't working.

Hiding the facts

The concept of consumer sovereignty also rests on the assumption that consumers know everything relevant about the products they might buy and so can make informed and rational buying decisions.

Of course, that's nonsense. Every part of the capitalist market is characterized by "information asymmetry"—the sellers have far more information than the buyers. Indeed, although economists rarely admit this, sellers routinely conceal important information from buyers.

In the United States during World War II, for example, price controls created a strong incentive for corporations to reduce the quality of food products in order to keep their profits up. When consumer groups campaigned for a simple A-B-C quality labeling system to allow comparisons of canned foods, the National Canners Association accused them of waging a "war" against brand names "in which our system of private enterprise is at stake." Congress obediently passed a law forbidding any such mandatory labeling system.[12]

More recently, North American agribusiness has successfully blocked demands for compulsory labeling of genetically modified foods. No matter what your opinion on GM foods is, it's obvious that shoppers can't vote with their wallets if they don't have the information.

But even labeling can't guarantee that people know what they are buying. Consider supposedly green products, the goods that consumers who wish to make ecologically responsible choices might buy. A study of the North American market, conducted in 2010 by the environmental consulting company Terrachoice, found 4,744 home and family products that claimed to be "green." More than 95 percent of those products made misleading or totally false claims about their environmental friendliness. Over 30 percent of the packages featured fake "certified green" labels. The producers of these products were guilty of "greenwashing," which Terrachoice defines as "the act of misleading consumers about the environmental practices of a company or the environmental benefits of a product or service." The greenwashed products included 100 percent of the toys studied and over 99 percent of the baby products.[13]

These are not exceptional cases. The balance of information and persuasion in the consumer goods marketplace is overwhelmingly weighted in favor of sellers and against buyers, for corporations and against consumers.

The throwaway economy

Marketing isn't just advertising and labeling; it comprises the entire ensemble of measures that corporations take to increase their sales, both absolutely and relative to their competitors. Two particularly destructive forms of marketing are planned obsolescence and throwaway products—the creation of products that are deliberately designed to have short lives and thus to force "overconsumption."

Capitalist corporations have always tried to introduce products that would drive competitors' products off the market, but planned obsolescence involves manufacturers' *deliberately making their own products obsolete.* The technique was brought to perfection in the mid-twentieth century by the automobile industry, which introduced superficially changed models every year. A 1962 study by three prominent economists concluded that since 1949 the US automobile industry had spent at least $5 billion a year on model changes alone, adding 25 percent to the average price of a car.[14]

The automobile industry's success was copied by almost every other corporation. Noted product designer Brooks Stevens explained why in a 1958 interview: "Our whole economy is based on planned obsolescence and everybody who can read without moving his lips should know it by now. We make good products, we induce people to buy them, and then next year we deliberately introduce something that will make those products old fashioned, out of date, obsolete. We do that for the soundest reason: to make money."[15]

What Stevens didn't say is that consumers don't automatically gravitate to the "new and improved" models. Planned obsolescence works only if coupled with intensive advertising, so it's no accident that in the United States five of the ten top spenders on advertising are car companies and that the automotive industry as a whole spends more than twice as much on ads as any other industry.[16]

The most extreme form of planned obsolescence is the throwaway product; it's been estimated that 80 percent of all products sold in the United States are designed to be used once and then thrown away.[17] The most egregious example is packaging, which has been called "garbage waiting to happen." In the United States, about 31 percent of all municipal solid waste is containers and packaging. A third of that by weight is paper or cardboard (made from trees) and 12 percent is plastic (made from petroleum). The production of packaging materials uses 3 percent of all US energy consumption.[18]

In recent decades electronics industries have become masters of planned obsolescence, designing and selling products that can't be upgraded or repaired and that are replaced by new models within months of introduction. The US Environmental Protection Agency estimates that in 2006–2007, 20.6 million television sets, 157.3 million computers, and 126.3 million cell phones were thrown out.[19] As the Computer TakeBack Campaign argues, this waste allows the electronics industry to offload its costs onto society at large.

> Discarded electronic equipment is one of the fastest growing waste streams in the industrialized world, due to the growing sales and rapid obsolescence of these products. Electronic equipment is also one of the largest known sources of heavy metals and organic pollutants in the waste stream. Without effective phase-outs of hazardous chemicals and the development of effective collection, reuse, and recycling systems, highly toxic chemicals found in electronics will continue to contaminate soil and groundwater as well as pollute the air, posing a threat to wildlife and people.
>
> The Computer TakeBack Campaign supports the guiding principle called Extended Producer Responsibility (EPR) for post-consumer electronics waste. The objective of EPR is to make brand name manufacturers and distributors financially responsible for their products when they become obsolete . . .
>
> This creates a powerful incentive for manufacturers of electronics to reduce such costs by designing products that are clean, safe, durable, reusable, repairable, upgradable, and easy to disassemble and recycle.[20]

The corporations that make disposable products are responsible and should bear the cost: that concept is obviously just and could easily be applied to other products than electronics, but populationists don't see it. All that garbage, they argue, just proves there are too many people. A college-level biology textbook puts it this way: "Humans are not only using up limited resources. We are also damaging air, water, and other renewable resources by polluting them with industrial waste, garbage, and sewage. The more of us there are, the more pollution we generate."[21]

The underlying assumption is that industry is just responding efficiently to consumer demands: garbage is inevitable, so the only variable is how many people buy and discard it. The authors ignore the simple fact that between 1960 and 2000, US garbage grew more than three times as fast as the population.[22] Obviously something other than the birth rate is driving the throwaway economy.

The case of the car

In the North, the automobile is usually a family's second most expensive and least environmentally friendly possession. In 2008, 17 percent of US greenhouse gas emissions came from passenger cars and light trucks,[23] which means that private cars are among the largest contributors to global warming. And that doesn't include the environmental damage caused by massively subsidized roads, highways, bridges, and parking lots. As a former counsel to the US Senate wrote in a 1974 report: "In terms of high energy consumption, accident rates, contribution to pollution, and displacement of urban amenities . . . motor vehicle travel is possibly the most inefficient method of transportation devised by modern man."[24]

It's not hard to conclude that we should all give up our cars, and books with titles like *Divorce Your Car* encourage us to do just that. But for most people, living without a car just isn't an option—not because they are addicted to automobiles but because there are no practical alternatives.

> Journalists never tire of pointing to the love of the automobile in the United States. But such "love" is more often than not a kind of desperation in the face of extremely narrow options. The ways in which cars, roads, public transport systems (often notable by their absence), urban centers, suburbs, and malls have been constructed mean that people often have virtually no choice but to drive if they are to work and live.[25]

The hurricane that devastated New Orleans in 2005 provided a particularly appalling demonstration of how indispensable cars are in America today.

> Among the many unpleasant realities exposed by Hurricane Katrina and its aftermath . . . [was] our nearly total dependence on automobiles. Nowhere was this clearer than in the exodus from New Orleans itself. The difference between those who escaped with their lives and loved ones, and those who did not, often came down to access to a car and enough money for gas. Now, in the recovery stage, many of those who were left behind have been evacuated to trailer-park camps, where they are likely to be worse off than they were before, in part because they cannot get to where the jobs are.[26]

North America's automobile-intensive society is the product of a deliberate, decades-long campaign by the oil and automobile industries, aided by compliant politicians, to close down or restrict public transit systems, kill passenger trains, pour billions of public dollars into building roads and highways, enforce zoning restrictions, and promote home construction programs that encouraged urban sprawl—and at the same time market the car as the quintessential symbol of success, freedom, and modernity.

The very design of modern cities has imposed car dependency on most people.

> While we can choose to buy hybrids or cut down on trips to the grocery store, the hard truth is that, in a suburbanized country, there is only so much Americans can do to reduce their car usage. To make a living, they have to work. And to get to work, the vast majority of Americans have to drive . . .
>
> Two-thirds of residents in metropolitan areas live in the suburbs, and two-thirds of new jobs are located there as well. It's no surprise that 88 percent of workers drive their cars to their jobs.[27]

Focusing on "consumer choice" as the cause of car dependency trivializes the issue and makes it harder to find real solutions. The few cities that have reduced automobile use have done so not by lecturing

More than advertising

"An immense amount of effort, including the formation of a vast advertising industry, has been put into influencing and manipulating the wants, needs and desires of human populations to ensure a potential market. But something more than just advertising is involved here. What is required is formation of conditions of daily life that necessitate the absorption of a certain bundle of commodities and services in order to sustain it. Consider, for example, the development of the wants, needs and desires associated with the rise of a suburban lifestyle in the United States after the Second World War. Not only are we talking about the need for cars, gasoline, highways, suburban tract houses and shopping malls, but also lawn mowers, refrigerators, air-conditioners, drapes, furniture (interior and exterior), interior entertainment equipment (the TV) and a whole mass of maintenance systems to keep this daily life going. Daily living in the suburbs required the consumption of at least all of that. The development of suburbia turned these commodities from wants and desires into absolute needs. The perpetual bringing-forth of new needs is a crucial precondition for the continuity of endlessly expanding capital accumulation."
—David Harvey, *The Enigma of Capital*

consumers but by investing in improved and affordable public transit and by abandoning the automobile-centric policies that dominate most city planning. Without such changes and more, the automobile will continue its environmentally destructive role.

The limits of choice

We are not saying that individual use of goods and services is not implicated in environmental problems. Of course it is—but those activities must be understood in their economic, social, and political context. Simply blaming "consumers" or "consumption" leads to wrong conclusions, and wrong prescriptions for action.

The case of the car illustrates the central problem with the idea that consumer sovereignty drives the economy. Individuals and families can decide which car to buy out of the hundreds of models on sale, but the choice of equally convenient public transit is rarely if ever available. Buyers face a "proffered world of micro-choices, where Ford versus Chevy is a live issue, but cars versus trains is most certainly not."[28]

If persuasion and education were all it took to change behavior, the environmental crisis would be easily solved; we have never met anyone who *wants* to pollute the earth or generate ever more greenhouse gases. But the hard fact is this: *most people have no real choice.* As Kim Humphery writes in his critique of anticonsumerism politics:

> More than a few contemporary commentators equate the need to deal with the realities of overconsumption by being overly censorious; diagnosing, chastising or simply lampooning the apparently woeful materialism of the conditioned masses . . .
>
> There is a dire need to re-emphasize within current debates the degree to which, as consumers and workers living in capitalist economies, we are systemically impelled to live, earn, spend, and overspend in certain ways. In terms of economic and social action, our options as subjects of capitalism are limited—and these options differ significantly across the categories of class, gender, race, age, sexuality, and physical and mental ability. We are to varying degrees compelled to work at certain jobs and for given hours, to live in certain types of housing and use particular types of transport, to consume or overconsume various kinds of products and services, to shop in various places, and to map out our life-course in structured ways.[29]

"Ironically," Murray Bookchin wrote, "most ordinary people and their families cannot afford to live simply."[30] For hundreds of millions of people, doing without a car would mean doing without a job, without access to shopping and food, without the ability to take children to recreation and friends.

The areas in which most individuals can easily switch to ecologically responsible products or behavior have limited impact on their lives and on society. As Tim Jackson writes, the biggest problems require *social solutions*.

> It's clear that changing the social logic of consumption cannot simply be relegated to the realm of individual choice. In spite of a growing desire for change, it's almost impossible for people to simply choose sustainable lifestyles, however much they'd like to. Even highly-motivated individuals experience conflict as they attempt to escape consumerism. And the chances of extending this behavior across society are negligible without changes in the social structure.[31]

"In the end," writes environmental policy professor Thomas Princen, "the idea of consumer sovereignty doesn't add up. It is a myth convenient for those who would locate responsibility for social and environmental problems on the backs of consumers, absolving those who truly have market power and who write the rules of the game and who benefit the most."[32]

13: The Military-Corporate Polluter Complex

Our Blue Planet . . . is being held hostage to the tyranny of the bottom line. It is falling increasingly under the domination of those who rule from on high, those who are deciding much of the world's fate from the sanctuary of their executive suites and board rooms.
—Joshua Karliner[1]

I n 2000, the world's two hundred largest corporations employed less than 1 percent of the world's population, but their sales equaled 27.5 percent of the world's GDP.[2] In 2008, there were 166 entities in the world with annual sales or GDP of $50 billion or more: only 60 of them were countries; 106 were corporations.[3]

And yet most books that attribute the environmental crisis to overpopulation have little or nothing to say about the role of corporations. Even the word *corporation* appears only three times in passing (once in a footnote) in the Ehrlichs' *The Population Explosion*; only twice, both times as part of an organization's name, in Brian O'Neill's *Population and Climate Change*; and not at all in James Lovelock's *The Ages of Gaia*.

Focusing on the abstraction of "population" draws attention away from the *social and institutional causes* of the global crisis. The impact of the super-rich on the environment results not primarily from their individual greedy gluttony but from their ownership and control of organizations and institutions whose ecocidal activities far exceed those of any individual or group of individuals.

As an example, consider . . .

The case of Ira Rennert

At some point near the top of the income ladder, *quantitative* increases in income lead to *qualitative* changes in social power, exercised not through consumption but through ownership and control of profit-making institutions, as the case of Ira Rennert illustrates.

If you wanted to start a campaign focusing on individual overconsumption as an environmental crime, then Mr. Rennert, who is number 144 on the 2010 *Forbes* list of the world's richest people, would be an appropriate poster boy. *Forbes* pegs his net worth at $5.3 billion.

Just over ten years ago Rennert built (more accurately, paid other people to build for him) a new vacation home in the Hamptons, on Long Island, New York. There are many absurdly large homes in the area, but Rennert's place, dubbed Fair Field, is believed to be the largest contemporary residence in America.

In addition to three swimming pools, a $150,000 hot tub, and a 164-seat movie theater, it features

> 25 bedrooms and as many full bathrooms, 11 sitting rooms, three dining rooms, and two libraries; a servants' wing with 4 more bedrooms; a power plant big enough to run a large municipal high school or shopping mall; a 10,000-square-foot "playhouse" with two bowling alleys and tennis, squash, and basketball courts; and a multi-story, 17,000-square-foot garage capable of accommodating perhaps 100 cars.[4]

The total area of the buildings at Fair Field is over 100,000 square feet, 40 percent larger than Bill Gates's more famous home in Washington State and almost twice as big as the White House.

Rennert travels in a private Gulfstream 5 jet, perhaps to save time commuting to his other homes. He owns one of the most expensive private homes in Jerusalem, a palatial property he bought for a rumored $4 million in 1996 and then had completely renovated, including installing what are said to be the most advanced electrical, climate-control, and water-filtration systems in Israel. That's in addition to his luxurious duplex apartment on Park Avenue in New York City, which is near the twin $30 million apartments he bought for his daughters as gifts.[5]

Obviously, no one is going to accuse Ira Rennert of living a green lifestyle, but where ecocide is concerned, Rennert the consumer is a piker compared to Rennert the capitalist.

Rennert's wealth comes from his 95 percent ownership of Renco Group, a private holding company whose principal subsidiaries are the only primary magnesium producer in the United States—US Magnesium LLC (MagCorp)—and the largest primary lead producer in the Western world, Doe Run Resources Corporation.

In 1996 the Environmental Protection Agency named MagCorp the number one polluting industrial facility in the United States. As recently as April 2010, the EPA said that investigations on the company's Utah site found

> high levels of environmental contamination . . . [including] arsenic, chromium, mercury, copper, and zinc; acidic waste water; chlorinated organics; polychlorinated biphenyls (PCBs); dioxins/furans, hexachlorobenzene (HCB); and polycyclic aromatic hydrocarbons (PAHs). These wastes are being released into the environment and are largely uncontrolled.

Wastewater ditches around MagCorp's plant are reported to be contaminated with dioxin at levels as high as 170 parts per billion: EPA rules require immediate cleanup action at one part per billion.[6]

Doe Run has frequently been cited by the EPA for exceeding legal emission limits, as well as polluting roads and soils around its facilities in Missouri. In February 2002, health officials found that 56 percent of children living near the Doe Run smelter had high blood-lead levels. An October 2009 EPA report says that soil on one-third of properties situated within a mile of the company's lead smelter contains lead at levels exceeding the legal threshold for mandatory removal and replacement. An EPA administrator said that Doe Run's emission reduction efforts "clearly fall short of what was necessary."[7]

Like many polluters in the North, Renco has in recent years shifted its focus to countries where there are fewer regulations, weak enforcement, and many poor people who desperately need jobs. In 1997 it bought a lead, silver, gold, copper, and zinc operation in the Andean city of La Oroya from the Peruvian government for $126 million; as part of the deal, Doe Run Peru was required to lend $126 million to Renco, interest free, which means that Rennert bought the operation with its own money.

That cash could have been used to live up to another part of the deal: Rennert promised to modernize the smelter and clean up the environment, but an environmental study six years later found that concentrations of lead, sulfur dioxide, and arsenic in the air had increased since the takeover. Renco says it can't afford the promised upgrades.

In March 2005, 99 percent of children tested in La Oroya had blood-lead levels that vastly exceeded EPA and World Health Organization limits.

In 2007, the UK *Guardian* sent prizewinning journalist Hugh O'Shaughnessy to La Oroya.

> The quality of air sampled in the neighborhood by three Peruvian voluntary agencies showed 85 times more arsenic, 41 times more cadmium and 13 times more lead than is safe. In parts of the town the water supply contains 50 per cent more lead than levels recommended by the World Health Organization. The untreated waters of the Mantaro river are contaminated with copper, iron, manganese, lead and zinc and are not suitable for irrigation or consumption by animals, according to the standards supposed to be legally enforced in Peru. The water coming out of the nearby Huascacocha lake contains more than four times the legal limit of manganese.[8]

In August 2009, the Inter-American Commission on Human Rights agreed to hear a case that accuses Peru's pro-business government of "violating the rights to life, personal integrity, and to information and access to justice, due to toxic pollution from Doe Run Peru's multi-metal smelter in La Oroya, Peru."[9]

The Blacksmith Institute and Green Cross Switzerland have identified La Oroya as one of the ten worst polluted places on earth, a list that also includes Chernobyl.[10]

The case of Ira Rennert offers important lessons for anyone who wants to understand the causes of environmental destruction.

One is the cruel absurdity of using "per capita" averages to determine the impact that individuals have on the environment. None of the poisons in Oroya, none of the lead dust in Missouri or the dioxins in Utah were caused by Peruvian or American working people, or by consumers anywhere. Ira Rennert and a handful of high-paid executives made all of the polluting decisions, and only they should be held responsible.

But a more important point is the distinction between consumption and power.

As an individual consumer, Rennert represents hyperconsumption at its worst. His way of living is a gross insult to the earth. But as the owner of the Renco Group Inc., he has shortened the lives of tens of thousands of people and laid waste to entire ecosystems.

As a consumer, Rennert lives an excessively wasteful life. As a capitalist, he has power over the way that other people live—and the way that they die.

That fundamental difference can't be reduced to too many people consuming too much.

A question of power

Environmental sociologist Alan Schnaiberg and his colleagues point out that consumers may decide what to buy from among the products that capitalists put on offer, but they can't choose what is produced or how those products are made—and those are the decisions that have the greatest environmental impact.

> While individual consumers may be the ultimate purchasers of *some* of the products of the new technologies, decisions about the allocation of technologies is the realm of production managers and owners . . . [I]t is within the production process where the initial interaction of social systems with ecosystems occurs and where the key decisions about the nature of social system-ecosystem relationships are made . . .
>
> The decision of which *alternative* forms of production will be offered consumers is not in their hands. It remains in the hands of a small minority of powerful individuals . . . who are empowered by their access to production capital. It is in those decisions where social systems (the producers' access to capital and labor, and their assessment of potential liability, profitability, and marketability) and ecosystems (the producers' access to natural resource inputs and ecosystem waste sinks) first interact.[11]

Michael Dawson makes a similar point: "Ordinary product users remain shut out of major economic decisions. Corporations plan, design, and sell goods and services according to their own profit requirements, without providing any means of subjecting basic productive priorities to popular debate and vote."[12]

As David Coleman commented on the Greenpeace ads that blamed consumers for the *Exxon Valdez* disaster: "This perspective completely overlooks the fact that it was Exxon that chose to use single-hulled ships, that failed to manage the drinking habits of its ship captain, that has worked and lobbied persistently to maintain America's need for a large supply of petroleum, and that pressed to open up the Alaskan oil fields in the first place against the protests of environmentalists."[13]

Similarly, we can reply to those who blamed BP's Gulf of Mexico disaster on our supposed addiction to oil: even if we accept the far-fetched idea that oil companies drill new wells only to please consumers, no one can reasonably suggest that consumers somehow forced BP to cut every possible corner, suborn regulators, or violate safety guidelines. Those decisions were made in BP's executive offices, and consumers had no say.

BP is not an exceptional case. Brian Wolf, an expert on environmental crime, tells us:

> The most widespread perpetrators of environmental crimes are corporations. As most pollution and toxics are emitted at the point of production for private gain, most environmental crimes are committed on behalf of corporations. A recent study found that nearly two-thirds of a sampling of manufacturing corporations had committed some kind of serious environmental offense over a six-year period.[14]

Wolf cites a number of well-known cases of corporate environmental crimes, including Hooker Chemical dumping toxic chemicals into Love Canal for thirty years, the Union Carbide chemical explosion that killed thousands in Bhopal, India, in 1984, the *Exxon Valdez* oil spill, and the conviction of Carnival Cruise Lines for repeatedly dumping waste at sea in the 1990s. "Nothing about any of these incidents suggests that they were accidental events; instead, each of these crimes was the result of premeditated cost-cutting measures that circumvented both environmental laws and common sense."[15]

Business as usual

It's important to expose the arrogance and indifference to human life that lead to criminal acts such as the Bhopal and Love Canal disasters, but it's even more important to understand that corporate environmental destruction doesn't typically involve outright lawbreaking. In most cases, polluting is *business as usual.*

The British consulting firm Trucost advises investors who are concerned about their "exposure" to environmental damage—that is, to the possibility that the corporate stocks they own might lose value if the corporations are required to pay for environmental damage. A recent Trucost report prepared for the United Nations found that the three thousand largest publicly listed companies cause $2.15 trillion worth of environmental damage every year, and the total is rising.[16]

Outrageously large as that figure is—only six countries have a GDP greater than $2.15 trillion—the study substantially understates the damage these companies cause. Trucost's calculations exclude costs that would result from "potential high impact events such as fishery or ecosystem collapse," nor do they include "external costs caused by product use and disposal, as well as companies' use of other natural resources and release of further pollutants through their operations and suppliers."[17]

In the case of BP, for example, the damages would include direct harm, emissions, and the like, caused by normal operations, but not the deaths and destruction caused by global warming, not the damage caused by worldwide use of its products, and not the multibillions of dollars in cleanup and legal costs resulting from oil spills. Nor would it include Shell's massive destruction of ecosystems in the Niger River Delta, or the immeasurable damage that Chevron has caused to Ecuador's rainforests.

So the environmental damages caused by just three thousand corporations engaging in business as usual are certainly much higher than $2.15 trillion a year—probably many times that amount.

Looking just at global warming, another Trucost report examined "Carbon Risks and Opportunities in the S&P 500"—the potential financial impact of a mandatory carbon cap-and-trade program on the five hundred largest companies whose shares are traded on the two largest US stock exchanges. Such a program would require corporations to purchase permits for each ton of greenhouse gas emissions their operations produce. The study found that the permits would cost those companies, *on average*, between 5.5 percent and 20 percent of their pretax profits[18]—the lower figure if permits sell for

$28.24/ton, as provided in a bill then before the US Congress, the higher figure if they sell for $105/ton, the "social cost of carbon" calculated by the Environmental Protection Agency.[19]

Emissions, however, aren't evenly distributed through the five hundred biggest companies: just five companies (Exxon Mobil, Chevron, American Electric Power, Southern Company, and ConocoPhillips) account for 22 percent of them. Even using Trucost's lowest estimate for the price of permits, seventy-one big emitters, mainly electrical utilities and oil and gas producers, would see their earnings fall by 10 percent or more if they had to pay to emit greenhouse gases.

As well, the Trucost report notes, permit prices might have to be as high as $200 to $500 a ton—two to five times as high as the highest permit price Trucost analyzed—to produce the investments in low-carbon technology that cap-and-trade is supposed to cause. In fact, many observers, including us, don't think cap-and-trade will work at any price, but let's leave that aside: the point is that actually paying for emissions could wipe out the profits of many of the largest US companies.

We draw attention to these Trucost studies not because they accurately measure the environmental damage routinely caused by large corporations—they likely don't even come close—but because they highlight the emptiness of any environmental analysis that focuses on counting people rather than investigating the impact of the corporate destroyers. Fossil fuels aren't a side issue in the corporate world; they are the very basis of its power.

> High levels of carbon-based energy are central to virtually every productive and reproductive process within the system—not just to manufacturing industry, but to food production and distribution, the heating and functioning of office blocks, getting labor power to and from workplaces, providing it with what it needs to replenish itself and reproduce. To break with the oil-coal economy means a massive transformation of these structures, a profound reshaping of the forces of production and the immediate relations of production that flow out of them.[20]

That's why the United States, the richest country on earth, has systematically sabotaged every attempt to reach a binding agreement to cut greenhouse gas emissions, while simultaneously spending hundreds of billions of dollars a year to ensure its continuing access to the world's oil.

The world's worst polluter

In 2009, the US military used 5.7 trillion gallons of oil, just under 16 million gallons a day. Its operations produced an estimated 73 million tons of greenhouse gases.[21] Nevertheless, the military gets even less attention from populationists than corporations. It's as though the biggest polluter on earth just doesn't exist.

Every war in history has left devastated environments in its wake, and no military organization is a force for sustainability or ecological good. The toxic horrors left behind by the armed forces of the Soviet Union have been well documented. But those disasters, appalling as they are, pale beside the ecocidal record of the US Department of Defense.

As Barry Sanders found when researching his book on the environmental costs of militarism,[22] it is impossible to get comprehensive data on US military pollution: the Pentagon treats even the most elementary statistics as top secret, and US negotiators prevented inclusion of overseas military emissions in the greenhouse gas inventory reports that all industrialized nations are supposed to publish. Any estimates are at least partly speculative, and as Sanders found, they usually understate the case. Nevertheless, there are a few broadly reliable studies.

For example, a report published in 2008 focused on the greenhouse gas emissions produced by the US war in Iraq between 2003 and 2007.[23] Among other things, the researchers found:

- The war had been responsible for at least 141 million metric tons of CO_2 emissions. That's equivalent to 25 million cars.

- Between March 2003 and October 2007 the US military in Iraq purchased more than 4 billion gallons of fuel. Burning these fuels has directly produced nearly 39 million metric tons of CO_2.
- If the war were ranked as a country in terms of annual emissions, it would rank ahead of 139 countries.
- US spending on the Iraq war could cover all of the global investments in renewable power generation that are needed between now and 2030 in order to halt current warming trends.

The US military is the largest user of petroleum in the world and thus is one of the largest emitters of greenhouse gases. It produces more hazardous waste than the five largest US chemical companies combined. It has rained down tons of radioactive waste in the form of "depleted uranium" on Iraq and Afghanistan.

The military's environmental impacts are also felt within the United States, where the commanders of military bases have ignored environmental regulations for decades. In 2004, the newspaper *USA Today* reported that "about one in 10 Americans—nearly 29 million—live within 10 miles of a military site that is listed as a national priority for hazardous-waste cleanup under the federal Superfund program." Over 10 percent of all Superfund sites are on military bases.[24]

It's been estimated that storing and disposing of the hazardous wastes left behind in the United States by nuclear weapons programs *alone* will cost between $300 and $400 billion—and that's assuming no cost overruns, which typically average 60 percent on military cleanup projects.[25]

◇

"The hidden hand of the market," writes the pro-globalization writer Thomas Friedman, "will never work without a hidden fist."

McDonald's cannot flourish without McDonnell Douglas, the

builder of the F-15. And the hidden fist that keeps the world safe for Silicon Valley's technologies is called the United States Army, Air Force, Navy, and Marine Corps.[26]

What US president Eisenhower famously dubbed the "military-industrial complex" isn't an alliance—it is a single system. Military destruction and corporate production/destruction are two sides of one coin, of an economic, social, and political system that for more than half a century has been dependent on military spending to maintain profits and growth, and on massive military force to maintain its global dominance.

Those who claim slowing population growth will stop or slow environmental destruction are ignoring these real and immediate threats to life on our planet. Corporations and armies aren't polluting the world and destroying ecosystems because there are "too many people," and they won't stop if the birth rate is reduced.

If Afghan women have fewer babies, the US military won't stop firing shells made of depleted uranium into their villages. Nor will military bases in Afghanistan stop dumping toxic wastes into open burn pits.

If Iraq's birth rate falls to zero, the US military will not use one gallon of oil less.

If the United States and Australia block all immigration, energy companies will continue burning coal to produce electricity.

If the world's population growth stops tomorrow, Ira Rennert's companies will still poison indigenous children in Peru, Shell will continue killing people in the Niger Delta, and Alberta's tar sands will still be the worst ecological crime on earth.

If we want an ecologically sound society, we must confront the real environmental criminals. We can't stop them unless we understand and address the real causes of the environmental crisis.

14: A System of Growth and Waste

> Liberal environmentalism suffers from a consistent refusal to see
> that a capitalistic society based on competition and growth for its
> own sake must ultimately devour the natural world, just like an
> untreated cancer must ultimately devour its host...An economy that
> is structured around the maxim, "Grow or Die," must *necessarily*
> pit itself against the natural world and leave ecological ruin in its
> wake as it works its way through the biosphere.
> —Murray Bookchin[1]

A 2010 report from the UK-based New Economics Foundation
offers this succinct summary of the environmental crisis:

> Globally we are consuming nature's services—using resources and
> creating carbon emissions—44 percent faster than nature can re-
> generate and reabsorb what we consume and the waste we produce.
> In other words, it takes the Earth almost 18 months to produce
> the ecological services that humanity uses in one year...
>
> Growth forever, as conventionally defined, within fixed,
> though flexible, limits isn't possible. Sooner or later we will hit the
> biosphere's buffers. This happens for one of two reasons. Either a
> natural resource becomes over-exploited to the point of exhaustion,
> or more waste is dumped into an ecosystem than can be safely ab-
> sorbed, leading to dysfunction or collapse. Science now seems to
> be telling us that both are happening, and sooner, rather than later.[2]

Despite near-unanimity among scientists that urgent action is
needed to reduce and reverse the activities that are destabilizing the

global environment, the corporations that cause most environmental damage are blithely continuing with business as usual.

The obvious question is *why*? But as Curtis White writes, environmentalists tend to steer away from that question.

> There is a fundamental question that environmentalists are not very good at asking, let alone answering: "Why is this, the destruction of the natural world, happening?" We ordinarily think of environmentalists as people who care about something called nature or (if they're feeling a little technocratic, and they usually are) the "environment." They are concerned, as well they should be, that the lifestyle and economic practices of the industrialized West are not sustainable, and that nature itself may experience a "system collapse." But as scientifically sophisticated as environmentalism's thinking about natural systems can be (especially its ability to measure change and make predictions about the future based on those measurements), its conclusions about human involvement in environmental degradation tend to be very reductive and causal. Environmentalism's analyses tend to be about "sources." Industrial sources. Nonpoint sources. Urban sources. Smokestack sources. Tailpipe sources. Even natural sources (like the soon-to-be-released methane from thawing Arctic tundra). But environmentalism is not very good at asking, "Okay, but *why do we have all of these polluting sources?*"[3]

The top managers and shareholders who control corporations have to live on the same planet as the rest of humanity. If you ask any of them individually, they would undoubtedly say that they want their children and grandchildren to live in a stable and sustainable world. So why do their actions contradict their words? Why do they seem determined, in practice, to leave their children and grandchildren a world of poisoned air and water, a world of floods and droughts and escalating climate disasters? Why do they create ever more polluting sources?

Why do the politicians whose campaigns are financed by corporate donations support economic policies that lead to destructive growth and waste? Why have they repeatedly sabotaged international efforts to reduce greenhouse gas emissions? Why do they always support "solutions" that do not work, that cannot possibly work?

Many in the environmental movement attribute the antiecological actions of the rich and powerful to mistaken ideas. Clive Hamilton, for example, says that politicians are "in the thrall of the growth fetish . . . The parties may differ on social policy, but there is unchallengeable consensus that the overriding objective of government must be growth of the economy."[4]

Other writers blame economic theory: mainstream economists have failed to include environmental costs in their formulas, so those costs are ignored. Adopting new environmental economic theories would fix things. Robert Nadeau writes:

> We must use scientifically valid measures of the damage done to the global environment by our economic activities as a basis for assessing the costs of this damage in economic terms and develop means and methods for including these costs in the economic system.
>
> If this could be accomplished within the framework of neoclassical economics, we could quickly begin to posit viable economic solutions to environmental problems.[5]

Many writers blame such commonly used measures of prosperity as gross domestic product or gross national product, because they treat all economic activity as positive, which leads to ludicrous results.

> Economic accounting counts many costs of economic growth as economic gains, even though they clearly reduce rather than increase our well-being . . . For example, the costs of cleaning up the *Exxon Valdez* oil spill on the Alaska coast and the costs of repairing damage from the terrorist bombing of the World Trade Center in New York both counted as net contributions to economic output. According to this distorted logic, disasters that are tragic for the people and the environment are beneficial to society.[6]

Some environmentalists argue that the environmental crisis could have been avoided if governments had only replaced GDP and GNP with an alternative economic measure that incorporates the costs of environmental damage, such as the Happy Planet Index or the Index of Sustainable Economic Welfare.

Such proposals are well-meaning, but they confuse cause and effect. Mainstream economic theory and measures such as GDP don't determine policy—they reflect the reality of the capitalist system. GDP and GNP are measures of economic activity in capitalist society, *from the viewpoint of capitalists*. In essence, GDP is the sum of corporate balance sheets, and from that perspective, the $2.15 trillion in annual environmental damage that Trucost attributes to the three thousand largest corporations simply doesn't count.

The growth imperative

What Hamilton calls a "fetish" is actually an economic imperative for a system in which capital is king. Capital has no conscience and no children. Capital has only one imperative: it must grow.

> The extraction of profit from labour and nature isn't some accidental part of what capitalism is. It's what makes the thing go. Similarly, growth and GDP aren't just bells and whistles that can be removed from some stripped-down, enviro-friendly version of the beast. Growth is why people invest. Without profit or growth, there would be no capitalists.[7]

In the box on pages 181–82, Richard Smith explains why "the growth imperative is virtually a law of nature built into any conceivable capitalism. Corporations have no choice but to seek to grow. It is not 'subjective.' It is not just an 'obsession' or a 'spell.' And it cannot be exorcised."[8]

Economist Samuel Bowles offers a concise explanation of capitalism's growth imperative:

> If a firm is not making a profit, it cannot grow: zero profit means zero growth. And if a firm does not grow, others that do grow will soon outpace it. In a capitalist economy, survival requires growth, and growth requires profits. This is capitalism's law of the survival of the fittest . . .
>
> Capitalism is differentiated from other economic systems by

Capitalism's imperative: grow or die

"1. Producers are dependent upon the market: Capitalism is a mode of production in which specialized producers (corporations, companies, manufacturers, individual producers) produce some commodity for market but do not produce their own means of subsistence. Workers own no means of production, or insufficient means to enter into production on their own, and so have no choice but to sell their labor to the capitalists. Capitalists as a class possess a monopoly ownership of most of society's means of production but do not directly produce their own means of subsistence. So capitalists have to sell their commodities on the market to obtain money to obtain their own means of subsistence and to purchase new means of production and hire more labor, to re-enter production and carry on from year to year. So in a capitalist economy, everyone is dependent upon the market, compelled to sell in order to buy, to buy in order to sell to re-enter production and carry on.

"2. Competition is the motor of economic development: When producers come to market they're not free to sell their particular commodity at whatever price they wish because they find other producers selling the same commodity. They therefore have to 'meet or beat' the competition to sell their product and stay in business. Competition thus forces producers to *reinvest much of their profit* back into productivity-enhancing technologies and processes (instead of spending it on conspicuous consumption or warfare without developing the forces of production as ruling classes did for example under feudalism): Producers must constantly strive to *increase the efficiency* of their units of production by *cutting the cost of inputs*, seeking cheaper sources of raw materials and labor, by *bringing in more advanced labor-saving machinery and technology* to boost productivity, or by *increasing their scale of production* to take advantage of economies of scale, and in other ways, to *develop the forces of production*.

"3. 'Grow or die' is a law of survival in the marketplace: In the capitalist mode of production, most producers . . . have no choice but to live by the capitalist maxim "grow or die.' First, as Adam Smith noted, the ever increasing division of labor raises productivity and output, compelling producers to find more markets for this growing

---

Capitalism's imperative: grow or die (continued)

output. Secondly, competition compels producers to seek to expand their market share, to defend their position against competitors. Bigger is safer because, *ceteris paribus*, bigger producers can take advantage of economies of scale and can use their greater resources to invest in technological development, so can more effectively dominate markets. Marginal competitors tend to be crushed or bought out by larger firms (Chrysler, Volvo, etc.). Thirdly, the modern corporate form of ownership adds irresistible and unrelenting pressures to grow from owners (share-holders). Corporate CEOs do not have the freedom to choose not to grow or to subordinate profit-making to ecological concerns because they don't own their firms even if they own substantial shares. Corporations are owned by masses of shareholders. And the shareholders are not looking for 'stasis'; they are looking to maximize portfolio gains, so they drive their CEOs forward." (italics in the original)

—Richard Smith, "Beyond Growth or Beyond Capitalism"

---

its drive to accumulate, its predisposition toward change, and its built-in tendency to expand.[9]

The result of this "built-in tendency to expand," write Marxist environmentalists John Bellamy Foster, Brett Clark, and Richard York, is a system that is increasingly at war with the world around it.

Capitalism has remained essentially (if not more so) what it was from the beginning: an enormous engine for the ceaseless accumulation of capital, propelled by the competitive drive of individuals and groups seeking their own self-interest in the form of private gain. Such a system recognizes no absolute limits to its own advance. The race to accumulate, the real meaning of economic growth under the system, is endless . . .

Ecologically, the system draws ever more destructively on the limited resources and absorptive capacity of nature, as the economy continually grows in scale in relation to the planetary system. The result is emerging and expanding ecological rifts that are turning into planetary chasms.

The essential nature of the problem resides in the fact that there is no way out of this dilemma within the laws of motion of a capitalist system, in which capital accumulation is the primary goal of society.[10]

The only reason capitalists spend money to buy stock, launch a corporation, build a factory, or drill an oil well is to get more money back than they invested. That doesn't always happen, of course—some investments fail to produce profits, and as we have seen since 2008, periodically the entire system goes into freefall, wiping out jobs and livelihoods and destroying capital. But that doesn't contradict the fact that the drive for profit, the drive to make capital grow, is a fundamental feature of capitalism. Without it, the system would rapidly collapse.

Under capitalism, the only measure of success is how much profit is made every day, every week, every year. It doesn't matter if the profit comes from selling products that are directly harmful to both humans and nature, or that many commodities cannot be produced without spreading disease, destroying the forests that produce the oxygen we breathe, demolishing ecosystems, and treating our water, air, and soil as sewers for the disposal of industrial waste. All of that contributes to profits, and thus to the growth of capital—and that's what counts.

As the *Belem Ecosocialist Declaration* says, "The insatiable need to increase profits cannot be reformed away. Capitalism can no more survive limits on growth than a person can live without breathing."[11]

A system based on waste

In *Capital*, Marx wrote that from a capitalist's perspective, raw materials such as metals, minerals, coal, and stone are "furnished by Nature gratis." The wealth of nature doesn't have to be paid for or replaced when it is used—it is there for the taking. That's true not only of raw materials but also of what are sometimes called "envi-

Capitalism versus nature

"Capitalism, like any other mode of production, relies upon the beneficence of nature. The depletion and degradation of the land and of so-called natural resources makes no more sense in the long run than the destruction of the collective powers of labor since both lie at the root of the production of all wealth. But individual capitalists, working in their own short-term interests and impelled by the coercive laws of competition, are perpetually tempted to take the position of *après moi le déluge* with respect to both the laborer and the soil. Even without this, the track of perpetual accumulation puts enormous pressures on the supply of natural resources, while the inevitable increase in the quantity of waste products is bound to test the capacity of ecological systems to absorb them without turning toxic."

—David Harvey, *The Enigma of Capital*

ronmental services"—the water and air that have been absorbing capitalism's waste products for centuries. They have been treated as free sewers and free garbage dumps, "furnished by Nature gratis."

If capitalists had to pay the real cost of replacing or restoring that natural wealth, their profits would fall, and in many cases would be completely wiped out.

The pressure of competition from other capitalists and the demands from investors for higher profits constantly force corporations to seek new ways to "externalize" ever more costs onto others. A major part of this involves dumping the waste products of production into the environment.

In 2000, the World Resources Institute (WRI) published a major study of "the materials that flow from the human economy back into the environment at every stage of economic activity, from commodity extraction or harvest, through processing and manufacturing, product use, and final disposal,"[12] in five industrialized countries. Rather than study cash flows as most economic studies do, the WRI examined material flows—what happens to actual materials in the course of production and distribution of goods.

It found that "one half to three quarters of annual resource inputs to industrial economies are returned to the environment as wastes within a year."

> Material outputs to the environment from economic activity in the five study countries range from 11 metric tons per person per year in Japan to 25 metric tons per person per year in the United States.
>
> When "hidden flows" are included—flows which do not enter the economy, such as soil erosion, mining overburden, and earth moved during construction—total annual material outputs to the environment range from 21 metric tons per person in Japan to 86 metric tons per person in the United States.[13]

Those figures understate the actual volume of waste, because the study did not include the use and disposal of water, which the authors say is so great that it would "completely dominate all other material flows."[14]

The WRI study confirms the judgment of pioneering environmental economist William Kapp, who wrote that "capitalism must be regarded as an economy of unpaid costs," because "a substantial portion of the actual costs of production remain unaccounted for in entrepreneurial outlays; instead they are shifted to, and ultimately borne by, third persons or by the community as a whole."[15]

Capitalism's claims of efficiency and productivity are based on what Kapp called "the omitted truth of social costs." Such claims are "nothing more than an institutionalized cover under which it is possible for private enterprise to shift part of the costs to the shoulders of others and to practice a form of large-scale spoliation which transcends everything the early socialists had in mind when they spoke of the exploitation of man by man."[16]

In short, pollution and waste are not accidents and are not market failures. They are the way the system works.

Capitalism combines an irresistible drive to grow with an irresistible drive to create waste and pollution. If nothing stops it, capitalism

The Logic of Cancer

"*System-change, not climate-change!* More and more, this demand has emerged in response to the overwhelming signs of environmental destruction around us. It reflects a growing understanding of the incompatibility of capitalism and life. However, many do not understand this. Many people concerned about what is happening to the planet think that what is necessary are regulations which can check the destructiveness of current patterns. Measures which try to limit carbon emissions by offering big carrots and small sticks, which propose taxes to encourage rational economic actors to choose less harmful options, which offer subsidies for forms of power generation deemed less harmful to the environment—all these efforts to patch up the problems which have emerged remain the first choice of those who look upon themselves as realists in the real world.

"The idea that we can regulate abuses within capitalism is not unique to environmental issues. We see the same pattern when it comes to the current financial crisis of capitalism. New regulations, new limits, new forms of oversight are seen as a solution to abuse and excess. They are proposed as ways to encourage good behavior on the part of the actors who have created the situation. Bad capitalists rather than capitalism itself are identified as the evil. And the problem of the newly homeless, the unemployed? Everywhere the same approach: protect those who are being evicted, protect the victims of the system, repair the excesses and all will go (more or less) well.

"The common element is the failure to understand the system, the failure to grasp the very nature of capital and capitalism. It is the failure to recognize that the logic of capital is the logic of cancer—the tendency to expand without limits."

—Michael Lebowitz, "Change the System, Not Its Barriers"

will try to extend both processes infinitely. But the earth is not infinite. The atmosphere and oceans and forests are very large, but ultimately they are finite, limited resources—and capitalism is now pressing against those limits.

In the face of capital's growth imperative, the idea that reducing birth rates will protect the environment seems even more absurd.

Radical ecologist Murray Bookchin once posed a simple question: if the population of the United States were halved today, would US corporations reduce their output and their ecological destruction by the same amount?[17] The answer, of course, is no. The problem isn't people, it's profit, and no population control program will change that.

15: Populationism or Ecological Revolution?

If we want to save the planet earth to save life and humanity, we are
obliged to end the capitalist system. The grave effects of climate
change, of the energy, food and financial crises, are not a product of
human beings in general, but rather of the capitalist system as it is,
inhuman, with its idea of unlimited industrial development.
—Evo Morales, president of Bolivia

The environmental crisis demands rapid and decisive action, but
we can't act effectively unless we clearly understand what is
causing the crisis. If we misdiagnose the illness, at best we will
waste precious time on ineffective cures; at worst, we will do even
more damage.

The "too many babies" argument is an important case in point.
It misdiagnoses the problem, directing the attention and efforts of
sincere activists to programs that will not have any substantial effect.
At the same time, it weakens efforts to build an effective global
movement against ecological destruction by dividing our forces, by
penalizing the principal victims of the crisis for problems they did
not cause.

Above all, it diverts attention from the real sources of the crisis:
an irrational economic and social system that has gross waste and destruction built into its DNA. The capitalist system, not population
size, is the root cause of today's ecological crisis.

◇

For more than two centuries, the idea that the world's ills are caused by poor people having too many babies has been remarkably successful at preventing change by blaming the victims of the existing social order for poverty and injustice. Adding environmental destruction to the crimes of the overbreeding poor continues that process, diverting attention from the real environmental vandals.

Populationism has also long been a weapon of those who seek to provoke division among the oppressed and hatred of those who are "different." Some of the loudest supporters of populationist policies today are anti-immigrant and racist groups for whom "too many people" is code for "too many foreigners" or "too many nonwhite people."

But many activists who honestly want to build a better world and are appalled by the racists of the far right are also attracted to populationist arguments. In our experience, three related factors help to explain why the "too many people" explanation is attractive to some environmentalists.

1. *Populationism identifies an important issue.* Some writers, on both the left and the right sides of the political spectrum, have tried to refute populationism by denying that population growth poses any social, economic, or ecological problems. Such arguments ignore the fact that human beings require sustenance to live and that unlike other animals, we don't just *find* our means of life, we use the earth's resources to *make* them.

If nothing else changes, more food must be produced to feed more people, and that will use resources. That's a fundamental fact of material existence, one that no society can possibly escape.

The claim made by right-wingers such as Julian Simon and Jacqueline Kasun, that a growing population poses no problems because the "free market" will magically provide whatever is needed, is refuted by the reality of twenty-first-century capitalism, which produces enough food to feed everyone, but starves the billions who can't afford to buy it.

It is also obvious that the global hypergrowth of cities is not ecologically sustainable. Over 160 years ago, Marx and Engels called for "the abolition of the antagonism between town and country," and the need for that is even more obvious today, when more than a billion people have been forced off the land into the mega-slums of the South. There are now twenty-three cities with more than ten million inhabitants, and there will likely be thirty-six by 2015.

Society must confront and resolve the gross imbalance that exists between resources and human needs, including the absurd distribution of population that crowds millions into cities while converting productive farmland into biofuel plantations.

Populationists are right that this is an important issue, but they are wrong to blame the imbalance on human numbers, and they are wrong about the measures needed to solve it. Populationists assume that the social and economic context won't change; we insist that it must.

For example, the populationist argument assumes that the only way to feed more people is to grow more food. Since modern agriculture is ecologically destructive, feeding more people will cause more destruction, so the only ecologically sound approach is to stop and reverse population growth.

But as we showed in chapter 6, ecologically sound agriculture can produce more than enough food to feed the expected population growth. And even before that transformation is carried out, *existing food production* is more than enough to feed many more people, as studies by Vaclav Smil and others have demonstrated.

> Food losses equivalent to 10–15 percent of total supply may be unavoidable, but there is no excuse for the enormous losses in affluent countries. If the rich world's food losses could be held to 20 percent of the overall supply, the annual savings (assuming that animal foods provide about 25 percent of all food energy) would be equivalent to . . . nearly half of all cereals on the world market.[1]

In other words, just by reducing the food wasted in rich countries to reasonable levels, we could feed billions more people, or we could help reduce greenhouse gas emissions by reforesting excess farmland. (The saving could be much greater than Smil's figures suggest, because he has not included redirecting the corn now used for biofuels and industrial cattle raising to human consumption.)

Food production isn't unique: gross excess and wastefulness are endemic to global capitalism. In that context, the impact of population growth as such is small.

2. *Populationism reduces complex social issues to simple numbers.* In 1798, Thomas Malthus argued that the imbalance between people and food is a permanent fact of life because population increases geometrically while subsistence increases only arithmetically. He had no evidence for that claim, and history has decisively proved him wrong, but he showed that appeals to the immutable laws of mathematics can be very effective. All populationist arguments since then have been rooted in the idea that our numbers determine our fate, that demography is destiny. Hunger, poverty, and environmental destruction are presented as natural laws: surely no reasonable person can argue when *science* says population growth is leading us to inevitable disaster.

> Among the many explanations of poverty—genetic, cultural, environmental, etc.—which depend for their credibility on a superficial and opportunistic reading of history, none ever has managed to achieve the effect of the Malthusian argument because, in presenting over-population as the root cause of most human ills, it could always threaten us with such apocalyptic scenarios that reasoned debate about alternative explanations has been consistently overwhelmed.[2]

Numeric explanations seem to be scientific and objective, and they seem to be easy to understand, but as we've seen, that's often an illusion; statistics can mislead, and in populationist writing they often do.

But even the best population numbers can't by themselves explain the environmental crisis, because *quantitative* measures can't take the decisive *qualitative* issues into account. Knowing the number of people in a city or country tells us nothing about the relationships of gender, race, class, oppression, and power that define our connections with each other and our world.

Lourdes Arizpe, a founding member of the Mexican Academy of Human Rights and former assistant director general of UNESCO, poses the issue very clearly:

> The concept of population as numbers of human bodies is of very limited use in understanding the future of societies in a global context. It is what these bodies do, what they extract and give back to the environment, what use they make of land, trees, and water, and what impact their commerce and industry have on their social and ecological systems that are crucial.[3]

3. Populationism promises easy solutions that don't require social change. "Part of the reason that worldwide attention is increasingly focused on the population issue," writes demographer George Martine, "stems from its painless simplicity. Attacking environmental issues from a demographic standpoint seems immensely easier than trying to deal with the causes of global environmental damage that are rooted in our very model of civilization."[4]

Noted populationist Frederick Myerson has offered exactly that justification for fighting climate change by reducing birth rates rather than trying to reduce greenhouse gas emissions.

> Just stabilizing total emissions at current levels, while keeping pace with population growth, would require reducing global per-capita emissions by 1.2 percent each year. We haven't managed to decrease per-capita emissions by 1 percent in the last 38 years combined . . .
>
> I think it will be easier to reduce unintended pregnancies and births, which we know how to do successfully through improved reproductive health services and education, than to reduce per-capita emissions, where our track record is poor.[5]

Myerson is more forthright than most of his co-thinkers, but there is no question that he is expressing a common populationist belief—or, more accurately, a common *lack of belief* in the possibility of a better world. The assumption that there is no possible alternative to the present social order is so deeply embedded in the populationist worldview that he and others who share his perspective rarely mention even the *possibility* of deep-going social change. If reducing emissions is impossible, then getting rid of the system that causes them is completely inconceivable.

There is an old joke about a drunk who lost his car keys on First Avenue but was searching for them on Main Street "because the light is better here." The populationist view that we should target birth rates because that is easier than changing society makes the same mistake. Only major social and economic change can save the earth—so focusing on "easier" birth rates is as pointless as searching where the light is good instead of where the keys are.

Getting to the root

Because it separates population growth from its historical, social, and economic context, the population explanation boils down to *big is bad and bigger is worse*, and its solutions are just as simplistic.

Two hundred years ago, radical essayist William Hazlitt identified the fundamental flaw in Malthus's theory: that population growth made poverty inevitable. Malthus, he wrote, viewed the specific social problems and structures of his time as laws of nature.

> Mr. Malthus wishes to confound the necessary limits of the produce of the earth with the arbitrary and artificial distribution of that produce according to the institutions of society, or the caprice of individuals, the laws of God and nature with the laws of man.[6]

Modern populationists are more likely to justify the "too many people" argument by reference to the laws of thermodynamics than to the laws of God, but Hazlitt's criticism still applies. The global economic system within which human beings live, work, consume, and reproduce is grossly inefficient, inequitable, and wasteful. It cannot create without destroying, cannot survive without mindlessly devouring ever more human and natural resources. Blaming shortages of food and overuse of resources on human numbers confuses sociology with biology: in Hazlitt's words, it treats the "institutions of society" as "laws of God."

Populationist responses to environmental problems search for solutions within a system that, as John Bellamy Foster writes, is inherently hostile to all such solutions.

> Logically, in order to be physically sustainable, an ecohistorical formation has to meet three conditions: (1) the rate of utilization of *renewable* resources has to be kept down to the rate of their regeneration; (2) the rate of utilization of *nonrenewable* resources cannot exceed the rate at which alternative sustainable resources are developed; and (3) pollution and habitat destruction cannot exceed the "assimilative capacity of the environment." Yet to achieve these ends, according to current ecological knowledge, we must not simply slow down present economic growth trends but reverse them. Nothing in the history of capitalism suggests that this will happen.[7]

Recognition that *the system is itself the problem* leads to a different approach, the pursuit of an ecological revolution that will refashion the economy and society, restore and maintain the integrity of ecosystems, and improve human welfare.

Reducing population will not solve ecological problems, but replacing the system can make it possible to reduce population pressure where it does exist. As Frederick Engels argued in 1881:

> There is, of course, the abstract possibility that the number of people will become so great that limits will have to be set to their increase. But if at some stage communist society finds itself obliged to regulate the production of human beings, just as it has already come to regulate the production of things, it will be precisely this society, and this society alone, which can carry this out without dif-

ficulty. It does not seem to me that it would be at all difficult in such a society to achieve by planning a result which has already been produced spontaneously, without planning, in France and Lower Austria. At any rate, it is for the people in the communist society themselves to decide whether, when, and how this is to be done, and what means they wish to employ for the purpose. I do not feel called upon to make proposals or give them advice about it. These people, in any case, will surely not be any less intelligent than we are.[8]

More recently, ecosocialist Joel Kovel made a similar point: "Human beings have ample power to regulate population so long as they have power over their social existence. To me, giving people that power is the main point, for which purpose we need a world where there are no lower classes, and where people are in control of their lives."[9]

A movement to save the planet

There are known solutions to the ecological crisis. Many books and reports have explained in great detail how to eliminate greenhouse gas emissions, how to feed the world using ecological agriculture, how to restore broken ecosystems to life, and how humans can live in harmony with the rest of nature. In book after book, report after report, the authors blame the failure to make the needed changes on "the lack of political will."

Political will is lacking, it's true—because the politicians themselves are part of an economic and social system that cannot abandon its pursuit of short-term growth and short-term profits, even if that leads to the destruction of civilization. The ecological tyranny of the bottom line keeps real solutions from even being considered, let alone carried out.

The biggest obstacle to the transition to an ecological society is not lack of technology or too little money, much less too many people.

Socialism, ecology, and ecosocialism

"You advocate a social ecology which you call ecosocialism. What is an ecosocialist? And how does he or she differ from a 'plain and simple' ecologist or socialist?

"Daniel Tanuro: An ecosocialist differs from an ecologist in that he analyzes the 'ecological crisis' not as a crisis of the relationship between humanity in general and nature but as a crisis of the relationship between an historically determined mode of production and its environment, and therefore in the last analysis as a manifestation of the crisis of the mode of production itself.

"In other words, for an ecosocialist, the ecological crisis is in fact a manifestation of the crisis of capitalism (not to overlook the specific crisis of the so-called 'socialist' societies, which aped capitalist productivism).

"A result is that, in his fight for the environment, an ecosocialist will always propose demands that make the connection with the social question, with the struggle of the exploited and oppressed for a redistribution of wealth, for employment, etc.

"However, an ecosocialist differs from the 'pure and simple' socialist, as you say, in that, for him, the only anticapitalism that is valid today is one that takes into account the natural limits and the operational constraints of the ecosystems. This has many implications: a break with productivism and consumerism, of course, within the perspective of a society in which, the basic needs having been satisfied, free time and social relations constitute the real wealth. "

—From an interview with Belgian ecosocialist Daniel Tanuro, in L'écologithèque.com, September 22, 2010, translated by Richard Fidler for climateandcapitalism.com

The barriers are *political and economic*—governments and big industry are blocking serious action. Indifference to the environment is not a choice that capitalists make, not a policy error, not the result of mistaken economic theories; endless pursuit of immediate gain, regardless of long-term consequences, is *the way the system works*.

As individual capitalists are engaged in production and exchange for the sake of the immediate profit, only the nearest, most immediate results must first be taken into account. As long as the individual manufacturer or merchant sells a manufactured or purchased commodity with the usual coveted profit, he is satisfied and does not concern himself with what afterwards becomes of the commodity and its purchasers. The same thing applies to the natural effects of the same actions . . . In relation to nature, as to society, the present mode of production is predominantly concerned only about the immediate, the most tangible result.[10]

The only long-term alternative to such irrationality is what Marx and Engels described as a society in which "the free development of each is the condition for the free development of all," and in which workers and farmers "govern the human metabolism with nature in a rational way."[11]

The politics of ecological revolution are distinguished from the politics of populationism above all by a commitment to confront the powerful corporate interests that stand in the way of change and to democratically refashion human society to function in harmony with the natural world. And that requires a fundamental break with the politics and parties of corporate power and ecological destruction.

In every country, we need governments that break with the existing order, that are answerable only to working people, farmers, the poor, indigenous communities, and immigrants—in a word, to the *victims* of ecocidal capitalism, not its beneficiaries and representatives.

Such governments would move immediately to transform the most destructive features of capitalism:

- rapidly phasing out fossil fuels and biofuels, replacing them with clean energy sources such as wind, geothermal, wave, and, above all, solar power
- actively supporting farmers to convert to ecological agriculture; defending local food production and distribution; working actively to restore soil fertility while eliminating

factory farms and polluting agribusinesses

- introducing free and efficient public transport networks, and implementing urban planning policies that radically reduce the need for private trucks and cars
- restructuring existing extraction, production, and distribution systems to eliminate waste, planned obsolescence, pollution, and manipulative advertising, placing industries under public control when necessary, and providing full retraining to all affected workers and communities
- retrofitting existing homes and buildings for energy efficiency, and establishing strict guidelines for green architecture in all new structures
- ceasing all military operations at home and elsewhere; transforming the armed forces into voluntary teams charged with restoring ecosystems and assisting the victims of floods, rising oceans, and other environmental disasters
- ensuring universal availability of high-quality health services, including birth control and abortion
- launching extensive reforestation and biodiversity programs

An ecological revolution—we would also call it an *ecosocialist* revolution—is the only way to permanently resolve the environmental crisis. But we can't just wait until such governments can be established: the crisis is pressing down on us, and action is needed *now*. The most important immediate task facing *all* serious environmentalists is the building of strong, broad, and inclusive movements for ecological defense, to slow capitalism's ecocidal drive as much as possible and to reverse it where we can, to win every possible victory over the forces of destruction.

As the 2009 Copenhagen Klimaforum argued, building a movement to fight for immediate changes is an essential part of the long-term fight for a comprehensive ecological revolution.

> There is an urgent need to build a global movement of movements dedicated to the long-term task of promoting a sustainable transition of our societies. Contrary to the prevailing power structures, this movement must grow from the bottom and up. What is needed is a broad alliance of environmental movements, social movements, trade unions, farmers, and other aligned parties that can work together in everyday political struggle on the local as well as national and international level.[12]

In April 2010, some thirty-five thousand activists, many of them indigenous leaders, gathered in Cochabamba, Bolivia, for the World People's Conference on Climate Change and the Rights of Mother Earth. The "People's Agreement" they adopted places responsibility for the climate crisis on the capitalist system and on the rich countries that "have a carbon footprint five times larger than the planet can bear." Its key demands include the following:

- cut greenhouse gas emissions by at least 50% by 2017
- protect the rights of indigenous peoples and of people who are forced to migrate due to climate change
- create an International Climate Justice Tribunal to penalize nations and corporations that flout international law
- oppose all procapitalist, promarket "solutions" such as carbon trading and markets for the forest homes of indigenous people
- repay the massive ecological debt that rich countries owe poor nations

The Cochabamba People's Agreement established a powerful basis for organizing the global movement that is so desperately needed, a movement that resists ecological destruction in every possible way today, while mobilizing the forces that will make permanent solutions possible tomorrow. The full text is online at http://pwccc .wordpress.com/support.

◇

Most liberal-minded populationists genuinely want to find solutions to the planetary crisis, but despite their good intentions, the policies they support would turn the environmental justice movement in the North in the wrong direction, both by focusing our attention on the wrong targets, and by preventing us from uniting with the radical movements in the South that are leading the global struggle. Populationist arguments aren't just wrong, they are harmful, because they identify our most important allies as a major part of the problem.

The animating spirit of the ecological revolution is human solidarity. Its overriding goal is sustainable human development. It aims, in Vandana Shiva's words, to "power down energy and resource consumption [and] power up creative, productive human energy and collective democratic energy to make the necessary transition."[13]

It recognizes, in the words of the Cochabamba People's Agreement, that "in order for there to be balance with nature, there must first be balance among human beings."[14] Sustainable environmental development is possible only if we open the road to sustainable human development as well.

Raising living standards globally, eradicating hunger and poverty, improving health care, providing access to education, and achieving full equality for women: all are necessary if we are to win a safe climate and global environmental justice. The scale of the crisis itself limits our options.

> With the increasing scale of the world economy, the human-generated rifts in the earth's metabolism inevitably become more severe and more multifarious . . . There is nothing in the nature of the current system, moreover, that will allow it to pull back before it is too late. To do that, other forces from the bottom of society are required.[15]

The path of ecological revolution will not be easy, and there is no guarantee that it will be successful. But it has the great advantage that, unlike populationism, it addresses the real causes of ecological destruction. We live in a time of extreme consequences, so it's crucial to fight for changes that can actually make a difference.

The ecological revolution aims to transform the way humans interact with nature. Populationism aims to reduce the number of humans who interact with nature in the same, unsustainable way. The choice should be easy to make.

Appendix 1: The Malthus Myth

The view that social problems are caused by excess population is back in vogue. The front cover of the May–June 2010 *Mother Jones* magazine asks us, in large bold type: "Who is to blame for the population crisis?" It offers three possible answers: the Vatican, Washington, or You.

The article warns us that the earth is in "ecological overshoot"—we're using resources faster than the earth can replenish them—and that the problem isn't social or economic, it is biological. "The only known solution to ecological overshoot is to decelerate our population growth faster than it's decelerating now and eventually reverse it—at the same time we slow and eventually reverse the rate at which we consume the planet's resources."[1]

If we believe the author, slowing population growth and cutting consumption are like the miracle elixirs peddled at old-time medicine shows—they will cure everything that ails us. She writes: "Success in these twin endeavors will crack our most pressing global issues: climate change, food scarcity, water supplies, immigration, health care, biodiversity loss, even war."[2]

(Adapted from the text of a class given by Ian Angus at an educational conference sponsored by the International Socialist Organization in Chicago, June 19, 2010.)

Such arguments have long been the standard fare of reactionaries, who use "overpopulation" as justification for cutting off aid to poor countries, eliminating welfare, and blocking immigration from the third world to wealthy countries.

But we should not assume that everyone who holds such views is a reactionary. Overpopulation is also a staple of liberal thinking about the environment. For example, the Sierra Club, the largest environmental organization in the United States, is sponsoring a program called "Population Justice" that promotes birth control in the third world as a way to fight climate change.

And beyond the organized groups, populationist views are very common among well-meaning, honest people who really want to stop climate change and save the planet. So socialists need to have answers to their questions and concerns.

Let's take a look at the man who is usually credited with founding populationist theory two hundred years ago, to see where these ideas came from and what social purpose they served. As you'll see, his views are often misrepresented.

The Reverend Thomas Robert Malthus was not the first person to attribute poverty to population growth, but he was definitely the most effective. His two *Essays on the Principle of Population*, published in 1798 and 1803, were among the most influential political statements of the 1800s.

But despite his long-continuing influence, Malthus's views are today quite consistently misrepresented. If he is mentioned in an article or book, nine times out of ten the author will say that Malthus predicted that one day the human population would outgrow the world's ability to sustain us. His timing was off, but he warned that if population growth isn't stopped, there will eventually be too many people and everyone will starve. These comments on Malthus are typical:

- *Lester Brown, Worldwatch Institute*: "Malthus foresaw massive food shortages and famine as an inevitable consequence of population growth. Critics of Malthus point out that his pessimistic scenario never unfolded. His supporters believe he was simply ahead of his time."[3]

- *Andrew Ferguson, Optimum Population Trust*: 'There was an inescapable truth in the logic of what Malthus said, namely that *unchecked* population growth would outstrip increase in food supply. How world population would change without severe restrictions on growth was clear to Malthus, and became empirically demonstrated around 1950."[4]

- *Jill Curnow, Sustainable Population Australia*: "Malthus has always been right. All species, including humans, tend to out-breed their means of subsistence . . . In the long term the planet can support only few humans at a high standard of living."[5]

That's the common view of Malthus—and it is wrong. Malthus did not predict what's been called the population explosion, and he didn't believe that it was desirable or even possible to slow population growth.

In fact, he explicitly said the idea that population growth would run up against an absolute limit on our ability to produce more was a "total misconception." In the second edition of his *Essay*, he wrote:

Poverty, and not absolute famine, is the specific effect of the principle of population . . . *even if we were arrived at the absolute limit to all further increase of produce, a point which we shall certainly never reach*.[6] (emphasis added)

Elsewhere he wrote:

The power of the earth to produce subsistence is certainly not unlimited, but it is strictly speaking indefinite; that is, its limits are not defined, and *the time will probably never arrive* when we shall be able to say, that no farther labour or ingenuity of man could make further additions to it.[7]

In short, Malthus believed it would always be possible to increase production, and he didn't believe population growth would lead to "absolute famine"—that is, to what some modern populationists call a die-off, a radical reduction in the human population.

Malthus's theory, which he called the "Principle of Population," can be summarized in three sentences.

1. Population will always increase to use up all of the food that is produced, until most people are living in poverty, on the edge of starvation.
2. At that point the increase in population will stop, either because the poor will delay marriage and so have fewer babies or because infant mortality and other forms of premature death will increase, or both.
3. If food production increases above the necessary minimum, the poor will have more babies and their children will live longer, so the population will increase again until a new limit of subsistence is reached.

So Malthus did not say that *someday* the world will be overpopulated. He said population is *always* at the limit or rising to a new limit. As Frederick Engels pointed out, taken logically his theory implied that the world was already overpopulated when there was only one human being on earth.

Contrary to the attempts of modern writers to claim him as some kind of pioneer ecologist, Malthus had no interest in protecting the environment from human overpopulation or protecting people from starvation. His goal was very different: to prove that most people will always be poor and that no social or political change could ever alter that. Nearly two hundred years before Margaret Thatcher declared that *there is no alternative* to capitalism, Malthus won the British ruling class to that very idea.

◇

In 1798, the year in which Malthus's first *Essay on the Principle of Population* was published, the self-confidence of the English ruling class was at a low ebb. Just fifteen years earlier, Britain's rulers had been profoundly shaken by the loss of the thirteen colonies in the American Revolution, a defeat that left them with a much-reduced empire and a public debt so large that many, including the economist Adam Smith, believed England was on the verge of bankruptcy.

In 1793, England and other countries had launched a war against France, aiming to overthrow the revolutionary government and restore the monarchy, but the war went badly. By 1798, Britain's allies had abandoned the fight, and the French army had captured Egypt, a move the English feared was a prelude to an assault on British-controlled India. The war, which was supposed to produce quick victory for England and its allies, lasted more than two decades.

Even more shocking to the British government in the 1790s, many people at home opposed the war—and many were inspired by the French Revolution to demand similar changes in Britain. The reform movement began with middle-class petitions for moderate reforms but quickly led to unprecedented mass working-class political activity and demands for comprehensive democratic change as a step toward radical social reforms. Millions of people in England and elsewhere believed that political change would transform their lives, ending poverty and inequality forever.

Malthus's goal was to refute that dangerous idea. The full title of his book shows his purpose clearly: *An Essay on the Principle of Population, as It Affects the Future Improvement of Society, with Remarks on the Speculations of Mr. Godwin, M. Condorcet, and Other Writers.*

As that title shows, Malthus's essay was not fundamentally a scientific study of population: it was a *political polemic* against social improvement, and in particular against William Godwin and Nicolas de Condorcet, both authors of popular books that said society could improve, that everyone could live in comfort, that an egalitarian society was possible.

In later editions of his book, Malthus replaced the criticisms of Condorcet and Godwin with attacks on the radical democrat Tom Paine and on the utopian socialist Robert Owen.

As we've seen, Malthus didn't predict an "overpopulation crisis." What's more, he didn't think there was any way to prevent the constant pressure of population on subsistence. He had two reasons.

First, he argued that the "passion between the sexes" is so strong that people are unable to resist it, so they will always have as many babies as possible.

Second, he believed that birth control, including all forms of nonreproductive sex, was so sinful that it was worse than having too many children. Malthus was so horrified by nonreproductive sex that he couldn't bring himself to discuss it directly, referring only to "improper arts" and to "vicious customs with respect to women."

In the second edition of his *Essay*, published in 1803, Malthus said that people could avoid having large families by "moral restraint," by which he meant not marrying until they had sufficient wealth to support children and remaining celibate until that time. He believed, however, that most of the poor didn't have the self-control required. As he had written in the First Essay, that was why they were poor:

> The laboring poor . . . seem always to live from hand to mouth. Their present wants employ their whole attention, and they seldom think of the future. Even when they have an opportunity of saving, they seldom exercise it, but all that is beyond their present necessities goes, generally speaking, to the ale house.[8]

In short, the "moral restraint" argument allowed Malthus and the English ruling class to blame poverty on the moral failures of the poor.

Malthus's success as a polemicist came not from facts or logic—there was little of either to be found in his *Essay*—but in the political conclusions he drew from his "principle of population."

If Malthus was right, then all attempts to build a better society are doomed. Prior to Malthus, Edmund Burke had issued a sweeping denunciation of all proposals to improve society, but Burke's attack was crudely reactionary: the old ways were better, all change is bad.

Burke said equality was a bad idea. Malthus said it would be wonderful, but it is impossible; the population principle won't allow it. "From the inevitable laws of our nature," he wrote, "some human beings must suffer from want."[9]

What Malthus did—and this was really his most important contribution to capitalist ideology—was to replace a moral argument against social change with a *natural law* argument, that human problems are caused by *biology*, by the laws of nature. He wrote:

> In every society that has advanced beyond the savage state, a class of proprietors and a class of laborers must necessarily exist.[10]

And later:

> No improved form of government, no plans of emigration, no benevolent institutions, and no degree or direction of national industry, can prevent the continued action of a great check to population in some form or other; it follows that we must submit to it as an inevitable law of nature.[11]

Malthus didn't just say that society couldn't get better, he argued that trying to ease the suffering of the poor actually made things worse. The Poor Laws, which since 1500 had required communities to provide food and other help to the destitute, just enabled the poor to have more babies and so increased poverty. The parts of his essay arguing for abolition of the Poor Laws have a very modern feel: they are virtually identical to the arguments we hear today against welfare.

This illustrates the central danger of all populationist theories. They are not and have never been politically neutral. No policy based on such views has ever involved reducing the number of rich people. Again and again, for over two centuries, the "too many people" argument has meant "too many poor people"—and most often it has meant "too many poor nonwhite people."

As the noted Marxist geographer David Harvey writes: "Whenever a theory of overpopulation seizes hold in a society dominated by an elite, then the non-elite invariably experience some form of political, economic, and social repression."[12]

Malthus, as we have seen, was opposed to the use of "improper arts," by which he meant birth control. In addition to his moral objection, he argued that if the poor could avoid having babies by artificial means, they would not have the stimulus of poverty to make them work hard, and that of course would harm the rich.

Modern populationist thought, by contrast, argues that the world would be a better place if smart rich people could convince the ignorant poor to stop overbreeding by using birth control.

That shift was initiated in the 1820s by Francis Place, who really deserves to be considered the father of modern populationism. Place had been a radical working-class organizer, but at some point he concluded that organizing unions would always fail so long as the number of workers exceeded the number of jobs available. Anyone who truly wants to raise living standards, he concluded, should educate the poor in the importance of restricting their numbers by using birth control.

This view, often called neo-Malthusianism, was widely considered outrageous and immoral when Place proposed it, but it gained adherents, and today it is universally accepted by populationists.

However, both classical Malthusianism and neo-Malthusianism went into decline by the early twentieth century, for two closely related reasons.

First, working people in many countries were able, through organization and struggle, to win real long-term gains in their standard of living. They provided a practical refutation of Malthus's assertion that the "principle of population" made subsistence-level poverty inevitable.

Second, the birth rate in some European countries started to fall. In France, for example, the birth rate in 1913 was half of what it was in 1800. The causes of the change are complex and not well understood, but it is clear that women were finding ways to control their own fecundity, as part of their broader struggle against economic and social oppression. In so doing, they proved conclusively that biology is not destiny.

The decline in birth rates that began in Europe in the 1800s was interrupted by the postwar "baby boom," but what is now called the "demographic transition" resumed in the 1970s, and it has spread to most of the world. The rate of population increase peaked in the late 1960s. Today the world's total population continues to grow, but at a substantially reduced rate. Most demographers believe the total world population will peak in this century.

For our purposes, there are two key points to note.

The first point is that the demographic transition directly contradicts Malthus. He said the birth rate would go up if the poor had enough to eat—in fact it has fallen fastest and farthest in rich countries.

The second point is that the demographic transition undermines a common assumption made by populationists—that high birth rates are the result of ignorant poor people not knowing about birth control. Birth rates started falling dramatically in Europe before modern birth control devices were available, even in countries where any form of birth control was illegal.

Obviously, as socialists and humanists, we are in favor of making all forms of birth control and maternal health services available to women everywhere. But we also need to beware of the racism, conscious and unconscious, that is embedded in the assumption that poor women in the third world have large families because they don't know any better.

Peasants in Africa today are not more ignorant of their bodies than the peasants of France and Italy before World War II. They continue to have large families because children are essential to personal and social survival. Subsistence farming requires many workers, and the absence of anything resembling a social safety net means that aging parents need the economic and social support of their children. Birth rates in those countries will undoubtedly stabilize when working people win secure and adequate living standards.

In short, high birth rates aren't the cause of third world poverty—they are an effect of poverty, and building birth control clinics, however important that is for other reasons, won't eliminate the underlying causes.

For anyone who really wants to understand the causes of environmental destruction, Marxism offers vastly more insight than populationism.

Today, Marxism is fighting an uphill battle. But in this battle for the minds of green activists, we have one great weapon on our side: an explanation that actually explains. As John Bellamy Foster wrote:

> Where threats to the integrity of the biosphere as we know it are concerned, it is well to remember that it is not the areas of the world that have the highest rate of population growth but the areas of the world that have the highest accumulation of capital, and where economic and ecological waste has become a way of life, that constitute the greatest danger.[13]

Helping greens to understand that is a crucial part of building the movement for socialism in the twenty-first century.

Appendix 2: Donella Meadows Reconsiders IPAT

Who Causes Environmental Problems?

To a small but influential bunch of global thinkers the abbreviation IPAT (pronounced "eye-pat") says volumes. It summarizes all the causes of our environmental problems.

IPAT comes from a formula originally put forth by ecologist Paul Ehrlich and physicist John Holdren:

Impact equals Population times Affluence times Technology

Which is to say, the damage we do to the earth can be figured as the number of people there are, multiplied by the amount of stuff each person uses, multiplied by the amount of pollution or waste involved in making and using each piece of stuff.

A car emits more pollution than a bicycle, and so the 10 percent of the world's people rich enough to have cars cause more environmental impact in their transport than do the much more numerous bicycling

For many years, Dr. Donella Meadows, a lead author of The Limits to Growth *(1972),* Beyond the Limits *(1992), and* The Limits to Growth: The 30 Year Up-date *(2004), accepted IPAT as a framework for understanding environmental problems. As this 1995 article shows, she reconsidered that position after attending a conference on global environmental policy. We are grateful to The Sustainability Institute (http://www.sustainer.org) for permission to republish it.*

poor. But a car with a catalytic converter is less polluting than a car without one, and a solar car even less. So technology can counter some of the impact of affluence.

The IPAT formula has great appeal in international debates, because it spreads environmental responsibility around. The poor account for 90 percent of global population increase—so they'd better get to work on P. Rich consumers need to control their hedonistic A. The former Soviets with their polluting factories, cars, and buildings obviously should concentrate on T.

I didn't realize how politically correct this formula had become, until a few months ago when I watched a panel of five women challenge it and enrage an auditorium full of environmentalists, including me.

IPAT is a bloodless, misleading, cop-out explanation for the world's ills, they said. It points the finger of blame at all the wrong places. It leads one to hold poor women responsible for population growth without asking who is putting what pressures on those women to cause them to have so many babies. It lays a guilt trip on Western consumers, while ignoring the forces that whip up their desire for ever more consumption. It implies that the people of the East, who were oppressed by totalitarian leaders for generations, now somehow have to clean up those leaders' messes.

As I listened to this argument, I got mad. IPAT was the lens through which I saw the environmental situation. It's neat and simple. I didn't want to see any other way.

IPAT is just what you would expect from physical scientists, said one of the critics, Patricia Hynes of the Institute on Women and Technology in North Amherst, Massachusetts. It counts what is countable. It makes rational sense. But it ignores the manipulation, the oppression, the profits. It ignores a factor that scientists have a hard time quantifying and therefore don't like to talk about: economic and political POWER. IPAT may be physically indisputable. But it is politically naive.

I was shifting uneasily in my seat.

There are no AGENTS in the IPAT equation, said Patricia Hynes, no identifiable ACTORS, no genders, colors, motivations. Population growth and consumption and technology don't just happen. Particular people make them happen, people who shape and respond to rewards and punishments, people who may be acting out of desperation or love or greed or ambition or fear.

Unfortunately, I said to myself, I agree with this.

Suppose we wrote the environmental impact equation a different way, said the annoying panel at the front of the auditorium. Suppose, for example, we put in a term for the military sector, which, though its Population is not high, commands a lot of Affluence and Technology. Military reactors generate 97 percent of the high-level nuclear waste of the US. Global military operations are estimated to cause 20 percent of all environmental degradation. The Worldwatch Institute says that "the world's armed forces are quite likely the single largest polluter on earth."

Suppose we added another term for the two hundred largest corporations, which employ only 0.5 percent of all workers but generate 25 percent of the gross world product—and something like 25 percent of the pollution. Perhaps, if we had the statistics, we would find that small businesses, where most of the jobs are, produce far less than their share of environmental impact.

Suppose we separate government consumption from household consumption, and distinguish between household consumption for subsistence and for luxury, for show, for making us feel better about ourselves. If we had reliable numbers, which we don't, we might be able to calculate how much of the damage we do to the earth comes from necessity and how much from vanity.

An equation was beginning to form in my head:

*Impact equals Military plus Large Business plus Small Business
plus Government plus Luxury Consumption
plus Subsistence Consumption*

Each of those terms has its own P and A and T. Very messy. Probably some double counting and some terms left out. But no more right or wrong, really, than IPAT.

Use a different lens and you see different things, you ask different questions, you find different answers. What you see through any lens is in fact there, though it is never all that is there. It's important to remember, whatever lens you use, that it lets you see some things but it prevents you from seeing others.

———————————

Appendix 3:
Eugene V. Debs on Immigration

My Dear Brewer:

Have just read the majority report of the Committee on Immigration. It is utterly unsocialistic, reactionary, and in truth outrageous, and I hope you will oppose with all your power. The plea that certain races are to be excluded because of tactical expediency would be entirely consistent in a bourgeois convention of self-seekers, but should have no place in a proletariat gathering under the auspices of an international movement that is calling on the oppressed and exploited workers of all the world to unite for their emancipation . . .

Away with the "tactics" which require the exclusion of the oppressed and suffering slaves who seek these shores with the hope of bettering their wretched condition and are driven back under the cruel lash of expediency by those who call themselves Socialists in the name

---

Eugene V. Debs (1855–1926) was a founding member of the Industrial Workers of the World and five-time candidate of the Socialist Party of America for president of the United States. In this letter, dated July 1910, he defended traditional socialist policy against an attempt by the party's right wing to adopt a policy against Asian immigration. His correspondent was George Brewer, a leader of the SPA in Kansas who wrote for the socialist newspaper Appeal to Reason.

of a movement whose proud boast it is that it stands uncompromisingly for the oppressed and downtrodden of all the earth. These poor slaves have just as good a right to enter here as even the authors of this report who now seek to exclude them. The only difference is that the latter had the advantage of a little education and had not been so cruelly ground and oppressed, but in point of principle there is no difference, the motive of all being precisely the same, and if the convention which meets in the name of Socialism should discriminate at all it should be in favor of the miserable races who have borne the heaviest burdens and are most nearly crushed to the earth.

Upon this vital proposition I would take my stand against the world and no specious argument of subtle and sophistical defenders of the civic federation unionism, who do not hesitate to sacrifice principle for numbers and jeopardize ultimate success for immediate gain, could move me to turn my back upon the oppressed, brutalized, and despairing victims of the old world, who are lured to these shores by some faint glimmer of hope that here their crushing burdens may be lightened, and some star of promise rise in their darkened skies.

The alleged advantages that would come to the Socialist movement because of such heartless exclusion would all be swept away a thousand times by the sacrifice of a cardinal principle of the international socialist movement, for well might the good faith of such a movement be questioned by intelligent workers if it placed itself upon record as barring its doors against the very races most in need of relief, and extinguishing their hope, and leaving them in dark despair at the very time their ears were first attuned to the international call and their hearts were beginning to throb responsive to the solidarity of the oppressed of all lands and all climes beneath the skies.

In this attitude there is nothing of maudlin sentimentality, but simply a rigid adherence to the fundamental principles of the International proletarian movement. If Socialism, international, revolutionary Socialism, does not stand staunchly, unflinchingly, and uncompromisingly for the working class and for the exploited and oppressed masses of all lands, then it stands for none and its claim is a false pretense and its profession a delusion and a snare.

Let those desert us who will because we refuse to shut the international door in the faces of their own brethren; we will be none the weaker but all the stronger for their going, for they evidently have no clear conception of the international solidarity, are wholly lacking in the revolutionary spirit, and have no proper place in the Socialist movement while they entertain such aristocratic notions of their own assumed superiority.

Let us stand squarely on our revolutionary, working-class principles and make our fight openly and uncompromisingly against all our enemies, adopting no cowardly tactics and holding out no false hopes, and our movement will then inspire the faith, arouse the spirit, and develop the fiber that will prevail against the world.

Yours without compromise,
Eugene V. Debs

Appendix 4: Climate Justice and Migration

As members of the Climate Justice and Migration Working Group of the Mobilization for Climate Justice, we represent national and international faith-based, human rights, and immigrant rights organizations concerned with climate change and its effect on migration around the world.

We acknowledge the implications of the ways in which governmental policies and corporate practices impact communities around the world, especially those most vulnerable. We also acknowledge and are concerned about national responses to the increasing phenomena of global migration that prioritize national security concerns and immigration restrictions, including for those who are forced to migrate.

It is estimated that between 25 and 50 million people have already been displaced due to environmental factors, and that number could rise to 150 million by 2050. These "environmental refugees" suffer from the repercussions of our environmental practices and policies.

This position statement, issued on December 12, 2009, by the Climate Justice and Migration Working Group of the Mobilization for Climate Justice, is published here with their permission. For more information on the Working Group, email Michelle Knight of the Columban Center for Advocacy and Outreach at mmknight@columban.org.

For example, desertification has severely threatened traditional agricultural practices of indigenous communities. People will migrate when land can no longer sustain the nutritional needs of their communities. The United Nations Convention to Combat Desertification (UNCCD) representative Massimo Candelori has reported that the combined effect of climate variation and unsustainable agricultural practices causes erosion and soil depletion, which leads to meager harvests.

Chacaltaya, a "dead glacier" in Bolivia that as recently as a decade ago was the highest ski slope in the world, has now melted into rocky soil that cannot support the traditional farming practices of its inhabitants. A staple food made by crushing and freeze-drying potatoes has become difficult to make without the low temperatures necessary for this process. Instead of being able to sustain themselves with their crops and sell the surplus, these Bolivian farmers face hunger as their harvests diminish: a casualty of climate change. This and similar phenomena affect the traditional lifestyles of a range of citizens, and have led to the movement of peoples throughout Latin America.

In sub-Saharan Africa, climate change may cut the amount of available food by 500 calories per person by 2050, a 21 percent decline that will cause malnutrition for 19 million children. This strain on health care facilities and economy will come from the failing rice, wheat, and maize yields, which may decline by up to 14 percent, 22 percent and 5 percent, respectively, as a result of climate change. Africa will be especially vulnerable to these environmental strains because it lacks the resources and infrastructure to adapt traditional agricultural practices to new weather patterns and soil conditions.

Most of African agriculture is rain-fed rather than irrigated, so it is vulnerable to both floods and droughts caused by climate change. Instead, individuals who can no longer feed themselves and their families will seek new land to cultivate. This process is already well under way in Sudan, where the expanding desert has pushed communities to neighboring territories. There, they are perceived as a burden on the already-strained local economies and are susceptible to the violent conflict intensified by competition for increasingly scarce resources.

Sri Lankans report unpredictable weather patterns induced by climate change; these have caused droughts in the southeast while the western regions suffer from heavy rainfall and monsoons.

Extreme weather conditions, such as the flash floods that hit the Vavuniya and Mannar districts of Sri Lanka in August 2009, threaten the economic and personal well-being of those who must consider relocating. Camps hold 260,000 Sri Lankans who are already displaced by ethnic war and who must relocate for a second time. The flooding and close quarters also severely increase the risk of infectious disease. Indeed, these extreme weather conditions threaten the economic and personal well-being of all Sri Lankans.

As the sea level rises, it threatens to engulf entire island nations. In the Carteret Islands the sea is now contaminating scarce fresh water resources, and the residents are more reliant on imports and foreign aid for food. The food they receive has a high sugar content, which has led to serious health concerns, such as diabetes. Climate change has already had an effect on the health and economies of residents in many regions. Bangladesh and coastal cities are especially vulnerable to increases in sea level.

These repercussions, disproportionately caused by wealthy nations, take their highest toll on the poorest nations. For example, Anwarul Karim Chowdhury, the UN High Representative for Least Developed Countries, Landlocked Developing Countries and Small Island Developing States, estimated in 2007 that about one-third of Least Developed Countries are threatened by rising sea levels and have large proportions of their populations living in low-elevation coastal areas. Often these countries do not have the capacity to cope with the destabilizing factors of climate change.

Understanding that climate change jeopardizes the traditional homes, lifestyles, health, and means of survival for many around the world, we call for:

- The international protection of the human rights of people displaced due to environmental factors, including recognition of refugee status and guarantee of all corresponding rights and accommodations achieved through support and expansion of international rights agreements on refugees, the internally displaced and migrants, as well as the formulation of multilateral migration agreements.
- Recognition of the right of human mobility.
- Increased policy and public awareness of environmental refugee and migration issues, including investment in further research drawing the link between environmentally degrading practices, climate change, and migration.
- Provision of a legal framework and financial assistance to allow migrants displaced from their home countries entrance to other countries.
- International recognition of the ways in which climate change has impinged on the rights of nations, as outlined by United Nations conventions.
- Provision for nations whose security is threatened by the disappearance of habitable land. As these "disappearing states" lose territory, we affirm the right of every nation to sovereignty.
- A reduction of domestic carbon emissions, mindful of the ways in which our energy use endangers the environment internationally. We ask that the US and other developed nations model environmental responsibility by adhering to the Intergovernmental Panel on Climate Change's suggestions, which indicate that the global community

must reduce emissions by between 25 and 40 percent by 2020 and by a minimum of 80 percent by 2050, below a 1990 baseline, in order to remain sustainable.

The issue of migration and displacement due to climate change continues to grow in its importance. We have already witnessed its effects and we will continue to see its consequences in the years to come. Action must be taken now to reduce the negative results and produce positive outcomes for current and potential environmental refugees.

Notes

Introduction

1. Athanasiou, "Green Romantics," 603.
2. Hansen, "Coal-Fired Power Plants."
3. Union of Concerned Scientists, "1992 World Scientists' Warning."
4. Flannery et al., "IQ² Debate." (A tonne, also known as a "metric ton," is 1,000 kilograms or 2,200 pounds.)
5. Huang, "10 Reasons."
6. Commoner, *The Closing Circle*, 255.

1. Are People the Problem?

1. Quoted in Athanasiou, *Divided Planet*, 5.
2. McCormick, *Reclaiming Paradise*, 48.
3. Paul Ehrlich was identified as the sole author of *The Population Bomb*, but he described Anne as "virtually a co-author." Most of their subsequent works have been co-signed, and we will refer to them as "the Ehrlichs" unless only one of them is meant.
4. Paddock and Paddock, *Famine—1975!* 56, 206, 222.
5. Udall, *The Quiet Crisis*, 239.
6. Egan, *Barry Commoner*, 120.
7. Ehrlich and Ehrlich, *Population Resources Environment*, 44.
8. Ehrlich and Holdren, "Population and Panaceas," 1070–71.
9. Egan, *Barry Commoner*, 93.
10. Ibid., 118–19.
11. Ibid., 130.
12. Ibid., 125.

13. Ehrlich and Holdren, "Critique"; Commoner, "Response."

14. Ehrlich and Ehrlich, *Population Resources Environment*, 272.

15. Millennium Ecosystem Assessment Board, *Living beyond Our Means*, 16.

16. United Nations, "Crude Death Rate."

17. Ehrlich and Ehrlich, *The Population Explosion*, 9–10.

2: Varieties of Populationism Today

1. Bookchin, "The Population Myth," 30.

2. Quoted in Lee, *Earth First!* 62.

3. Quoted in Bookchin, *Re-enchanting Humanity*, 107.

4. Quoted in Egan, *Barry Commoner*, 229–30.

5. Foreman, *Confessions*, 218–19.

6. PAI and PJP, "Population and the Environment." The previous quotations in this section are also from this source.

7. Mazur, *A Pivotal Moment*, 9.

8. Mazur, "The Population Debate Is Screwed Up."

9. All quotations in this section were on OPT's website, www.optimumpopulation.org, in January 2011. In February 2011, OPT announced that it was changing its working name, though not its legal name, to Population Matters, and launched a new website, http://populationmatters.org. In cases where we could locate the documents on the new website, we have updated the URLs in the bibliography.

10. OPT, "OPT Population Policy Proposals."

11. McDougall, "Too Many People," 4.

12. Nicholson-Lord, "Population-Based Climate Strategy," 1.

13. OPT, "OPT Population Policy Proposals."

14. OPT, "Think-Tank Urges Population Inquiry."

15. Duguid and Ferguson, "International Migration," 19.

16. Lovelock, *The Revenge of Gaia*, 3, 7; *The Vanishing Face*, 110.

17. Lovelock, *The Vanishing Face*, 141.

18. Lovelock, *The Revenge of Gaia*, 68.

19. Ibid., 13.

20. Ibid., 247–48.

21. Sachs, *Common Wealth*, 180.

22. Ibid., 177.

23. Ibid., 160.

24. SPA, "Aims and Objectives."

25. SPA, "Global Population Reduction."

26. SPA, "Aims and Objectives."

27. SPA, "Population Policy."

28. ABC News, "Australia Needs One-Child Policy."

29. Berger, "The Population Myth."
30. Australian Conservation Foundation, "Population and Demographic Change," 4.

3: Dissecting Those "Overpopulation" Numbers

1.   Gould, *The Mismeasure of Man*, 106.
2.   McDougall, "Too Many People."
3.   Global Population Speak Out, "Talking Points."
4.   Ryerson, *Population*, 1.
5.   All Party Parliamentary Group, *Return of the Population*, 18.
6.   Gould, *The Mismeasure of Man*, 272.
7.   Steffen et al., *Executive Summary: Global Change*, 18.
8.   Marx, *Grundrisse*, 100.
9.   Satterthwaite, "The Implications of Population Growth."
10. IIED, "Study Shatters Myth."
11. United Nations Statistical Division, "CO_2 Emissions in 2006."
12. Pearce, *Peoplequake*, 122.
13. Ibid., 242.
14. Schnaiberg, *The Environment*, 69–70.
15. Nicholson-Lord, "A Population-Based Climate Strategy."
16. Wire, *Fewer Emitters, Lower Emissions*.
17. Quoted in Angus, "Do Consumers Cause Climate Change?"
18. Brown, Gardner, and Halweil, *Beyond Malthus*, 47.
19. Sachs, *Common Wealth*, 23.
20. Hartman, *The Population Fix*, 78–79.
21. Courtice, "I=PAT Proves Nothing."
22. Holdren and Ehrlich, "Human Population and the Global Environment," 291.
23. Meyer and Turner, "Human Population Growth," 52.
24. Dietz and Rosa, "Rethinking," 278
25. O'Neill, MacKellar, and Lutz, *Population and Climate Change*, 119, 123.
26. Hynes, *Taking Population Out of the Equation*, 8–9.
27. Ibid., 24.
28. IIASA, "Population Change: Another Influence."
29. O'Neill et al., "Global Demographic Trends."
30. PAI and PJP, "Population and the Environment"; Engelman, *Population, Climate Change, and Women's Lives*, 25.
31. Hansen, *Storms of My Grandchildren*, 81.
32. Meadows et al., *The Limits to Growth*, 23.
33. Freeman, "Malthus with a Computer," 7–8.
34. Ibid., 8–9.
35. Smith, *Econned*, 20.

4: Is the World Full?

1. Marx, *Grundrisse*, 606.
2. Simon, *The Ultimate Resource 2*, 36.
3. Ibid., 12, 97.
4. Simon and Kahn, introduction to *The Resourceful Earth*, 338.
5. Ibid., 266.
6. Kasun, *The War against Population*, 74.
7. Catton, *Overshoot*, 4.
8. Price, "Carrying Capacity Reconsidered," 9.
9. Seidl and Tisdell, "Carrying Capacity Reconsidered," 407.
10. Cohen, "Population Growth and Earth's Human Carrying Capacity."
11. Cohen, *How Many People Can the Earth Support?* 11, 17.
12. Ibid., 232.
13. Ibid., 262.
14. Cohen, "Beyond Population," 23.

5: The Bomb That Didn't Explode

1. Krause, "From Explosion to Implosion."
2. Ehrlich and Ehrlich, *The Population Explosion*, 15–16.
3. PAI, "Population—Facts and Figures."
4. Ekins, *The Living Economy*, 12.
5. Cohen, *How Many People Can the Earth Support?* 84.
6. Hardin, *Stalking*, 243, 245; Ehrlich and Holdren, "Critique," 26.
7. Kinsella and He, *An Aging World*, 139.
8. Pearce, *Peoplequake*, 117.
9. Cohen, *How Many People Can the Earth Support?* 109–10.
10. Bandarage, "Population and Development," 35–36.

6: Too Many Mouths to Feed?

1. Sen, *Poverty and Famines*, 1.
2. Brown, "Improving Food Security."
3. Brown, "The Great Food Crisis of 2011."
4. Paddock and Paddock, *Famine—1975!* 9, 56, 97.
5. Brown, *World on the Edge*, 163.
6. Lappé, Collins, and Rosset, *World Hunger: Twelve Myths*, 8.
7. Ehrlich, Ehrlich, and Daily, "Food Security, Population, and Environment," 17, 25.
8. Lappé, Collins, and Rosset, *World Hunger: Twelve Myths*, 8.
9. UN Millennium Project, *Halving Hunger*, 6.
10. Hildyard, "Too Many for What?"

11. Paillard, Treyer, and Dorin, *Agrimonde*, 57.
12. Magdoff and Tokar, "Agriculture and Food in Crisis," 12.
13. Lundqvist, de Fraiture, and Molden, "Saving Water," 22.
14. Patnaik, "Origins of the Food Crisis."
15. Fairlie, *Meat: A Benign Extravagance*, 33.
16. Mitchell, "A Note on Rising Food Prices."
17. Lynas, "How the Rich Starved the World."
18. Brown, *World on the Edge*, 61.
19. Lynas, "How the Rich Starved the World."
20. Worldwatch Institute, *State of the World 2011*, 101.
21. Gooch, Felfel, and Marenik, "Food Waste in Canada."
22. Stuart, *Waste*, 193.
23. Pfeiffer, *Eating Fossil Fuels*, 39–40.
24. Giampietro and Pimentel, "The Tightening Conflict."
25. Pimentel et al., "Natural Resources and an Optimum Human Population."
26. Avery, "Losing the Organic Debate."
27. Rosset, "Lessons of Cuban Resistance," xviii.
28. Badgley et al., "Organic Agriculture and the Global Food Supply," 91.
29. Pretty et al., "Resource-Conserving Agriculture."
30. Paillard, Treyer, and Dorin, *Agrimonde*.
31. For more complete accounts, see Conway, *The Doubly Green Revolution*; and Griffon, *Nourrir la planète*.
32. Paillard, Treyer, and Dorin, *Agrimonde*, 222.
33. Ibid, 238.

7: The Populationist War against the Poor

1.   Harvey, "The Political Implications of Population-Resources Theory."
2.   Connelly, *Fatal Misconception*, xi.
3.   Bandarage, *Women, Population and Global Crisis*, 74.
4.   Mamdani, *The Myth of Population Control*, 18.
5.   Bandarage, *Women, Population and Global Crisis*, 10.
6.   Ibid., 11.
7.   Connelly, *Fatal Misconception*, xii.
8.   Goldberg, *The Means of Reproduction*, 230.
9.   US Department of State, *United States Relations with China*, iv–v.
10. Weissman, "Why the Population Bomb," 47.
11. Mamdani, *The Myth of Population Control*, 21.
12. Connelly, *Fatal Misconception*, 202–3.
13. Ibid., 205.
14. Bandarage, *Women, Population and Global Crisis*, 82.

15. Quoted in Cultural Survival, "Population Control."
16. Goldberg, *The Means of Reproduction*, 80.
17. Connelly, *Fatal Misconception*, 258.
18. Ibid., 221.
19. Ibid., 254.
20. Ibid., 318.
21. Ibid., 218.
22. Ibid., 322.
23. Bandarage, *Women, Population and Global Crisis*, 75.
24. Connelly, *Fatal Misconception*, 229.
25. Ibid., 322.
26. Ibid., 325.
27. Bandarage, *Women, Population and Global Crisis*, 77.
28. Ibid., 75.
29. Connelly, *Fatal Misconception*, 341–42.
30. Ibid., 342.
31. Ibid., 347.
32. Bandarage, *Women, Population and Global Crisis*, 79.
33. Ibid., 73.
34. Ibid., 98.
35. Quoted in Goldberg, *The Means of Reproduction*, 172.
36. Pearce, *Peoplequake*, 172.
37. Connelly, *Fatal Misconception*, 378.
38. Harvey, "The Political Implications."

8: Control without Coercion?

1. Nikoukari, "Gradations of Coercion," 50.
2. Mazur, "Population and Environment."
3. Feenberg, "The Commoner-Ehrlich Debate," 267.
4. Pérez, "Between Radical Theory and Community Praxis," 92–93.
5. Hartmann, *Reproductive Rights and Wrongs*, 71–72.
6. Oldham, "Rethinking the Link," 3, 5.
7. Lappé, Collins, and Rosset, *World Hunger: Twelve Myths*, 37.
8. Nikoukari, "Gradations of Coercion," 65.
9. Mazur, "The World Needs Population Justice."
10. Hartmann, "The Changing Faces of Population Control," 262.
11. Shiva and Shiva, "Was Cairo a Step Forward?"
12. Petchesky, *Global Prescriptions*, 41.
13. Hartmann, *Reproductive Rights and Wrongs*, 135.
14. Ibid., 135–36.

15. Goldberg, *The Means of Reproduction*, 234.
16. Mazur, "The World Needs Population Justice."
17. Hartmann, "The Changing Faces of Population Control," 263.
18. OPT, "Gaia Scientist to Be OPT Patron."
19. Martine, "Population Dynamics," 13.
20. Ibid., 14.
21. Hartmann, *Reproductive Rights and Wrongs*, 303.
22. Martine, "Population Dynamics," 13.
23. Lutz, "World Population Trends," 59.
24. Martine, "Population Dynamics," 15.
25. Hansen et al, "Target Atmospheric CO_2."
26. Hansen, *Storms of My Grandchildren*, 282.
27. Martine, "Population Dynamics," 16.

9: Lifeboat Ethics

1. Athanasiou, *Divided Planet*, 82.
2. Goldsmith et al., "A Blueprint for Survival," 14.
3. Hardin, *Biology: Its Human Implications*, 611–12.
4. See Angus, "The Myth of the Tragedy of the Commons," for a critique of Hardin's argument about common ownership.
5. Hardin, "The Tragedy of the Commons."
6. Hardin, "Everybody's Guilty," 45.
7. Hardin, "Lifeboat Ethics."
8. Hardin, "The Survival of Nations," 1297.
9. Commoner, *The Closing Circle*, 297.
10. Gottlieb, *Forcing the Spring*, 258.
11. Ehrlich, Bilderback, and Ehrlich, *The Golden Door*, 325.
12. Ehrlich and Ehrlich, *The Population Explosion*, 62, 64.
13. Ehrlich and Ehrlich, *One with Nineveh*, 108.
14. Røpke, "2006 Migration and Sustainability," 192.
15. Neumayer, "The Environment," 204.
16. Pope, "Moving On: Lessons of the Immigration Debate."
17. Martin, "Immigration, Energy," 7.
18. Staples and Cafaro, "Environmental Argument," 14.
19. NumbersUSA, "Immigration Numbers."
20. Bierich and Botok, *The Nativist Lobby*, 4.
21. FAIR, "If Washington Won't, Arizona Will."
22. Wessler, "The Far-Right Movement."
23. Bierich and Potok, *The Nativist Lobby*, 4.
24. Kolankiewicz and Camarota, "Immigration to the United States," 7.

25. Ibid., 3.
26. Beck, *The Case against Immigration*, 12.
27. All of the quotes in this section are from the CCIPR website, accessed February 17, 2011: http://www.immigrationreform.ca.
28. Poswolsky and M., "Anti-immigrant Leader Admits."
29. *Occidental Quarterly*, "Statement of Principles."
30. Reimers, *Unwelcome Strangers*, 60.
31. Center for New Community, "American Bigfoot."

10: Allies, Not Enemies

1.   Commoner, *The Closing Circle*, 292.
2.   Athanasiou, *Divided Planet*, 304.
3.   Hartmann, "Conserving Racism."
4.   Hamilton and Turton, "Population Growth and Environmental Degradation," 21, 34.
5.   Daly, "Population, Migration, and Globalization," 189.
6.   Pimentel and Pimentel, "Global Environmental Resources," 197.
7.   Rees, "Globalization, Trade and Migration," 223.
8.   Lohmann, "Re-imagining the Population Debate."
9.   Bullard et al., *Toxic Wastes and Race at Twenty*. The original 1987 report is available online at http://urbanhabitat.org/node/5346.
10. Bullard, "Anatomy of Environmental Racism," 15.
11. Gottlieb, *Forcing the Spring*, 266.
12. Ibid., 269.
13. People of Color Environmental Justice, "Principles of Working Together."
14. Tactaquin, "Environmentalists and the Anti-immigrant Agenda," 8.
15. Heilbroner, *21st Century Capitalism*, 56.
16. Biel, *The New Imperialism*, 78.
17. Toussaint, *Your Money or Your Life*, 31.
18. Carnegie Institution, "Carbon Emissions 'Outsourced' to Developing Countries."
19. Vidal, "Nigeria's Agony."
20. http://chevrontoxico.com.
21. Watts, *When a Billion Chinese Jump*, 388–89.
22. Bello, "The Environmental Movement in the Global South."
23. Mimi, "Anti-dam Protests Get Louder in Northeast India."
24. La Vía Campesina, "Declaration in Cancún."

11: Too Many Consumers?

1.   Dorling, *Injustice*, 252.

2. Ehrlich and Ehrlich, *The Population Explosion*, 273.
3. Simms et al, *The Consumption Explosion*, 11.
4. Morales, "Let Us Respect Our Mother Earth."
5. Durning, *How Much Is Enough?* 23.
6. PBS, "Affluenza."
7. de Geus, *The End of Over-consumption*, 13.
8. Diamond, "What's Your Consumption Factor?"
9. Wallis, "Capitalist and Socialist Responses," 33.
10. Makower and Pike, *Strategies for the Green Economy*, 112.
11. Natural Resources Canada, *Energy Efficiency Trends*, 34.
12. Stern, *The Economics of Climate Change*, 196.
13. Hamilton, *Growth Fetish*, xi.
14. Ehrenreich, *Nickel and Dimed*, 25–26.
15. Perelman, "Some Economics of Class," 19.
16. US Census Bureau, "Median and Average Sales Prices."
17. Warren, "The Middle Class on the Precipice."
18. Natural Resources Canada, *Energy Efficiency Trends*, 13.
19. Warren, "The Middle Class on the Precipice."
20. Mishel, Bernstein, and Shierholz, *The State of Working America*, 286.
21. Gordon, *Fat and Mean*, 101.
22. Wolff, "Recent Trends in Household Wealth," 44, 46.
23. Mackenzie, Messinger, and Smith, *Size Matters*, 4.
24. Ibid.
25. Lovelock, *The Ages of Gaia*, 211.
26. Adapted from Phillips, "How Wealth Defines Power," 146.
27. Shaw and Stone, "Tax Data Show Richest 1 Percent," 2–3.
28. Kapur, Macleod, and Singh, "Plutonomy: Buying Luxury," 1.
29. Frank, *Richistan*, 151.
30. Merrill Lynch Global Wealth Management and Capgemini, *World Wealth Report, 2010*, 4.
31. Miller and Kroll, "World's Billionaires 2010."
32. Dorling, *Injustice*, 252.
33. Kempf, *How the Rich Are Destroying the Earth*, 46.
34. Wolff, "Recent Trends in Household Wealth," 52.
35. Lind, "Is America a Plutonomy?"
36. Calculation courtesy of Dick Nichols. The eleven are the ten men and one woman from Australia on the *Forbes* list of the world's billionaires. The 800,000 households are the poorest decile (10 percent) according to the Australian Bureau of Statistics.
37. Toussaint, *Your Money or Your Life*, 34.
38. Monbiot, "The Population Myth."

12: The Myth of Consumer Sovereignty

1. Jameson, *Postmodernism*, 266.
2. Quoted in Coleman, *Ecopolitics*, 38.
3. Coeckelbergh, "We're All to Blame."
4. Perry, "Consumer, Not Corporate."
5. Potter, *Society and the Social Sciences*, 90–91.
6. Löwy, "Advertising Is a 'Serious Health Threat.'"
7. Galbraith, *The Essential*, 34–35.
8. Galbraith, *The New Industrial State*, 247.
9. Ibid., 259–60.
10. Dawson, *The Consumer Trap*, 1, 134.
11. Galbraith, *The New Industrial State*, 259–60.
12. Cotton, *A Consumers' Republic*, 69.
13. Terrachoice, "Terrachoice 2010 Sins"; Terrachoice, *The Sins of Greenwashing*, 20.
14. Fisher, Griliches, and Kaysen, "Costs of Automobile Model Changes," 450.
15. Ibid., 153.
16. Nielsen Company, "U.S. Ad Spending."
17. Rogers, *Gone Tomorrow*, 6.
18. EPA, "Municipal Solid Waste," 6.
19. EPA, "Statistics on the Management."
20. Computer TakeBack Campaign, "Platform."
21. Tobin and Dusheck, *Asking about Life*, 592.
22. According to the US Census Bureau, population grew 50 percent, from 179 million to 281 million. According to the Environmental Protection Agency, municipal solid waste grew 170 percent, from 88 million to 239 million tons.
23. Environmental Protection Agency, "Inventory of U.S. Greenhouse Gas Emissions," tables ES-2 and 2–15.
24. Snell, "American Ground Transport."
25. Foster, *Ecology against Capitalism*, 101.
26. Waller, "Auto-mobility," 19.
27. Ibid., 20.
28. Dawson, *The Consumer Trap*, 144.
29. Humphery, *Excess*, 7, 133.
30. Bookchin, "On Growth and Consumerism."
31. Jackson, *Prosperity without Growth*, 153.
32. Princen, "Consumer Sovereignty and Sacrifice," 152.

13: The Military-Corporate Pollution Complex

1. Karliner, *The Corporate Planet*, 3.
2. Anderson and Cavanaugh, "Top 200."

3. Rothkopf, *Superclass*, 34.
4. Shnayerson, "Sand Simeon."
5. Thornton, "Ira Rennert's House of Debt"; Hellman, "Rennert Redux."
6. EPA, "Superfund Program"; Allan, "DOJ Files Civil Action."
7. Garrison, "Doe Run Lead Smelter."
8. O'Shaughnessy, "Poisoned City."
9. Inter-American Association for Environmental Defense, "IACHR Will Examine Case."
10. Blacksmith, "Top 10 Most Polluted Places 2007."
11. Gould, Pellow, and Schnaiberg, *The Treadmill of Production*, 20, 22.
12. Dawson, *The Consumer Trap*, 144.
13. Coleman, *Ecopolitics*, 38.
14. Wolf, "Environmental Crime," 91.
15. Ibid., 91.
16. Trucost, "Universal Ownership," 2.
17. Ibid., 6.
18. More precisely, EBITDA earnings before interest, taxes, depreciation, and amortization.
19. Trucost, "Carbon Risks," 22–23.
20. Harman, *Zombie Capitalism*, 311.
21. Karbuz, "DoD Energy Use in 2009."
22. Sanders, *The Green Zone*.
23. Reisch and Kretzmann, *A Climate of War*.
24. Eisler, "Pollution Cleanups."
25. Schwartz, "Atomic Audit," 2; Durant, *The Greening of the US Military*, 21.
26. Quoted in McNally, *Another World Is Possible*, 233.

14: A System of Growth and Waste

1. Bookchin, *Remaking Society*, 15.
2. Simms, Johnson, and Chowla, *Growth Isn't Possible*, 5.
3. White, "The Barbaric Heart."
4. Hamilton, *Growth Fetish*, 2.
5. Nadeau, *Wealth of Nature*, 113.
6. Korten, *When Corporations Rule the World*, 46.
7. Travis, "Sustainable Capitalism?" 99.
8. Smith, "Beyond Growth or beyond Capitalism?" 30–31.
9. Bowles, Roosevelt, and Richards, *Understanding Capitalism*, 152.
10. Foster, Clark, and York, *The Ecological Rift*, 28–29.
11. Ecosocialist International Network, "Belem Ecosocialist Declaration."
12. Matthews et al., *The Weight of Nations*, 2.

13. Ibid., xi.
14. Ibid., 8.
15. Kapp, *Social Costs of Private Enterprise*, 231.
16. Ibid., 62.
17. Bookchin, *Re-enchanting Humanity*, 83.

15: Populationism or Ecological Revolution?

1. Smil, *Feeding the World*, 210.
2. Ross, *The Malthus Factor*, 7.
3. Arizpe and Velázquez, "The Social Dimensions of Population," 18.
4. Martine, "Population Dynamics and Policies," 13.
5. Myerson, "Population Growth Is Easier to Manage."
6. Hazlitt, *Political Essays*, 426.
7. Foster, *The Vulnerable Planet*, 132.
8. Engels, letter to Karl Kautsky, February 1, 1881.
9. Kovel, *The Enemy of Nature*, 10.
10. Engels, "The Part Played by Labour," 463.
11. Marx and Engels, *The Manifesto of the Communist Party*, 506; Marx, *Capital*, 3: 959.
12. Klimaforum09, "System Change—Not Climate Change."
13. Shiva, *Soil Not Oil*, 4.
14. Cochabamba Conference 2010, "People's Agreement."
15. Magdoff and Foster, "What Every Environmentalist Needs to Know," 14–15.

Appendix 1: The Malthus Myth

1. Whitty, "The Last Taboo," 28.
2. Ibid.
3. Brown, Gardner, and Halweil, *Beyond Malthus*, 23.
4. Ferguson, "Malthus."
5. Curnow, "Malthus Wrong? Never!"
6. Malthus, Second Essay, 70.
7. Ibid., 341.
8. Malthus, First Essay, 40.
9. Ibid., 85.
10. Ibid., 118.
11. Malthus, Second Essay, 207.
12. Harvey, "The Political Implications."
13. Foster, *Ecology against Capitalism*, 152.

Bibliography

"10 Principles for Just Climate Change Policies in the U.S." http://www.ejnet.org/ej/ climatejustice.pdf. ABC News. "Australia Needs One-Child Policy." April 22, 2009. http://www.abc.net.au/news/stories/2009/04/22/2549917.htm.

Allan, Sterling D. "DOJ Files Civil Action against MagCorp for PCB Violations." *Pure Energy Systems News*, May 12, 2005. http://pesn.com/2005/05/12/6900093 _MagnesiumCorporation_of_America/.

All Party Parliamentary Group on Population, Development and Reproductive Health. *Return of the Population Growth Factor*. UK. 2007. http://www.appg-popdevrh .org.uk/.

Anderson, Sarah, and John Cavanaugh. "Top 200: The Rise of Corporate Global Power." Institute for Policy Studies, December 4, 2000. http://www.globalpolicy .org/component/content/article/221/47211.html.

Angus, Ian. "And You Thought Carbon Offsets Couldn't Get Worse!" *Climate and Capitalism*, December 28, 2009. http://climateandcapitalism.com/?p=1473.

———. "Dissecting Those 'Overpopulation' Numbers, Part One—Population Where?" *Climate and Capitalism*, April 28, 2010. http://climateandcapitalism .com/?p=2270.

———. "Do Consumers Cause Climate Change?" *Climate and Capitalism*, February 20, 2010. http://climateandcapitalism.com/?p=1748.

———, ed. *The Global Fight for Climate Justice: Anticapitalist Responses to Global Warming and Environmental Destruction*. Winnipeg: Fernwood Publishing, 2010.

———. "The Myth of the Tragedy of the Commons." In Angus, *The Global Fight for Climate Justice*.

Arizpe, Lourdes, M. S. Stone, and D. C. Major, eds. *Population and Environment: Rethinking the Debate*. Boulder: Westview Press, 1994.

———. "Conclusions: Rethinking the Population-Environment Debate." In Arizpe, Stone, and Major, *Population and Environment*.

Arizpe, Lourdes, and Margarita Velázquez. "The Social Dimensions of Population." In Arizpe, Stone, and Major, *Population and Environment*.

Athanasiou, Tom. *Divided Planet: The Ecology of Rich and Poor*. New York: Little, Brown, 1996.

———. "Green Romantics." *The Nation*, May 1, 1995, 603.

Australian Conservation Foundation. "Population and Demographic Change." ACF Policy Statement 51, amended July 2009. http://www.acfonline.org.au/uploads/res/51_-_Population_and_Demographic_Change_Jul_09__2_.pdf.

———. "Population Boom Will Bust Environment and Quality of Life." September 22, 2009. http://www.acfonline.org.au/articles/news.asp?news_id=2469.

Avery, Dennis. "Losing the Organic Debate." Center for Global Food Issues, April 21, 2010. http://www.cgfi.org/2010/04/losing-the-organic-debate-by-dennis-t-avery/.

Badgley, Catherine, J. Moghtader, E. Quintero, E. Zakem, M. J. Chappell, K. Avilés-Vázquez, A. Samulon, and I. Perfecto. "Organic Agriculture and the Global Food Supply." *Renewable Agriculture and Food Systems* 22, no. 2: 86–108.

Bandarage, Asoka. "Population and Development: Toward a Social Justice Agenda." In *Dangerous Intersections: Feminism, Population and the Environment*, edited by Jael Silliman and Ynestra King. London: Zed Books, 1994.

———. *Women, Population and Global Crisis: A Political-Economic Analysis*. London: Zed Books, 1997.

Barry, Tom. "The Politics and Ideologies of the Anti-immigration Forces." *Counterpunch*, June 25–26, 2005. http://www.counterpunch.org/barry06252005.html.

Bartlett, Albert A. "The Most IMPORTANT Video You'll Ever See." YouTube video posted by "wonderingmind42," June 16, 2007. http://www.youtube.com/watch?v=F-QA2rkpBSY.

Beck, Roy. *The Case against Immigration: The Moral, Economic, Social, and Environmental Reasons for Reducing U.S. Immigration Back to Traditional Levels*. New York: W. W. Norton, 1996.

Behrman, J. R. "Why Micro Matters." In *Population Matters: Demographic Change, Economic Growth, and Poverty in the Developing World*, edited by Nancy Birdsall, A. Kelley, and S. W. Sinding. Oxford: Oxford University Press, 2001.

Bello, Walden. "The Environmental Movement in the Global South." *Climate and Capitalism*, November 5, 2007. http://climateandcapitalism.com/?p=239.

Berger, Charles. "The Population Myth." Australian Conservation Foundation, July 2010. http://www.acfonline.org.au/articles/news.asp?news_id=2952.

Biel, Robert. *The New Imperialism: Crisis and Contradiction in North/South Relations*. London: Zed Books, 2000.

Bierich, Heidi, and Mark Potok. *The Nativist Lobby: Three Faces of Intolerance*. Mont-

gomery, AL: Southern Poverty Law Center, 2009. http://www.Splcenter.org/
pdf/static/splc_nativistlobby_022009.pdf.

Blacksmith Institute. "Top 10 Most Polluted Places 2007." http://www.worstpol-
luted.org/projects_reports/display/41.

Bookchin, Murray. "On Growth and Consumerism." *Climate and Capitalism*, March
5, 2010. http://climateandcapitalism.com/?p=1814.

———. "The Population Myth." In *Which Way for the Ecology Movement?* San Francisco: AK Press, 1994.

———. *Re-enchanting Humanity*. New York: Cassell, 1995.

———. *Remaking Society: Pathways to a Green Future*. Boston: South End Press, 1990.

Bowles, Samuel, Frank Roosevelt, and Richard Edwards. *Understanding Capitalism:
Competition, Command, and Change*. New York: Oxford University Press, 2005.

Brown, Lester. "The Great Food Crisis of 2011." *Foreign Policy*, January 10, 2011.
http://www.foreignpolicy.com/articles/2011/01/10/the_great_food_crisis_of_2011.

———. "Improving Food Security by Strategically Reducing Grain Demand." 2010.
http://www.earth-policy.org/book_bytes/2010/pb4ch09_ss6.

———. *World on the Edge: How to Prevent Environmental and Economic Collapse*. New
York: W. W. Norton, 2011. Available online at http://www.earth-policy.org/
books/wote.

Brown, Lester, Gary Gardner, and Brian Halweil. *Beyond Malthus: Nineteen Dimensions of the Population Challenge*. New York: W. W. Norton, 1999.

Bullard, Robert D. "Anatomy of Environmental Racism and the Environmental Justice Movement." In *Confronting Environmental Racism: Voices from the Grassroots*,
edited by Robert D. Bullard. Cambridge, MA: South End Press, 1993.

Bullard, Robert D., Paul Mohai, Robin Saha, and Beverly Wright. *Toxic Wastes and
Race at Twenty: 1987–2007*. Cleveland: United Church of Christ, 2007. Available online at http://www.ucc.org/assets/pdfs/toxic20.pdf.

Carnegie Institution. "Carbon Emissions 'Outsourced' to Developing Countries." News
release, March 8, 2010. http://carnegiescience.edu/news/carbon_emissions
_outsourced_developing_countries.

Carrying Capacity Network (CCN). "What Is Carrying Capacity?" http://www
.carryingcapacity.org.

Catton, William R. *Overshoot: The Ecological Basis of Revolutionary Change*. Chicago:
Illinois University Press, 1982.

Center for New Community. "American Bigfoot: Immigration, Population Growth
and Racism." http://www.newcomm.org/content/view/2143/122.

Chase, Allen. *The Legacy of Malthus: The Social Costs of the New Scientific Racism*.
Champaign: University of Illinois Press, 1980.

Cochabamba Conference 2010. "People's Agreement on Climate Change and the
Rights of Mother Earth." *Climate and Capitalism*, April 26, 2010. http://

climateandcapitalism.com/?p=2255.

Coeckelbergh, M. "We're All to Blame for the Oil Spill." *Guardian*, June 9, 2010. http://www.guardian.co.uk/commentisfree/cifamerica/2010/jun/09/deepwater-horizon-oil-spill-responsibility-bp.

Cohen, Joel E. "Beyond Population: Everyone Counts in Development." Center for Global Development Working Paper 220, July 2010. http://www.cgdev.org/content/publications/detail/1424318/.

———. *How Many People Can the Earth Support?* New York: W. W. Norton, 1995.

———. "Population Growth and Earth's Human Carrying Capacity." *Science* 269, no. 5222 (July 21, 1995): 341–46.

Cole, H. S. D., Christopher Freeman, Marie Jahoda, and K. L. R. Pavitt, eds. *Thinking about the Future: A Critique of the Limits to Growth*. London: Sussex University Press, 1973.

Coleman, D. A. *Ecopolitics: Building a Green Society*. New Brunswick, NJ: Rutgers University Press, 1994.

Commoner, Barry. *The Closing Circle: Nature, Man, and Technology*. New York: Alfred A. Knopf, 1971.

———. "How Poverty Breeds Overpopulation (and Not the Other Way Around)." *Ramparts*, August–September 1975, 21–25, 58–59.

———. *The Poverty of Power: Energy and the Economic Crisis*. New York: Random House, 1976.

———. "Response." *Bulletin of the Atomic Scientists*, May 1972, 17 et seq.

Computer TakeBack Campaign. "Platform." n. d. http://www.grrn.org/e-scrap/take-back_platform.pdf.

Connelly, Matthew. *Fatal Misconception: The Struggle to Control World Population*. Cambridge, MA: Harvard University Press, 2008.

Conway, Gordon. *The Doubly Green Revolution: Food for All in the 21st Century*. Ithaca, NY: Cornell University Press, 1998.

Cotton, Lizabeth. *A Consumers' Republic: The Politics of Mass Consumption in Postwar America*. New York: Vintage Books, 2003.

Courtice, Ben. "I=PAT Proves Nothing." *Blind Carbon Copy*, March 17, 2010. http://bccwords.blogspot.com/2010/03/ipat-proves-nothing.html.

Cultural Survival. "Population Control." 2001. http://www.culturalsurvival.org/publications/cultural-survival-quarterly/thailand/population-control.

Curnow, Jill. "Malthus Wrong? Never!" Sustainable Population Australia, January 4, 2009. http://www.population.org.au/index.php/population/71-infosheets/163-malthus-wrong-never.

Daly, Herman E. "Population, Migration, and Globalization." *Ecological Economics* 59 (2006): 187–90.

Dawson, Michael. *The Consumer Trap: Big Business Marketing in American Life*. Urbana and Chicago: University of Illinois Press, 2005.

de Geus, Marius. *The End of Over-consumption: Towards a Lifestyle of Moderation and Self-Restraint*. Utrecht: International Books, 2003.

Desvaux, Martin. "Towards Sustainable and Optimum Populations." London: Optimum Population Trust, 2008. http://www.optimumpopulation.org/opt.optimum.html.

Diamond, Jared. "What's Your Consumption Factor?" *New York Times*, January 2, 2008. http://www.nytimes.com/2008/01/02/opinion/02diamond.html?pagewanted =1&_r=2.

Diesendorf, Mark. "Why Environmentalists Must Address Population as Well as Technology and Consumption." PowerPoint presentation, New South Wales, June 21, 2008. http://www.sustainabilitycentre.com.au/Population.pdf.

Dietz, Thomas, and Eugene Rosa. "Rethinking the Environmental Impacts of Population, Affluence and Technology." *Human Ecology Review* 1 (1994): 277–300.

Dorling, Daniel. *Injustice: Why Social Inequality Persists*. Bristol: Policy Press, 2010.

Duguid, James P., and Andrew R. B. Ferguson. "International Migration and Over-population." *Optimum Population Trust Journal* 92 (2009): 19–23.

Durant, Robert F. *The Greening of the U.S. Military: Environmental Policy, National Security, and Organizational Change*. Washington, D.C.: Georgetown University Press, 2007.

Durning, Alan. *How Much Is Enough? The Consumer Society and the Future of the Earth*. New York: W. W. Norton, 1992.

Ecosocialist International Network. "Belem Ecosocialist Declaration." 2009. http://www.ecosocialistnetwork.org/Docs.htm.

Egan, Michael. *Barry Commoner and the Science of Survival: The Remaking of American Environmentalism*. Cambridge, MA: MIT Press, 2007.

Ehrenreich, Barbara. *Nickel and Dimed: On (Not) Getting By in America*. New York: Holt, 2008.

Ehrlich, Paul. *The Population Bomb*. New York: Ballantine Books, 1968.

Ehrlich, Paul, Loy Bilderback, and Anne H. Ehrlich. *The Golden Door: International Migration, Mexico and the United States*. Updated ed. New York: Wideview Books, 1981.

Ehrlich, Paul, and Anne Ehrlich. *One with Nineveh: Politics, Consumption, and the Human Future*. Washington, DC: Island Press, 2004.

———. *The Population Explosion*. New York: Simon & Schuster, 1990.

———. *Population Resources Environment: Issues in Human Ecology*. 2nd ed. San Francisco: W. H. Freeman, 1972.

Ehrlich, Paul, Anne Ehrlich, and Gretchen Daily. "Food Security, Population, and Environment." *Population and Development Review* 19, no. 1 (March 1993): 1–32.

Ehrlich, Paul, and John Holdren. "Critique." *Bulletin of the Atomic Scientists*, May 1972, 16 et seq.

———. "Population and Panaceas: A Technological Perspective." *Bioscience* 19, no. 12 (1969): 1065–71.

Eisler, Peter. "Pollution Cleanups Pit Pentagon against Regulators." *USA Today*, October 14, 2004. http://www.usatoday.com/news/nation/2004–10–14-cover-pollution_x.htm.

Ekins, Paul. *The Living Economy: A New Economics in the Making.* London: Routledge & Kegan Paul, 1986.

Engelman, Robert. *Population, Climate Change, and Women's Lives.* Washington, DC: Worldwatch Institute, 2010.

Engels, Frederick. Letter to Karl Kautsky, February 1, 1881. In *Marx and Engels on Malthus*, edited by Ronald L. Meek. New York: International Publishers, 1954.

———. "The Part Played by Labour in the Transition from Ape to Man." In Karl Marx and Frederick Engels, *Collected Works*, vol. 25. New York: International Publishers, 1987.

EPA (Environmental Protection Agency). "Inventory of U.S. Greenhouse Gas Emissions and Sinks: 1990–2008." http://www.epa.gov/climatechange/emissions/usinventoryreport.html.

———. "Municipal Solid Waste Generation, Recycling, and Disposal in the United States: Facts and Figures for 2008." http://www.epa.gov/osw/nonhaz/municipal/pubs/msw2008rpt.pdf.

———. "Statistics on the Management of Used and End-of-Life Electronics." http://www.epa.gov/epawaste/conserve/materials/ecycling/manage.htm.

———. "Superfund Program: U.S. Magnesium." updated April 10, 2010. http://www.epa.gov/region8/superfund/ut/usmagnesium/index.html.

FAIR (Federation for American Immigration Reform). "If Washington Won't, Arizona Will: State Passes Tough, Sensible Illegal Immigration Laws to Protect Arizonans." April 14, 2010. http://www.fairus.org/site/News2?page=NewsArticle&id=22725.

Fairlie, Simon. *Meat: A Benign Extravagance.* White River Junction, VT: Chelsea Green Publishing, 2010.

Feenberg, Andrew. "The Commoner-Ehrlich Debate: Environmentalism and the Politics of Survival." In *Minding Nature: The Philosophers of Ecology*, edited by David Macauley. New York: Guilford Press, 1996.

Ferguson, Andrew. "Malthus over a 270 [sic] Year Perspective." *Optimum Population Trust Journal*, April 2008.

Fisher, Franklin M., Zvi Griliches, and Carl Kaysen. "The Costs of Automobile Model Changes since 1949." *Journal of Political Economy* 70, no. 3 (October 1962): 433–51.

Flannery, Tim. "Too Many People, Not Enough Resources." *Sydney Morning Herald*, September 16, 2009. http://www.smh.com.au/opinion/politics/too-many-people-not-enough-resources-20090916-fql2.html.

Flannery, Tim, Helen Hughes, John Sutton, and Tom Keneally. "IQ² Debate: Our Current Immigration Rates Are Too High." Audio file. 2009. http://mpegmedia .abc.net.au/rn/podcast/2009/09/fro_20090923_1810.mp3.

Foreman, Dave. *Confessions of an Eco-warrior*. New York: Harmony Books: 1991.

Foster, John Bellamy. *Ecology against Capitalism*. New York: Monthly Review Press, 2002.

———. *The Vulnerable Planet: A Short Economic History of the Environment*. New York: Monthly Review Press, 1999.

Foster, John Bellamy, Brett Clark, and Richard York. *The Ecological Rift: Capitalism's War on the Earth*. New York: Monthly Review Press, 2010.

Frank, Robert. *Richistan: A Journey through the American Wealth Boom and the Lives of the New Rich*. New York: Crown Publishers, 2007.

Freeman, Christopher. "Malthus with a Computer." In Cole, Freeman, Jahoda, and Pavitt, *Thinking about the Future*, 5–13.

Friends of the Earth Sydney. "A Statement on Population and Climate Change." n. d. http://www.sydney.foe.org.au/news/statement-population-and-climate-change.

Galbraith, John Kenneth. *The Essential Galbraith*. New York: Houghton Mifflin Harcourt, 2001.

———. *The New Industrial State*. Princeton, NJ: Princeton University Press, 2007.

Garrison, Chad. "Doe Run Lead Smelter Continues to Contaminate Herculaneum." *Riverfront Times*, October 27, 2009. http://blogs.riverfronttimes.com/dailyrft/ 2009/10/doe_run_lead_smelter_continues_to_contaminate_herculaneum.php.

Giampietro, Mario, and David Pimentel. "The Tightening Conflict: Population, Energy Use, and the Ecology of Agriculture." Negative Population Growth Forum Series, October 1993. http://www.npg.org/forum_series/tightening_conflict.htm.

Global Footprint Network (GFN). "World Footprint: Do We Fit on the Planet?" n. d. http://www.footprintnetwork.org/en/index.php/GFN/page/world_footprint/.

Global Population Speak Out. "Talking Points." 2010. http://gpso.wordpress.com/resources/.

Goldberg, Michelle. *The Means of Reproduction: Sex, Power, and the Future of the World*. New York: Penguin Books, 2010.

Goldsmith, Edward, Robert Allen, Michael Allaby, John Davoll, and Sam Lawrence. "A Blueprint for Survival." *The Ecologist* 21 (January 1972): 1–43.

Gooch, Martin, Abdel Felfel, and Nicole Marenik. "Food Waste in Canada." Value Chain Management Centre, November 2010. http://www.vcmtools.ca/pdf/ Food%20Waste%20in%20Canada%20120910.pdf.

Gordon, David M. *Fat and Mean: The Corporate Squeeze of Working Americans and the Myth of Managerial "Downsizing."* New York: Simon & Schuster, 1996.

Gottlieb, Robert. *Forcing the Spring: The Transformation of the American Environmental Movement*. Washington, DC: Island Press, 1993.

Gould, Kenneth A., David N. Pellow, and Allan Schnaiberg. *The Treadmill of Pro-*

duction: Injustice and Unsustainability in the Global Economy. Boulder: Paradigm Publishers, 2008.

Gould, Stephen Jay. The Mismeasure of Man. Rev ed. New York: W. W. Norton, 1996.

Griffon, Michel. Nourrir la planète: Pour une révolution doublement verte. Paris: Odile Jacob, 2006.

Hamilton, Clive. Growth Fetish. London: Pluto Press, 2004.

Hamilton, Clive, and Hal Turton. "Population Growth and Environmental Degradation: Sources and Trends in Greenhouse Gas Emissions." People and Place 7, no. 4 (2010): 42–62. http://elecpress.monash.edu.au/pnp/free/pnpv7n4/v7n4_8hamilton.pdf.

Hansen, James E. "Coal-Fired Power Plants Are Factories of Death." Climate and Capitalism, March 25, 2009. http://climateandcapitalism.com/?p=656.

———. Storms of My Grandchildren: The Truth about the Coming Climate Catastrophe and Our Last Chance to Save Humanity. New York: Bloomsbury USA, 2010.

Hansen, James E., Makiko Sato, Pushker Kharecha, David Beerling, Robert Berner, Valerie Masson-Delmotte, Mark Pagani, Maureen Raymo, Dana L. Royer, and James C. Zachos. "Target Atmospheric CO_2: Where Should Humanity Aim?" Open Atmospheric Science Journal 2 (2008): 217–31. http://benthamscience.com/open/openaccess.php?toascj/articles/V002/217TOASCJ.htm.

Hardin, Garrett. Biology: Its Human Implications. San Francisco: W. H. Freeman, 1949.

———. "Everybody's Guilty: The Ecological Dilemma." California Medicine 112, no. 5 (1970): 40–47.

———. "Lifeboat Ethics: The Case against Helping the Poor." Psychology Today, September 1974. http://www.garretthardinsociety.org/articles/art_lifeboat_ethics _case_against_helping_poor.html.

———. Stalking the Wild Taboo. 2nd ed. Los Altos, CA: William Kaufmann, 1978.

———. "The Survival of Nations and Civilization." Science 172 (1971): 1272.

———. "The Tragedy of the Commons." Science, December 13, 1968. http://www .garretthardinsociety.org/articles/art_tragedy_of_the_commons.html.

Harman, Chris. Zombie Capitalism: Global Crisis and the Relevance of Marx. London: Bookmarks, 2009.

Hartman, Edward C. The Population Fix: Breaking America's Addiction to Population Growth. Moraga, CA: Think Population Press, 2006.

Hartmann, Betsy. "The Changing Faces of Population Control." In Policing the National Body: Race, Gender, and Criminalization, edited by Jael Silliman and Anannya Bhattacharjee. Cambridge, MA: South End Press, 2002.

———. "Conserving Racism: The Greening of Hate at Home and Abroad." 2003. http://www.zcommunications.org/conserving-racism-the-greening-of -hate-at-home-and-abroad-by-betsy-hartmann.

———. "Liberal Ends, Illiberal Means: National Security, 'Environmental Conflict' and the Making of the Cairo Consensus." *Indian Journal of Gender Studies* 13, no. 2 (2006): 195–227.

———. "The 'New' Population Control Craze: Retro, Racist, Wrong Way to Go." *Climate and Capitalism*, January 17, 2010. http://climateandcapitalism .com/?p=1544.

———. *Reproductive Rights and Wrongs: The Global Politics of Population Control.* Rev ed. Boston: South End Press, 1995.

Harvey, David. *The Enigma of Capital and the Crises of Capitalism.* London: Profile Books, 2010.

———. "The Political Implications of Population-Resources Theory." *Climate and Capitalism*, May 23, 2010. http://climateandcapitalism.com/?p=2519.

Hazlitt, William. *Political Essays, with Sketches of Public Characters.* London: William Hone, 1819.

Heilbroner, Robert. *21st Century Capitalism.* New York: W. W. Norton, 1993.

Hellman, Peter. "Rennert Redux." *New York*, December 14, 1998. http://nymag.com/ nymetro/realestate/features/1718/.

Hildyard, Nicholas. "Too Many for What? The Social Generation of Food 'Scarcity' and 'Overpopulation.'" Corner House, November 1996. http://www .thecornerhouse.org.uk/resource/too-many-what.

Holdren, John, and Paul Ehrlich. "Human Population and the Global Environment." *American Scientist* 62 (1974): 282–92.

Huang, Patricia. "10 Reasons to Rethink the Immigration-Overpopulation Connection." 2009. http://popdev.hampshire.edu/projects/dt/59.

Humphery, Kim. *Excess: Anti-consumerism in the West.* Boston: Polity, 2009.

Hynes, Patricia. *Taking Population Out of the Equation: Reformulating I=PAT.* North Amherst, MA: Institute on Women and Technology, 1993. http:// readingfromtheleft.com/PDF/IPAT-Hynes.pdf.

IIASA (International Institute for Applied Systems Analysis). "Population Change: Another Influence on Climate Change." News release, October 11, 2010. http://www.iiasa.ac.at/Admin/INF/PR/2010/2010–10–11.html.

IIED (International Institute for Environment and Development). "Study Shatters Myth That Population Growth Is a Major Driver of Climate Change." News release, September 28, 2009. http://www.iied.org/human-settlements/ media/study-shatters-myth-population-growth-major-driver-climate-change.

Interamerican Association for Environmental Defense. "IACHR Will Examine Case against Peru for Violating the Human Rights of Residents of La Oroya, a City Extensively Contaminated by the Doe Run Peru Smelter." News release, August 19, 2009. http://www.aida-americas.org/en/node/1292.

Jackson, Tim. *Prosperity without Growth: Economics for a Finite Planet.* Sterling, VA:

Earthscan, 2009.

Jameson, Fredric. *Postmodernism, or The Cultural Logic of Late Capitalism*. Durham, NC: Duke University Press, 1991.

Jensen, Erik. "Right-Wing Genie Out of the Bottle." *Sydney Morning Herald*, July 5, 2009. http://www.smh.com.au/national/rightwing-genie-out-of-the-bottle -20090708-ddfk.html.

Kapp, K. William. *Social Costs of Private Enterprise*. Cambridge, MA: Harvard University Press, 1950.

Kapur, Ajay, Niall Macleod, and Narendra Singh. "Plutonomy: Buying Luxury, Explaining Global Imbalances." *Citigroup Industry Note*, October 16, 2005.

Karbuz, Sohbet. "DoD Energy Use in 2009." 2010. http://karbuz.blogspot.com/2010/ 07/dod-energy-use-in-2009.html.

Karliner, Joshua. *The Corporate Planet: Ecology and Politics in the Age of Globalization*. Sierra Club Book. San Francisco: University of California Press, 1997.

Kasun, Jacqueline. *The War against Population: The Economics and Ideology of World Population Control*. 2nd ed. San Francisco: Ignatius Press, 1999.

Kempf, Hervé. *How the Rich Are Destroying the Earth*. Translated by Leslie Thatcher. White River Junction, VT: Chelsea Green, 2007.

Kinsella, Kevin, and Wan He. *An Aging World: 2008*. Washington, DC: US Census Bureau, 2009.

Klimaforum09. "System Change—Not Climate Change." *Links International Journal of Socialist Renewal*, December 2009. http://links.org.au/node/1399.

Kolankiewicz, Leon. "Tribute to Garrett Hardin." 2003. http://www.garretthardinsociety .org/tributes/tr_kolankiewicz_2003oct.html.

Kolankiewicz, Leon, and Steven A. Camarota. "Immigration to the United States and World-Wide Greenhouse Gas Emissions." Center for Immigration Studies Backgrounder, August 2008. http://www.cis.org/articles/2008/back1008.pdf.

Korten, David C. *When Corporations Rule the World*. 2nd ed. San Francisco: Kumarian Press, 2001.

Kovel, Joel. *The Enemy of Nature: The End of Capitalism or the End of the World?* London: Zed Books, 2002.

Krause, Elizabeth L. "From Explosion to Implosion: A Call for Population Skepticism." *DifferenTakes* no. 46 (Spring 2007). http://popdev.hampshire.edu/projects/dt/46.

Lappé, Francis Moore, Joseph Collins, and Peter Rosset. *World Hunger: Twelve Myths*. New York: Grove Press, 1998.

Lebowitz, Michael A. "Change the System, Not Its Barriers." *Socialism and Democracy* 24, no. 3 (November 2010): 46–59.

Lee, Martha F. *Earth First! Environmental Apocalypse*. Syracuse, NY: Syracuse University Press, 1995.

Lewontin, Richard, and Richard Levins. *Biology under the Influence: Dialectical Essays on Ecology, Agriculture, and Health.* New York: Monthly Review Press, 2007.

Lind, Michael. "Is America a Plutonomy?" *Salon*, October 5, 2010. http://www
.salon.com/news/opinion/feature/2010/10/05/lind_america_plutonomy/index.html.

Lohmann, Larry. "Re-imagining the Population Debate." *Corner House Briefing* 28
(March 2003). http://www.thecornerhouse.org.uk/resource/re-imagining
-population-debate.

Lovelock, James. *The Ages of Gaia: A Biography of Our Living Planet.* New York: Ban-
tam Books, 1988.

———. *The Revenge of Gaia: Earth's Climate in Crisis and the Fate of Humanity.* New
York: Basic Books, 2006.

———. *The Vanishing Face of Gaia: A Final Warning.* London: Allen Lane, 2009.

Löwy, Michael. "Advertising Is a 'Serious Health Threat'—to the Environment."
Monthly Review 61, no. 8 (January 2010): 19–25. http://monthlyreview.org/
100101lowy.php.

Lundqvist, J., C. de Fraiture, and D. Molden. "Saving Water: From Field to Fork—
Curbing Losses and Wastage in the Food Chain." Stockholm International
Water Institute, 2008. http://www.siwi.org/documents/Resources/Policy_Briefs/
PB_From_Field_to_Fork_2008.pdf.

Lutz, W. "World Population Trends: Global and Regional Interactions between Population and Environment." In Arizpe, Stone, and Major, *Population and Environment.*

Lynas, Mark. "How the Rich Starved the World." *New Statesman*, April 17, 2008.
http://www.newstatesman.com/200804170025.

Mackenzie, Hugh, Hans Messinger, and Rick Smith. *Size Matters: Canada's Ecological
Footprint, by Income.* Montreal: Canadian Centre for Policy Alternatives, 2008.
http://www.policyalternatives.ca/publications/reports/size-matters.

Magdoff, Fred, and John Bellamy Foster. "What Every Environmentalist Needs to
Know about Capitalism." *Monthly Review* 61, no. 10 (March 2010): 1–30.
http://www.monthlyreview.org/100301magdoff-foster.php.

Magdoff, Fred, and Brian Tokar. "Agriculture and Food in Crisis: An Overview." In
Magdoff and Tokar, *Agriculture and Food in Crisis.*

———, eds. *Agriculture and Food in Crisis: Conflict, Resistance, and Renewal.* New
York: Monthly Review Press, 2010.

Makower, Joel, and Cara Pike. *Strategies for the Green Economy: Opportunities and
Challenges in the New World of Business.* New York: McGraw-Hill, 2008.

Malthus, Thomas. *An Essay on the Principle of Population* (First Essay). Edited by Ge-
offrey Gilbert. Oxford: Oxford University Press, 2004.

———. *An Essay on the Principle of Population* (Second Essay). Abridged variorum
ed., edited by Donald Winch. Cambridge: Cambridge University Press, 1992.

Mamdani, Mahmood. *The Myth of Population Control: Family, Caste, and Class in an*

Indian Village. New York: Monthly Review Press, 1972.

Martin, Jack. "Immigration, Energy and the Environment." Washington, DC: Federation of Americans for Immigration Reform (FAIR), 2009. http://www .fairus.org/site/docserver/energy_enviro.pdf?docid=2941.

Martine, George. "Population Dynamics and Policies in the Context of Global Climate Change." In *Population Dynamics and Climate Change*, edited by José Miguel Guzmán, George Martine, Gordon McGranahan, Daniel Schensul, and Cecilia Tacoli. New York: United Nations Population Fund, 2009.

Marx, Karl. *Capital: A Critique of Political Economy.* vol. 3. London: Penguin, 1993.

———. *Grundrisse: Introduction to the Critique of Political Economy.* Harmondsworth, UK: Penguin Books, 1973.

Marx, Karl, and Frederick Engels. *The German Ideology.* In Karl Marx and Frederick Engels, *Collected Works.* vol. 5. New York: International Publishers, 1976.

———. *The Manifesto of the Communist Party.* In Karl Marx and Frederick Engels, *Collected Works.* vol. 6. New York: International Publishers, 1976.

Matthews, Emily, Christof Amann, Stefan Bringezu, Marina Fischer-Kowalski, Walter Hüttler, René Kleijn, Yuichi Moriguchi, Christian Ottke, Eric Rodenburg, Don Rogich, Heinz Schandl, Helmut Schütz, Ester Vandervoet, and Helga Weisz. *The Weight of Nations: Material Outflows from Industrial Economies.* Washington, DC: World Resources Institute, 2000. http://pdf.wri.org/weight_of_nations.pdf.

Mazur, Laurie A., ed. *A Pivotal Moment: Population, Justice and the Environmental Challenge.* Washington, DC: Island Press, 2010.

———. "Population and Environment: A Progressive, Feminist Approach." *Climate and Capitalism*, January 17, 2010. http://climateandcapitalism.com/ ?p=1544.

———. "The Population Debate Is Screwed Up." *Alternet*, March 28, 2009. http://www.alternet.org/environment/133039/the_population_debate_is _screwed_up/.

———. "The World Needs Population Justice: A Reply to Ian Angus." *Climate and Capitalism*, March 7, 2010. http://climateandcapitalism.com/?p=1821.

McCormick, John. *Reclaiming Paradise: The Global Environmental Movement.* Bloomington: Indiana University Press, 1991.

McDougall, Rosamund. "Too Many People: Earth's Population Problem." London: Optimum Population Trust, 2010. http://www.optimumpopulation.org/opt .more.earth.pdf.

McNally, David. *Another World Is Possible: Globalization and Anti-capitalism.* 2nd ed. Winnipeg: Arbeiter Ring, 2006.

Meadows, Donella H., Dennis L. Meadows, Jorgen Randers, and William W. Behrens III. *The Limits to Growth.* New York: Universe Books, 1972.

Merrill Lynch Global Wealth Management and Capgemini. *World Wealth Report,*

2010. http://www.capgemini.com/insights-and-resources/by-publication/world
-wealth-report-2010.

Meyer, William B., and B. L. Turner II. "Human Population Growth and Land-
Use/Cover Change." *Annual Review of Ecology and Systematics* 23 (1992): 39–61.

Millennium Ecosystem Assessment Board. *Living beyond Our Means: Natural Assets
and Human Well-Being*. Washington, D.C.: Millennium Ecosystem Assessment,
2005. http://www.maweb.org/documents/document.429.aspx.pdf.

Miller, Matthew, and Luisa Kroll. "World's Billionaires 2010." *Forbes*, March 10,
2010. http://finance.yahoo.com/career-work/article/109029/worlds-billionaires-
2010.

Mimi, Raju. "Anti-dam Protests Get Louder in Northeast India." *World Rivers Review*, December 2010. http://www.internationalrivers.org/node/6049.

Mishel, Lawrence, Jared Bernstein, and Heidi Shierholz. *The State of Working America
2008–2009*. Ithaca, NY: Cornell University Press, 2009.

Mitchell, Donald. "A Note on Rising Food Prices—Abstract." World Bank Policy Research Working Paper 4682, July 2008. http://go.worldbank.org/X85VJWS610.

Monbiot, George. "The Population Myth." September 29, 2009. http://www.monbiot
.com/archives/2009/09/29/the-population-myth.

Morales, Evo. "Let Us Respect Our Mother Earth." *Climate and Capitalism*, September 25, 2007. http://climateandcapitalism.com/?p=203.

Myerson, Frederick A. B. "Population Growth Is Easier to Manage Than Per Capita
Emissions." *Bulletin of the Atomic Scientists Roundtable on Population and Climate
Change*, April 16, 2008. http://www.thebulletin.org/web-edition/roundtables/
population-and-climate-change.

Nadeau, Robert L. *The Wealth of Nature: How Mainstream Economics Has Failed the
Environment*. New York: Columbia University Press, 2003.

Natural Resources Canada. *Energy Efficiency Trends in Canada, 1990 to 2007*. September 2009. Ottawa, ON. http://oee.nrcan.gc.ca/publications/statistics/trends09/
pdf/trends.pdf.

Neumayer, Eric. "The Environment: One More Reason to Keep Immigrants Out?"
Ecological Economics 592 (2006): 204–07.

Nicholson-Lord, David. "A Population-Based Climate Strategy." London: Optimum
Population Trust, 2007. http://www.optimumpopulation.org/opt.sub.briefing
.climate.population.may07.pdf.

Nielsen Company. "U.S. Ad Spending Fell 2.6% in 2008, Nielsen Reports." News release, March 13, 2009. http://blog.nielsen.com/nielsenwire/wp-content/
uploads/2009/03/nielsen2008adspend-release.pdf.

Nikoukari, Mondana. "Gradations of Coercion: The Plight of Women of Color and
Their Informed Consent in the Sterilization Debate." *Connecticut Public Interest
Law Journal* 1, no. 1: 49–76. http://www.law.uconn.edu/system/files/private/

nikoukari.pdf

NumbersUSA. "Immigration Numbers—Talk about Numbers, Talk about Immigration." September 2008. http://www.numbersusa.com/content/resources/video/commercials/immigration-numbers-talk-about-numbers-talk-about-immigration.html.

Occidental Quarterly. "Statement of Principles." *Occidental Quarterly,* Winter 2004. Formerly at http://theoccidentalquarterly.com/archives/vol3no4/toq-editnote3-4.html.

Oldham, James. *Rethinking the Link: A Critical Review of Population-Environment Programs.* Amherst, MA: Political Economy Research Institute, 2006. http://www.peri.umass.edu/fileadmin/pdf/popenvt.pdf.

O'Neill, Brian C., Michael Dalton, Regina Fuchs, Leiwen Jiang, Shonali Pachauri, and Katarina Zigova. "Global Demographic Trends and Future Carbon Emissions." *Proceedings of the National Academy of Sciences* 107, no. 41 (October 12, 2010): 17521–26. http://www.pnas.org/content/107/41/17521.full.pdf.

———. "Supporting Information." *Proceedings of the National Academy of Sciences* 107, no. 41 (October 12, 2010). http://www.pnas.org/content/suppl/2010/10/01/1004581107.dcsupplemental/pnas.201004581si.pdf.

O'Neill, Brian C., F. Landis MacKellar, and Wolfgang Lutz. *Population and Climate Change.* Cambridge: Cambridge University Press, 2001.

OPT (Optimum Population Trust). "Gaia Scientist to Be OPT Patron." News release, August 26, 2009. http://populationmatters.org/2009/press/gaia-scientist-opt-patron.

———. "OPT Population Policy Proposals." 2002–2009. http://www.optimumpopulation.org/opt.policies.html.

———. "Think-Tank Urges Population Inquiry by Government." News release, January 5, 2009. http://populationmatters.org/2009/press/thinktank-urges-population-inquiry-government.

Osborne, Fairfield. *Our Plundered Planet.* London: Faber and Faber, 1948.

O'Shaughnessy, Hugh. "Poisoned City Fights to Save Its Children." *Guardian,* August 12, 2007. http://www.guardian.co.uk/world/2007/aug/12/environment.pollution.

Paddock, William, and Paul Paddock. *Famine—1975! America's Decision: Who Will Survive?* Boston: Little, Brown, 1967.

PAI (Population Action International). "Population—Facts and Figures." 2007. http://www.populationaction.org/Publications/Reports/Why_Population_Matters/Population_-_Facts_and_Figures.shtml.

PAI and PJP (Population Action International and Population Justice Project). "Population and the Environment: Where We're Headed and What We Can Do." 2010. http://www.populationaction.org/Publications/Fact_Sheets/Population_and_Environment/popenvguide.pdf.

Paillard, Sandrine, Sébastien Treyer, and Bruno Dorin, eds. *Agrimonde: Scenarios for Feeding the World in 2050*. Versailles: Éditions Quae, 2011.

Patnaik, Utsa. "Origins of the Food Crisis in India and Developing Countries." In Magdoff and Tokar, *Agriculture and Food in Crisis*.

PBS. "Affluenza: Test Your Consumption Quotient." n. d. http://www.pbs.org/kcts/affluenza/diag/what.html.

Pearce, Fred. *Peoplequake: Mass Migration, Ageing Nations and the Coming Population Crash*. London: Eden Project Books, 2010.

People of Color Environmental Justice. "Principles of Working Together." http://www.ejnet.org/ej/workingtogether.pdf.

Perelman, Michael. "Some Economics of Class." *Monthly Review* 58, no. 3 (July-August 2006): 18–28. http://www.monthlyreview.org/0706perelman.htm.

Pérez, Amara. "Between Radical Theory and Community Praxis." In *The Revolution Will Not Be Funded: Beyond the Non-profit Industrial Complex*, edited by Incite! Women of Color Against Violence. Cambridge, MA: South End Press, 2007.

Perry, Mark. "Consumer, Not Corporate, 'Greed' Is Ultimately behind Layoffs." Mackinac Center for Public Policy, January 7, 2002. http://www.mackinac.org/3931.

Petchesky, Rosalind P. *Global Prescriptions: Gendering Health and Human Rights*. London: Zed Books, 2003.

Pfeiffer, Dale Allen. *Eating Fossil Fuels: Oil, Food and the Coming Crisis in Agriculture*. Gabriola Island, BC: New Society Publishers, 2006.

Phillips, Kevin. "How Wealth Defines Power." In *The Wealth Inequality Reader*. 2nd ed., edited by Dollars & Sense Collective. Boston: Dollars & Sense Economic Affairs Bureau, 2008.

Pilger, John, ed. *Tell Me No Lies: Investigative Journalism and Its Triumphs*. London: Jonathan Cape, 2004.

Pimentel, David, and Marcia Pimentel. "Global Environmental Resources versus World Population Growth." *Ecological Economics* 59 (2006): 195–98.

Pimentel, David, Rebecca Harman, Matthew Pacenza, Jason Pecarsky, and Marcia Pimentel. "Natural Resources and an Optimum Human Population." Minnesotans for Sustainability, 1994. http://www.mnforsustain.org/pimentel_d_natural_resources_and_optimum_population.htm.

Pope, Carl. "Moving On: Lessons of the Immigration Debate." *Sierra Magazine*, July-August 1998. http://www.sierraclub.org/sierra/199807/ways.asp.

Poswolsky, Rebecca, and Dave M. "Anti-immigrant Leader Admits Using Climate Change for Political Gain." *Imagine2050*, February 23, 2010. http://imagine2050.newcomm.org.

Potter, David. *Society and the Social Sciences: An Introduction*. London: Routledge, 1989.

Pretty, J. N., A. D. Noble, D. Bossio, J. Dixon, R. E. Hine, F. W. T. Penning de Vries, and J. I. L. Morison. "Resource-Conserving Agriculture Increases Yields in Developing Countries." *Environmental Science & Technology* 40, no. 4 (2006): 1114–19.

Price, David. "Carrying Capacity Reconsidered." *Population and Environment* 21, no. 1 (September 1999): 5–26.

Princen, Thomas. "Consumer Sovereignty and Sacrifice: Two Insidious Concepts in an Expansionist Economy." In *The Environmental Politics of Sacrifice*, edited by Michael Maniates and J. M. Meyer. Cambridge, MA: MIT Press, 2010.

Princen, Thomas, Michael F. Maniates, and Ken Conca, eds. *Confronting Consumption.* Cambridge, MA: MIT Press, 2002.

Rees, William E. "Globalization, Trade and Migration: Undermining Sustainability." *Ecological Economics* 59 (2006): 220–25.

Reimers, David M. *Unwelcome Strangers: American Identity and the Turn against Immigration.* New York: Columbia University Press, 1998.

Reisch, Nikki, and Steve Kretzmann. *A Climate of War: The War in Iraq and Global Warming.* Advance ed. Oil Change International, March 2008. http://priceofoil.org/wp-content/uploads/2008/03/A%20Climate%20of%20War%20FINAL%20%28March%2017%202008%29.pdf.

Rogers, Heather. *Gone Tomorrow: The Hidden Life of Garbage.* New York: New Press, 2005.

Røpke, Inge. "2006 Migration and Sustainability Compatible or Contradictory?" *Ecological Economics* 592 (2006): 191–94.

Ross, Eric B. *The Malthus Factor: Poverty, Politics and Population in Capitalist Development.* London: Zed Books, 1998.

Rosset, Peter. "Lessons of Cuban Resistance." In *Sustainable Agriculture and Resistance: Transforming Food in Cuba*, edited by Fernando Funes, Luis García, Martin Bourque, Nilda Pérez, and Peter Rosset. Oakland, CA: Food First Books, 2001.

Rothkopf, David. *Superclass: The Global Power Elite and the World They Are Making.* Toronto: Penguin Canada, 2009.

Ryerson, William N. *Population: The Multiplier of Everything Else.* Santa Rosa, CA: Post Carbon Institute, 2010. http://www.postcarbon.org/report/131587-population-the-multiplier-of-everything-else.

Sachs, Jeffrey. *Common Wealth: Economics for a Crowded Planet.* New York: Penguin, 2008.

Sanders, Barry. *The Green Zone: The Environmental Costs of Militarism.* Oakland, CA: AK Press, 2009.

Satterthwaite, David. "The Implications of Population Growth and Urbanization for Climate Change." *Environment and Urbanization* 21, no. 2 (2007): 545–67.

Schnaiberg, Allan. *The Environment: From Surplus to Scarcity.* New York: Oxford University Press, 1980.

Schnaiberg, Allan, and Kenneth A. Gould. *Environment and Society: The Enduring Conflict.* New York: St. Martin's Press, 1994.

Schwartz, Stephen I. "Atomic Audit: The Costs and Consequences of U.S. Nuclear Weapons since 1940." http://www.ipb.org/Schwartz%20presentationText.pdf.

Seccombe, Wally. "Marxism and Demography." *New Left Review* 1, no. 137 (January-February 1983): 22–47.

Seidl, Irmi, and Clem A. Tisdell. "Carrying Capacity Reconsidered: From Malthus' Population Theory to Cultural Carrying Capacity." *Ecological Economics* 31 (1999): 395–408.

Sen, Amartya. *Poverty and Famines: An Essay on Entitlement and Deprivation*. Oxford: Oxford University Press, 1982.

Shaw, Hannah, and Chad Stone. "Tax Data Show Richest 1 Percent Took a Hit in 2008, but Income Remained Highly Concentrated at the Top." Center on Budget and Policy Priorities, October 21, 2010. Washington, DC. http://www.cbpp.org/files/10–21–10inc.pdf.

Shiva, Vandana. *Soil Not Oil: Environmental Justice in an Age of Climate Crisis*. Cambridge, MA: South End Press, 2008.

Shiva, Vandana, and Mira Shiva. "Was Cairo a Step Forward for Third World Women?" Posted on the ecofem listserv, March 20, 1995, by "Stefanie." http://www.mail-archive.com/ecofem@csf.colorado.edu/msg06397.html.

Shnayerson, Michael. "Sand Simeon." *Vanity Fair,* August 1998. http://www.vanityfair.com/magazine/archive/1998/08/sandsimeon199808.

Simms, Andrew, Victoria Johnson, and Peter Chowla. *Growth Isn't Possible*. London: New Economics Foundation (NEF), 2010. http://www.neweconomics.org/sites/neweconomics.org/files/Growth_Isnt_Possible.pdf.

Simms, Andrew, Victoria Johnson, Joe Smith, and Susanna Mitchell. *The Consumption Explosion: The Third UL Interdependence Report*. London: New Economics Foundation (NEF), September 2009. http://www.neweconomics.org/sites/neweconomics.org/files/The_Consumption_Explosion_1.pdf.

Simon, Julian L. *The Ultimate Resource 2*. Princeton, NJ: Princeton University Press, 1996.

Simon, Julian L., and Herman Kahn. Introduction to *The Resourceful Earth*. In *Population Matters: People, Resources, Environment, and Immigration*, edited by Julian L. Simon. New Brunswick, NJ: Transaction Publishers, 1996.

Smil, Vaclav. *Feeding the World: A Challenge for the Twenty-First Century*. Cambridge, MA: MIT Press, 2000.

Smith, Richard. "Beyond Growth or beyond Capitalism?" *Real-World Economics Review* 53 (June 26, 2010): 28–42. http://www.paecon.net/PAEReview/issue53/whole53.pdf.

Smith, Yves. *Econned: How Unenlightened Self-Interest Undermined Democracy and Corrupted Capitalism*. New York: Palgrave Macmillan, 2010.

Snell, Bradford. "American Ground Transport: A Proposal for Restructuring the Automobile, Truck, Bus & Rail Industries." 1974. http://www.worldcarfree.net/resources/freesources/American.htm.

SPA (Sustainable Population Australia). "Aims and Objectives." 2008. http://www.population.org.au/index.php/about-us/aims-a-objectives.

————. "Global Population Reduction: A 21st Century Strategy to Avoid Human Suffering and Environmental Devastation—Warning Bells Are Ringing." 2007. http://www.population.org.au/images/stories/Documents/gpr_spa_2007.pdf.

————. "Population Policy." 2005. http://www.population.org.au/images/stories/Documents/spa_population_policy.pdf.

Spratt, David. "Global Warming—No More Business as Usual: This Is an Emergency!" *Links International Journal of Socialist Renewal* (October 2008). http://links.org.au/node/683.

Staples, Winthrop, and Philip Cafaro. "The Environmental Argument for Reducing Immigration to the United States." Washington DC: Center for Immigration Studies, 2009. http://www.cis.org/articles/2009/back709.pdf.

Steffen, Will, Regina Angelina Sanderson, Peter D. Tyson, Jill Jäger, Pamela A. Matson, Berrien Moore III, Frank Oldfield, Katherine Richardson, Hans-Joachim Schellnhuber, Billie L. Turner II, and Robert J. Wasson. "*Executive Summary: Global Change and the Earth System: A Planet under Pressure.*" New York: Springer, 2004. www.igbp.net/documents/igbp_execsummary.pdf.

Stern, Nicholas. *The Economics of Climate Change.* Cambridge: Cambridge University Press, 2007.

Stuart, Tristram. *Waste: Uncovering the Global Food Scandal.* London: W. W. Norton, 2009.

Tactaquin, Cathi. "Environmentalists and the Anti-immigrant Agenda." *Race, Poverty & the Environment* 4, no. 2 (Summer 1993): 6–8.

Terrachoice. *The Sins of Greenwashing: Home and Family Edition 2010.* Ottawa: Terrachoice, 2010. http://sinsofgreenwashing.org/?dl_id=102.

————. "Terrachoice 2010 Sins of Greenwashing Study Finds Misleading Green Claims on 95 Per Cent of Home and Family Products." News release, October 26, 2010. http://www.terrachoice.com/Home/News/Media%20Releases.

Thornton, Emily. "Ira Rennert's House of Debt." *BusinessWeek*, February 17, 2003. http://www.businessweek.com/magazine/content/03_07/b3820069_mz020.htm.

Tobin, Allan J., and Jennie Dusheck. *Asking about Life.* 3rd ed. Belmont, CA: Brooks/Cole, 2005.

Toussaint, Eric. *Your Money or Your Life: The Tyranny of Global Finance.* Chicago: Haymarket Books, 2005.

Travis, David. "Sustainable Capitalism." In Angus, *The Global Fight for Climate Justice.*

Trucost. "Carbon Risks and Opportunities in the S&P 500." IRRC Institute and Trucost, June 2009. Boston, MA. http://www.trucost.com/_uploads/publishedResearch/

Carbon_Risks_&_Opportunities_S&P_500-LowRes.pdf.

———. "Universal Ownership: Why Environmental Externalities Matter to Institutional Investors." October 2010. http://www.unpri.org/files/6728_ES_report_environmental_externalities.pdf.

Udall, Stewart L. *The Quiet Crisis and the Next Generation.* Salt Lake City: Peregrine Smith Books, 1988.

Union of Concerned Scientists. "1992 World Scientists' Warning to Humanity." Cambridge, MA. http://www.ucsusa.org/about/1992-world-scientists.html.

United Nations Millennium Project. *Halving Hunger: It Can Be Done; Summary Version of the Report of the Task Force on Hunger.* New York: Earth Institute, Columbia University, 2005.

United Nations Population Division. "Crude Death Rate (per 1,000 population)." n. d. http://data.un.org/Data.aspx?d=PopDiv&f=variableID:65.

United Nations Statistical Division. "CO_2 Emissions in 2006." http://unstats.un.org/unsd/environment/air_co2_emissions.htm.

US Census Bureau. "Median and Average Sales Prices of New Homes Sold in United States." 1963–2009. http://www.census.gov/const/uspriceann.pdf.

US Department of State. *United States Relations with China: With Special Reference to the Period 1944–1949.* Washington, D.C.: US Govt. Printing Office, 1949.

La Vía Campesina. "Declaration in Cancún." December 2010. http://viacampesina.org/en/index.php?option=com_content&view=article&id=1018.

Vidal, John. "Nigeria's Agony Dwarfs the Gulf Oil Spill: The US and Europe Ignore It." *Guardian,* May 30, 2010. http://www.guardian.co.uk/world/2010/may/30/oil-spills-nigeria-niger-delta-shell.

Vogt, William. *Road to Survival.* New York: William Sloan Associates, 1948.

Waller, Margy. "Auto-mobility: Subsidizing America's Commute Would Reward Work, Boost the Economy, and Transform Lives." *Washington Monthly,* October-November 2005, 18–22.

Wallis, Victor. "Capitalist and Socialist Responses to the Ecological Crisis." *Monthly Review* 60, no. 6 (November 2008): 25–40. http://www.monthlyreview.org/081103wallis.php.

Warren, Elizabeth. "The Middle Class on the Precipice." *Harvard Magazine,* January-February 2006. http://harvardmagazine.com/2006/01/the-middle-class-on-the-html.

Watts, Jonathan. *When a Billion Chinese Jump: How China Will Save Mankind—or Destroy It.* London: Faber & Faber, 2010.

Weissman, Steve. "Why the Population Bomb Is a Rockefeller Baby." *Ramparts* 8, no. 11 (May 1970): 42–47.

Wessler, Seth. "The Far-Right Movement behind Arizona Copycat Bills." *Colorlines,* May 4, 2010. http://www.colorlines.com/archives/2010/05/the_farright_movement

_behind_arizona_copycat_bills.html.

White, Curtis. "The Barbaric Heart: Capitalism and the Crisis of Nature." *Orion Magazine,* May–June 2009. http://www.orionmagazine.org/index.php/articles/article/4680/.

Whitty, Julia. "The Last Taboo." *Mother Jones*, May–June 2010, 24-43.

Wire, Thomas. *Fewer Emitters, Lower Emissions, Less Cost: Reducing Future Carbon Emissions by Investing in Family Planning.* London: Optimum Population Trust, 2009. http://www.optimumpopulation.org/reducingemissions.pdf.

Wolf, Brian. "Environmental Crime." In *Encyclopedia of White-Collar Crime*, edited by Jurg Gerber and Eric L. Jensen. Westport, CT: Greenwood, 2007.

Wolff, Edward N. "Recent Trends in Household Wealth in the United States: Rising Debt and the Middle-Class Squeeze—An Update to 2007." Levy Economics Institute of Bard College, Working Paper 589, March 2010. http://www.levyinstitute.org/publications/?docid=1235.

Worldwatch Institute. *State of the World 2011: Innovations That Nourish the Planet.* New York: W. W. Norton, 2011.

Index

A

Abernethy, Virginia, 119
Abramovich, Roman, 148
Acheson, Dean, 85
advertising, 140–41, 153–58, 162, 199
Afghanistan, 36, 175–76
Africa, 40, 42, 49, 65, 68, 74, 126,
 212, 222
 See also Egypt, Niger, Nigeria
agriculture, 71–82, 138–39, 191, 196,
 198, 222
Agrimonde, 80–82
All Party Parliamentary Group on
 Population, 36
Allen, Paul, 148
Ambani, Mukesh, 148
American Electric Power, 173
American Enterprise Institute, 152
anticommunism, 85
anticonsumerism, 163
Apply the Brakes, 119
Arizpe, Lourdes, 193
Athanasiou, Tom, 1, 109, 123
Attenborough, David, 28

Australia, xxi, 5, 24, 47, 75, 137, 140
 Australia Institute, 123
 Australian Conservation
  Foundation, 34
 greenhouse gas emissions, 42
 immigration, 3, 29, 115, 125, 176
 inequality, 146, 149, 235n36
 Sustainable Population Australia
  (SPA), 33–34, 205
automobile, 15, 38–9, 140, 158, 160–62
Avery, Dennis, 78

B

Bandarage, Asoka, 70, 84, 93
Bangladesh, 43, 94, 223
Barclay, David and Frederick, 147
Bartlett, Albert, 64–65
Beck, Roy, 117
Belem Ecosocialist Declaration, 183
Bello, Walden, 132
Bhopal, 171
Biel, Robert, 129
Bilderback, Loy, 113
bin Rashid Al Maktoum, Mohammed,

259

About Ian Angus

Ian Angus is editor of *Climate and Capitalism*, an online journal focusing on capitalism, climate change, and the ecosocialist alternative. His previous books include *Canadian Bolsheviks* and *The Global Fight for Climate Justice*.

"The most reliable single source of information and strategic insights for climate justice is *Climate and Capitalism*, the website Ian Angus edits."
—Patrick Bond, director of the Centre for Civil Society, University of KwaZulu-Natal, South Africa

About Simon Butler

© Kate Ausburn

Simon Butler, a climate justice activist based in Sydney, Australia, is coeditor of *Green Left Weekly*, one of the country's leading sources of anti-capitalist news, analysis, discussion, and debate.

"Without *Green Left Weekly,* freedom of press and public
truth-telling in Australia would be gravely ill."
—John Pilger

Also from Haymarket Books

Ecology and Socialism
Solutions to Capitalist Ecological Crisis
Chris Williams • Around the world, consciousness of the threat to our environment is growing. The majority of solutions on offer, from using efficient light-bulbs to biking to work, focus on individual lifestyle changes, yet the scale of the crisis requires far deeper adjustments. *Ecology and Socialism* argues that time still remains to save humanity and the planet, but only by building social movements for environmental justice that can demand qualitative changes in our economy, workplaces, and infrastructure. ISBN: 978-1-60846-091-5

Kivalina
A Climate Change Story
Christine Shearer • For the people of Kivalina, Alaska, the price of further climate change denial could be the complete devastation of their lives and culture. Their village must be relocated to survive, and neither the fossil fuel giants nor the US government is willing to take full responsibility. ISBN: 978-1-60846-128-8

Field Notes on Democracy
Listening to Grasshoppers
Arundhati Roy • Combining fierce conviction, deft political analysis, and beautiful writing, this is the essential new book from Arundhati Roy. This series of essays examines the dark side of democracy in contemporary India. It looks closely at how religious majoritarianism, cultural nationalism, and neofascism simmer just under the surface of a country that projects itself as the world's largest democracy. ISBN: 978-1-60846-024-3

Fields of Resistance
The Struggle of Florida's Farmworkers for Justice
Silvia Giagnoni • Migrant farmworkers in the United States are routinely forced to live and work in unsafe, often desperate, conditions. In Immokalee, Florida, the tomato capital of the world—which has earned the dubious distinction of being "ground zero for modern slavery"—farmworkers organized themselves into the Coalition of Immokalee Workers and launched a nationwide boycott campaign that forced McDonald's, Burger King, and Taco Bell to recognize their demands for workers' rights. ISBN: 978-1-60846-093-9

The Meaning of Marxism

Paul D'Amato • In this lively and accessible introduction to the ideas of Karl Marx, with historical and contemporary examples, D'Amato argues that Marx's ideas of globalization, oppression, and social change are more important than ever. ISBN: 978-1-931859-29-5

No One Is Illegal

Fighting Racism and State Violence on the U.S.-Mexico Border
Justin Akers Chácon, Mike Davis • Countering the chorus of anti-immigrant voices, Mike Davis and Justin Akers Chacón expose the racism of anti-immigration vigilantes and put a human face on the debate over immigrants who risk their lives to cross the border to work in the United States. ISBN: 978-1-931859-35-6

Ours to Master and to Own

Workers' Control from the Commune to the Present
Immanuel Ness and Dario Azzellini • From the dawning of the industrial epoch, wage earners have organized themselves into unions, fought bitter strikes, and gone so far as to challenge the very premises of the system by creating institutions of democratic self-management aimed at controlling production without bosses. With specific examples drawn from every corner of the globe and every period of modern history, this pathbreaking volume comprehensively traces this often underappreciated historical tradition. ISBN: 978-1-60846-119-6

The Bending Cross

A Biography of Eugene Victor Debs
Ray Ginger, introduction by Mike Davis • Orator, organizer, self-taught scholar, presidential candidate, and prisoner, Eugene Debs maintained a lifelong commitment to the fight for a better world that is chronicled in this unparalleled biography by historian Ray Ginger. This moving story presents the definitive account of the life and legacy of the most eloquent spokesperson and leader of the US labor and socialist movements. ISBN: 978-1-931859-40-0

Breaking the Sound Barrier

Amy Goodman • The award-winning host of *Democracy Now!* breaks through the corporate media's lies, sound bites, and silence in this wide-ranging new collection of articles. In place of the usual suspects—the "experts" who, in Goodman's words, "know so little about so much, explain the world to us, and get it so wrong"—this accessible, lively collection allows the voices the corporate media exclude and ignore to be heard loud and clear. ISBN: 978-1-60846-007-6

About Haymarket Books

Haymarket Books is a nonprofit, progressive book distributor and publisher, a project of the Center for Economic Research and Social Change. We believe that activists need to take ideas, history, and politics into the many struggles for social justice today. Learning the lessons of past victories, as well as defeats, can arm a new generation of fighters for a better world. As Karl Marx said, "The philosophers have merely interpreted the world; the point, however, is to change it."

We take inspiration and courage from our namesakes, the Haymarket Martyrs, who gave their lives fighting for a better world. Their 1886 struggle for the eight-hour day, which gave us May Day, the international workers' holiday, reminds workers around the world that ordinary people can organize and struggle for their own liberation. These struggles continue today across the globe—struggles against oppression, exploitation, hunger, and poverty.

It was August Spies, one of the Martyrs targeted for being an immigrant and an anarchist, who predicted the battles being fought to this day. "If you think that by hanging us you can stamp out the labor movement," Spies told the judge, "then hang us. Here you will tread upon a spark, but here, and there, and behind you, and in front of you, and everywhere, the flames will blaze up. It is a subterranean fire. You cannot put it out. The ground is on fire upon which you stand."

We could not succeed in our publishing efforts without the generous financial support of our readers. Many people contribute to our project through the Haymarket Sustainers program, where donors receive free books in return for their monetary support. If you would like to be a part of this program, please contact us at info@haymarketbooks.org.

Shop our full catalog online at www.haymarketbooks.org or call 773-583-7884.